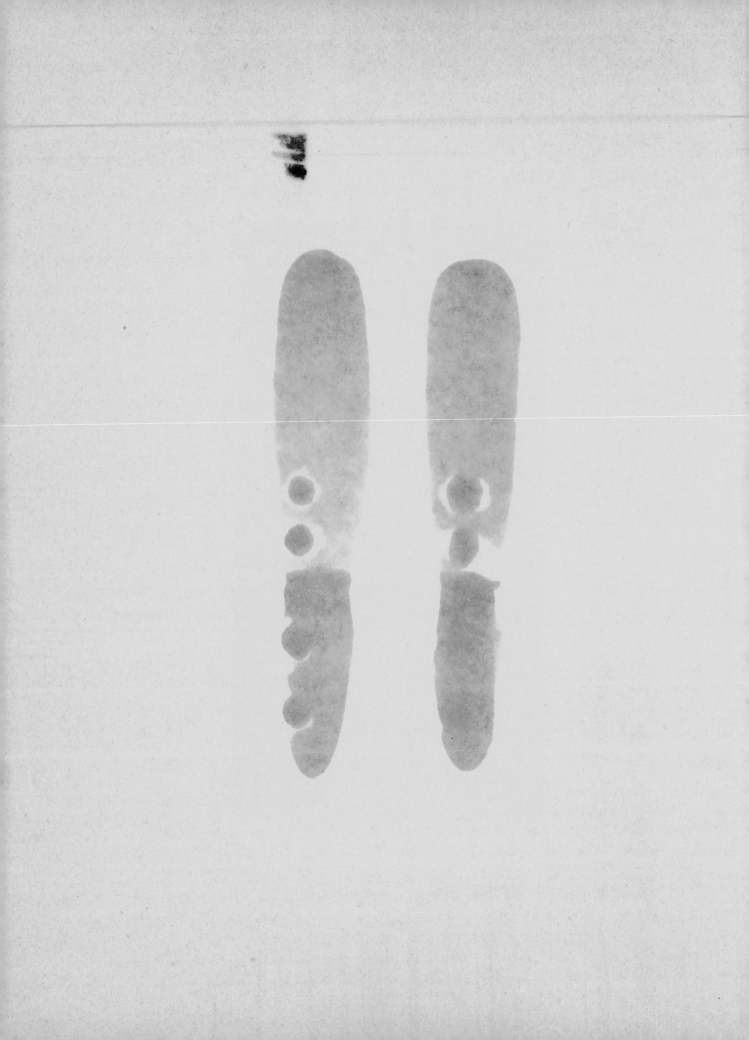

Theme Gardens

Theme Gardens

By Barbara Damrosch

Illustrations by Karl W. Stuecklen

A REGINA RYAN BOOK

WORKMAN PUBLISHING
NEW YORK

To my parents, Eleanor Southern Damrosch and Douglas Stanton Damrosch.

Library of Congress Cataloging in Publication Data

Damrosch, Barbara.
Theme gardens.

Includes index.
1. Gardens. 2. Gardens—Design. 3. Landscape gardening. I.
Title. II. Title: Theme gardens. III. Title: Theme gardens.
SB457.5.D35   1982   635.9   82-60062
ISBN 0-89480-218-6
ISBN 0-89480-217-8 (pbk.)

Art Direction and Cover design: Paul Hanson
Designer: Geoffrey Stevens
Cover photographs: Butterfly Garden, © Jo Brewer; Garden of Old
Roses, © Viki Ferreniea; Secret Garden, © Barbara Damrosch;
Victorian Garden, © Pamela Harper; Shakespeare Garden
© Lynne Meyer; Colonial Garden, © Emerick Bronson.

Workman Publishing Company, Inc.
1 West 39th Street
New York, N.Y. 10018

Printed in Hong Kong
First printing September 1982

10 9 8 7 6 5 4 3 2

Acknowledgment

Of the many people who helped with this book I would especially like to thank Regina Ryan who initiated the project and guided it throughout; my editor, Barbara Plumb; and the illustrator, Karl Stuecklen. The energetic staff of Workman Publishing—Peter Workman, Geoffrey Stevens, Sally Kovalchick, Paul Hanson and many others—were a pleasure to work with. Jim Harrison gave much skillful and patient assistance.

I am enormously indebted to T. H. Everett's encyclopedic knowledge and assistance. Other invaluable advisors were: Viki Ferreniea of the New Canaan Nature Center in Connecticut; Elizabeth Hall of the Horticultural Society of New York; Lily Shohan, Jo Brewer, Richard Lighty of Longwood Gardens; Frederick McGourty of the Brooklyn Botanic Garden; and Joan DeWind, Anne Damrosch, Gary Porwitzki and Henry Fisher. I would also like to thank the library at the Horticultural Society of New York; the Gunn Memorial Library in Washington, Connecticut; the library of The New York Botanical Garden; and Nancy Callaghan. Anne Daniels and Maggie Higgens gave unstinting secretarial aid. Other helpers were Margaret Dangler of the Hickory Stick Bookshop in Washington Depot, Connecticut, Caroline Ferriday, Rosemary Verey, Myra Hecht, Terry Stevens, Charles Reppenhagen, the New York Zendo, and the Sharon Audubon Society in Sharon, Connecticut.

Those who have given me help and advice in my horticultural work include my parents; my grandmother, Lucille Southern; Lee Bristol of the Lee Bristol Nursery in Sherman, Connecticut; Howard Kemmerer of the Cooperative Extension Service in Bethel, Connecticut; David Smith of White Flower Farm, Litchfield, Connecticut; Glenn Waruch of Claire's Garden Center in Patterson, New York.

I owe a personal debt to Edith Lewis Moss for many kindnesses; to my friends Susan Tilman and Denise Bryan; and finally to Chris and Ward for their support and patience.

—B.D.

Contents

Introduction 9

A Garden Primer 11

A Fragrance Garden 25

A Colonial Garden 37

A Butterfly Garden 53

A Moon Garden 67

A Children's Garden 77

A Garden of Old Roses 88

A Zen Garden 101

A Shakespeare Garden 111

A Gray Garden 127

A Garden of Love 138

A Hummingbird Garden 149

A Secret Garden 159

A Medieval Paradise Garden 169

A Grass Garden 181

A Victorian Garden 189

A Winter Garden 203

Appendix

   Plant Hardiness Zone Map 215

   Where to Order Plants 215

   For Further Reading 217

Index to Plants 221

Introduction

A Gardiner is never rich, yet he is ever raking together. His knowledge consists in the vegetative knowledge of plants. Like Adam, hee is put into some gentleman's garden to dresse the Trees, and to make it if he can, a Paradise of Pleasure, and for this he has yearly wages.

—WYE SALTONSTALL, *PICTURES DRAWN FORTH IN CHARACTERS,* 1635.

In the beginning there was a garden. Call it Eden if you like, or call it a vision of a time when our partnership with the earth was a simple and fruitful one. "God Almightie first planted a Garden," said Francis Bacon in his famous essay on gardening. "And indeed it is the Purest of Humane pleasures."

In the end, too, there is a garden. For the ancient Egyptians, life after death was an oasislike place that had running water, green plants and good things to eat. For the Greeks and Romans it was the flowery fields of Elysium. For Mahayana Buddhists it was the "western paradise" with its scents, birds and pools of lotus blossoms. Most of the world's religions have promised a haven of pleasure and bounty to their believers— the fortunate ones are allowed to return to the garden from whence they came.

Meanwhile, we plant gardens—"paradises of pleasure." Our word "paradise" comes, via the Greek *paradeisos,* from the Old Persian word *pairidaeza,* which simply meant a "walled enclosure" (originally a hunting park for the king). Historically, it seems, we first had gardens, then imagined heavenly ones. But it makes little difference which came first. The idea of the garden as paradise is always there, ready to be summoned by that part of our nature that seems to love it.

There is also a less primeval side to it all; gardening has been an art for several millennia, and our desire to make gardens comes also from a love of beauty—a desire to shape unruly nature into forms that please us more, from the Hanging Gardens of Babylon to the White House Rose Garden.

All this puts gardening into a rather grand frame of reference, considering the cozy, modest scale on which most of us practice it—as garden club members marching out with our civic petunias or as husbands surveying our kingdoms of lawn on Sunday afternoon. But gardening has always been a blend of the humble and the sublime. After a life of great deeds, many a ruler—from Kublai Khan to Winston Churchill—created a private garden world of which he was the Adam. A few, no doubt, even got their knees dirty, though others merely commanded squadrons of workers. There are, after all, two kinds of garden makers: those who love gardening and those who simply love gardens. For whatever the cosmic heritage of our gardens, they are gardens after the Fall. Like Adam, we delve; we get sore backs and mealybugs. For some people the sense of fulfillment from this labor is part of the garden of earthly delights; for others it is purgatory. But almost anyone who has a garden takes pride in it as his Eden.

The sense of "enclosure" in the word *pairidaeza* still persists in our idea of a garden, the "little paradises" in this book were designed with this in mind. Not all are enclosures in a literal sense, however, though some are designed to have hedges or fences around them. All are enclosed or defined, nonetheless, by a specific idea that gives them a special sense of place. Each carries out a single theme.

Some of the gardens are small glimpses of a historical period: a garden in the Victorian manner; a medieval "paradise," or "plesaunce," like those that castle-dwellers set within their walls; a Colonial garden; a garden that re-creates the world of Shakespeare. Two of them are sanctuaries for wildlife—one for butterflies, another for hummingbirds. Some are private refuges—for lovers, for children, for those who seek a tranquil place for meditation. Some are for the enjoyment of special plants: unusual grasses, old-fashioned roses, plants that grow well by the seashore if sheltered from the briny winds. One little enclosure traps the scents of flowers, another the winter sun. And one is filled with flowers that are beautiful by moonlight.

All these gardens are within the capabilities of the amateur gardener. They do not require enormous skill, great expenditures of money or large amounts of space. Each one, in fact, could be planted in a small backyard. For each I have given some historical or technical information, followed by a plan of the garden, and then instructions for growing the plants recommended. Some of the gardens are complemented by simple constructions such as arbors, terraces, walks or fences. Some gardens are more ambitious than others. I have also made suggestions for scaling things down if you wish something more modest, and ideas for expansion if you get caught up in a particular theme and want to take it further.

Every house is different; every garden site is different so you may find that you cannot—or prefer not to—copy these schemes in strict detail. You may have strong feelings about certain plants, colors or scents. I have tried to explain what my goals are in the designs, why the plants were chosen and placed in certain ways. You might want to take these general principles and use them to spark your own imagination, altering the plan to suit your preferences or the demands of the terrain you have to work with.

Geography is an important variable, too. All these gardens will work in the northeastern part of the United States and other cooler areas, but they can be adapted to other regions as well. I suggest ways of doing this at the end of each chapter under Additions and Substitutions. Your local nurserymen can give you additional guidance as to which varieties of plants will do best in your locality. I give zone numbers (which refer to the U.S. Department of Agriculture Zone Map on p. 215) for perennials in the Plant Lists, but I do it

with some reservations. Hardiness zones have not been conclusively established for all the plants we grow. Moreover, the zones indicate only hardiness with respect to cold, disregarding such factors as moisture content or acidity of soil, for example. Even winter hardiness can vary with factors such as altitude. It might be zone 5 on your hill but zone 6 in the neighboring valley; or zone 5 on your windy front lawn but zone 6 in your sheltered back patio. The numbers should merely be taken as a general guide to the hardiness of plants relative to one another.

Most of the plans in this book are for perennial gardens. Most of them also contain some annuals, foliage plants, bulbs, a few shrubs and an occasional tree. General guidelines for planting and maintenance are set forth in the Garden Primer, which follows this introduction. The illustrations in each chapter give you an idea of what the gardens might look like if all goes well, but bear in mind that there will always be plants that do not produce the dazzling mass of blooms or the lush foliage that you would like.

I have included plans that show you where to plant what. And in most cases there are two or three diagrams, showing the garden at different times in the blooming season. But as veteran gardeners know, a garden changes so rapidly that it has a different look almost every week.

For the names of plants I have, in most cases, used the common name first, though in some cases I have decided that the Latin name is more "common." Many people prefer common names because they are descriptive and charming. But the Latin ones are just as descriptive when you know, for example, that *repens* means "creeping" and *tomentosum* means "woolly" or "hairy." They are also downright useful when you want to know for sure which plant you are buying. Many common names apply to several different plants, whereas Latin names are used customarily, in the trade, to distinguish different genera, species and varieties, and nurserymen are usually familiar with them. In any case, do not be intimidated by the Latin names, or by any other plant lore. You are not studying to pass an examination, only trying to enter paradise. What could be easier?

A Garden Primer

Some gardens are planted as living works of art. They exist only to be looked at.

Useful gardens can be beautiful too, of course—a productive orchard in its spring bloom, or a utilitarian vegetable garden with its tidy rows of greenery dotted with the colors of ripening produce. But the gardens we plant for ornament, like the lilies of the field, "toil not, neither do they spin," even though their tenders might work like the very devil.

Gardens are also great battlegrounds between the real and the ideal. Anyone who has nurtured bright visions of phlox and dahlias in gloomy February, only to harvest weeds and aphids in dismal August, knows that gardens can fall short of one's expectations. Even the successful gardener whose beds glow with color finds that these beds change from day to day. And they are always thinking about a new plant to try or a new combination of colors.

There is no great mystery to the way these gardeners succeed. The more you learn about gardening and the harder you work at it, the more beautiful your garden will be.

THE GARDEN COMMUNITY

Did you ever consider the fact that every garden flower started as a wild flower somewhere? You can see the origins of many garden hybrids in the natural landscape around you. The purple and blue asters that grow along the New England roadsides in autumn *(Aster novae-angliae* and *A. novi-belgii)* are parents of most of our perennial garden asters. Our familiar garden phlox comes from a plant, *Phlox paniculata*, that grows wild in the southern United States. Gaillardias *(Gaillardia aristata)* cover our western meadows with bright blankets of flowers.

Other common garden flowers come from wild flowers of foreign lineage. Canterbury bells *(Campanula medium)*, foxgloves *(Digitalis purpurea)* and larkspur *(Delphinium ajacis)*, for example, are from European species. Others, such as peonies, have honorable ancestors in China. Many herbs such as sage, lavender, and rosemary are

A harmonious spring border composed of lily-flowered tulips, yellow doronicum and rose-colored pasque-flowers, with pansies and forget-me-nots in the foreground.

© PAMELA HARPER

from the dry hills of the Mediterranean region. Most annuals are from tropical or subtropical countries such as Mexico. Our shrubs, ornamental foliage plants, and vegetables have all been derived from a wild species or a combination of two and sometimes more.

When you consider the different growing conditions that all these plants prefer, to combine all of them in one garden seems like an act of faith comparable to the founding of the League of Nations. All must adapt to the common denominators of the soil in our gardens and the local vagaries of climate, even if the conditions stray far from what they would choose in nature. Fortunately, our ornamental plants have been bred to live in gardens. If we begin with a plant so that each plant has its proper space, then prepare plant and maintain the garden properly, the community will thrive.

For this we rely on a basic gardening science. No two gardens are alike. It's best to understand how plants grow, learn some simple guidelines, and then let your own garden teach you about its particular needs. More precious than the perfect recipe for compost is the ability of an experienced gardener to test the soil by feel. The fingers can learn to tell "good garden loam" as expertly as if those fingers themselves were probing roots. After fighting many battles, a veteran gardener can face the spring wise in the ways of weeds and pests, knowing who is friend and who is foe.

WHAT PLANTS NEED

Plants manufacture their own food and vitamins from simple inorganic substances by means of the process called photosynthesis. During this chain of chemical reactions, the plant takes in carbon dioxide and produces sugar (glucose) for food and oxygen as a byproduct. The energy for these reactions is provided by sunlight. Plants make their own enzymes, to aid digestion, and they manufacture hormones, which govern the "tropisms," which cause stems to lean toward light and roots to grope toward water.

Plants need sixteen different elements for life, growth and reproduction. Three of these—carbon, hydrogen and oxygen—are obtained through water and air. All the rest must be present in the soil, where they are absorbed by the root hairs. Of these, the three most important are nitrogen, phosphorus and potassium, followed by sulfur, calcium and magnesium. (The others, known as trace elements, must be there in small quantities.) To be skillful at feeding your plants, you must be aware of what the major elements do for them.

Soil Structure

Establishing a good soil is one of the chief goals in gardening. Few soils are perfect to begin with. When you start a garden, take a good look at the soil, decide what it needs and get it in proper shape before you plant.

Soil structure is the place to begin. Soils are classified according to the size of the particles of which they are composed; the smaller the particles, the "heavier" the soil. The lightest soil is coarse gravel, with particles larger than 5 mm; the heaviest is clay, with particles less than .005 mm. In between lie fine gravel, coarse sand, fine sand and silt. Most soils are mixtures of these types, and are called "sandy," "clay" or "silt" soils according to which type predominates. The ideal garden soil is "loam," which is roughly half sand and half silt or clay, combining the best features of both, together with an admixture of organic matter.

The virtues of light soil are that it drains well, warms up early in the spring, provides plenty of air, bacteria and other microorganisms and can be penetrated easily by roots. Its chief defect is its inability to hold water, which also means that nutrients leach out along with the moisture. Heavy soil holds water and nutrients very well, but it can become waterlogged, so that plant roots cannot get enough oxygen. Clay is also hard for roots to penetrate— and hard to till. Clay is a cold soil that warms slowly in spring. To find out what structure your own soil has, squeeze it. If it crumbles very easily or runs through your fingers it is sandy; if it holds together firmly it is clay.

Fortunately there is a simple way to create loam without having to change the proportion of sand or clay in your soil: add organic matter. Usually organic matter is added in the form of humus, which is plant or animal substances that have been partly or fully decomposed by the action of microscopic soil organisms, chiefly fungi and bacteria. Most soil already contains some humus, the result of accumulation from plants and animals that have lived and died there over the years. This is why the topsoil level is dark, whereas the subsoil, which does not contain organic matter, is light in color.

The beauty of humus is that it provides so many benefits at once. It gives the soil a "crumb" texture—clusters of particles that permit the free movement of air and water between them, making both available to the plant. It helps clay soils warm up and drains them of excess water. It helps sandy soils to retain water, holding in nutrients as well. When organic matter decomposes, it is broken down by soil bacteria and fungi; this process releases nutrients which the plant uses to manufacture its food.

There are many sources of organic matter: peat moss, leaf mold, rotted manure, leaves, grass clippings and compost. You can also plant a cover crop—a plant such as buckwheat or rye which is planted solely to be tilled under and incorporated into the soil. Usually the best source is the home compost heap—a pile of organic matter that you are constantly building from leaves, grass clippings, manure, weeds and other garden debris that is not diseased or pest-ridden. Kitchen garbage can also be used, but beware of meat wastes that attract rats and other predators, and wastes that are too tough to decompose quickly such as corn cobs or fruit rinds.

There are many ways to make compost. Some people just make neat piles; others fill bins with it; others collect it in pits dug in the ground. Plastic can be spread over it (to keep the sun from drying it out) or under it (to keep nutrients from leaching out). You can make it faster if your heap is accessible and easy to fork over from time to time, and if you keep it just moist enough to keep bacterial action going without losing nutrients. A compost shredder is a good investment if you do a lot of gardening, especially if you share the cost with other gardeners. It is particularly helpful if you are using maple leaves or other materials that would otherwise mat and decompose very slowly. Adding manure

This midsummer border on Martha's Vineyard has yellow yarrow in the foreground; behind it are red phlox and feathery pink astilbe. Tall shasta daisies stand against the fence, which provides a good backdrop.

will also speed up decomposition by activating the bacteria.

Soil Nutrients

Most soils contain the elements that plants need, but often not enough, and not in the right proportions. We fertilize to give plants an extra boost, to replace nutrients that have been lost through intensive gardening and to adjust the soil to specific growing needs. But with what?

Plants need sixteen different elements for life, growth and reproduction. Three of these—carbon, hydrogen and oxygen—are obtained through water and air. All the rest must be present in the soil, where they are absorbed by the root hairs. Of these, the three most important are nitrogen, phosphorus and potassium, followed by sulfur, calcium and magnesium. (The others, known as trace elements, must be there in small quantities). To be skillful at feeding your plants, you must be aware of what the major elements do for them.

Nitrogen is the element most responsible for the growth of leaves and stems. Its action is rapid, almost magical, as anyone knows who has greened up a brown lawn with a nitrogenous food, or who has given a stunted houseplant a dose of fish emulsion and watched it shoot across the ceiling. It is the element that is used up first, and most easily leached away, and it is not always available to plants in forms that they can use. Nitrogen contained in organic matter must be converted to nitrates by the action of the bacteria in order to be absorbed by plants. Plants cultivated chiefly for their foliage usually benefit from fairly frequent applications of nitrogenous fertilizer.

However, if you are growing a root crop, or trying to produce fruits or flowers, you do not want rapid stem and leaf growth. Or this kind of growth might be ill-timed—in early spring or late fall, for example, when tender new growth might be killed by cold. Rapid leaf and stem growth may also tend to be weak and soft, needing artificial support, and is more susceptible to disease. The action of nitrogen is a little like the action of sugar in the bloodstream—a rush of energy at the expense of permanent structural growth.

Phosphorus, on the other hand, produces good root growth, flowers and fruit. Use a fertilizer high in phosphorus when you first set a plant in the ground, so that the roots will grow quickly. This is especially true with fall planting, because root growth will continue well into the winter while the rest of the plant is dormant.

Potassium is also essential for root growth, and for the general well-being of the plant, especially in promoting its resistance to disease. If your plants show signs of poor general health—stunted growth, unsatisfactory color or disease—it might be due to a potassium deficiency.

There are many ways of adding these three elements to your soil. Nitrogen is abundant in animal manures, dried blood, cottonseed meal and fish emulsion. Phosphorus

is present in bone meal, in rock phosphate (natural deposits of calcium phosphate) and in the highly concentrated superphosphates, which have been made more soluble by the addition of sulfuric acid.

Most commercial fertilizers sold today are "complete" fertilizers, in that they contain a combination of nitrogen, phosphorus and potassium as well as some of the other nutrients and trace elements. Their labels must show the exact percentage of N (nitrogen), P (phosphorus) and K (potassium) that they contain, always in that order and separated by hyphens. Thus a bag of fertilizer marked 5-8-7 is 5 percent nitrogen, 8 percent phosphorus and 7 percent potassium. One marked 20-20-20 contains 20 percent of each.

When you buy these inorganic chemical fertilizers it is very easy to calculate how much of each nutrient you are giving your plant. They will go to work quickly, moreover, because the nitrogen is usually in an available form. Sometimes a commercial preparation will combine organic and inorganic nitrogen, so as to provide both a quick-acting and a slow-acting source in one application. Personally, I prefer a good compost because I like the process of recycling natural materials in my garden and because these make a more lasting contribution to the soil structure. When you are building your compost pile, you need a good nitrogen source such as manure, a phosphorus source such as bone meal and a potassium source such as wood ashes. It is best, however, to store ashes dry and add them directly to the soil at the time you apply your compost; potassium is very soluble and leaches easily.

Light

Most gardens need full sun. This means at least six hours of direct sunlight each day. Since afternoon sunlight is stronger than morning, your garden might get by on five hours of afternoon sun, but needs seven hours if most of it comes in the morning. Many flowering plants will grow perfectly well in the shade, but need sun in order to bloom profusely. Day lilies and azaleas are two examples. Others such as heliopsis are truly sunloving and even the shape of the plant will suffer in shady or partly shady situations;

CORRECTING POOR DRAINAGE

There are a number of reasons why your garden might drain poorly: clay soil, hardpan (an extremely compacted subsoil), a high water table or simply low ground with no exit for water that collects. Laying drainage tile will correct all these problems efficiently, permanently and invisibly. The tiles are usually made of red hard-baked clay, 4 to 6 inches in diameter and 1 foot long. Use 6-inch tile for an area larger than 500 square feet.

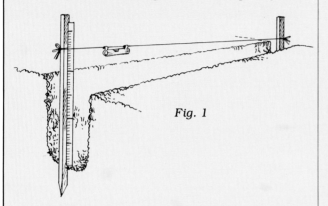

Fig. 1. Find a spot below the garden where the water can drain away without causing further problems, or where it can feed into a storm drain

or dry well. Dig a trench 2½ to 3 feet deep and 1 foot wide for 4-inch tile (1½ feet wide for 6-inch), from the lowest point of the problem area to the place where it will drain away. The trench should slope steeply enough for the water to drain off even if frost heaves the pipe a bit in the future; you should try for about 1 inch of drop every 10 feet. Stretch a level string on stakes, using a spirit level, and measure the amount of drop on the stakes.

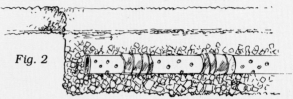

Fig. 2. Place gravel at the high point of the trench to cover the tile opening and to keep soil from entering; lay 3 inches of gravel along the bottom of the trench. Then lay tile on the gravel, sealing the joints by wrapping them in tar paper held in place with wire. Add more gravel, covering tile by 6 inches. Replace the subsoil, then topsoil, tamping as you fill, until trench is full.

the stems will become tall and ungainly, reaching out for more light.

When a garden plant is recommended for shady places, this nearly always means part shade. For these you can provide shade for part of the day, or dappled sunlight filtering through trees, or the high, bright shade cast by trees whose branches are far from the ground. You can achieve the second two conditions by judicious pruning. You may even want to cut some trees down if you have decided to grow flowers.

Many shade-loving plants such as astilbe, forget-me-not and impatiens can do very well in sunlight. The key is water. It is the sun's drying action that bothers them, not its light. If you grow them in sun, use a mulch, or water them in hot dry weather.

Water

Plants need water in order to absorb nutrients and to maintain the turgor (rigidity) of their leaves and stems. When they are too dry, they will let you know their displeasure by wilting or even dying. Plants' roots are hydrotropic—they move in the direction of water, whether it is right at the soil surface or deep below it. This is why a light sprin-

kling in hot weather may do more harm than good. The roots will grow upward to reach the water, then be parched by the sun. Most gardens need at least one inch of water per week—more in hot weather when evaporation is rapid. In many parts of the country rainfall provides enough water during most of the growing season, but in dry areas frequent watering or irrigation is necessary. You must also take into account the kinds of plants you are growing, and whether they like wet or dry conditions.

Gardeners sometimes disagree about when to water. Some claim that late watering will keep foliage from drying properly, thus encouraging fungus diseases. Others say that early watering causes the roots to come to the surface. The important thing is always to water thoroughly, whenever you do it. A soaker hose is a good way to achieve deep watering. If apprehensive about disease, water early enough in the day so that foliage is dry by nightfall.

Too much water is as bad as too little. If water sits in puddles in your garden, porous drainage tile that will drain the water off to a lower point (see above). You can also raise the bed above its original level, as shown in the box on page 45. Sometimes drainage problems can be corrected by simply grading the site with a rake and shovel so that the slope is in the right direction. But be sure you solve these problems before you plant your garden.

pH

The pH of the soil is the measure of its acidity or alkalinity. On a scale of 1 to 14, 7 is a "neutral" pH. As the numbers increase from 7 they indicate greater alkalinity; as they decrease they indicate greater acidity. Plants vary in their pH requirements, but most of our common garden plants prefer a slightly acid soil—that is, one with a pH between 6 and 6.8.

If you live in a region with a chalky, alkaline soil and your great love in life is the ericaceous group of plants—azaleas, rhododendrons, heathers etc.—all of which like acid soil, you can add a material such as ground sulfur to your soil every year, but you may have to forgo such plants if your soil is decidedly alkaline. If your soil is very acid, or if you have been using very acid materials such as bark for mulch, and you want to grow plants such as snapdragons, baby's breath, pinks, flax and Japanese anemones, then you should apply lime to your garden.

A simple soil test will tell you the pH of your soil and give you a sound basis from which to figure its needs. If you have a clay soil, lime improves soil texture by causing the fine particles to cling together and form "crumbs." To calculate the proper amount, add ten pounds of ground limestone per hundred square feet of garden to raise the soil one pH degree. The closer you can get to a pH of about 6.5, the more available mineral nutrients will be to your plants, and the more active soil organisms will be. But pH is not a big worry for most gardeners, because there is a considerable margin for error in either direction.

Temperature

Variation in temperature depends, of course, on the weather, and there is nothing you can do about that. But you can choose varieties that are hardy in your climate and control when and how they are planted. In a very cold winter with no snow cover, some of your less hardy or shallow-rooted plants won't survive. But if you have mulched them, their roots may not be killed and they may make it. A lot of freezing and thawing during the winter and early spring may heave out perennials if you have planted them late in the fall and they have not had time to root in sufficiently. Here again, mulch might have saved them.

The function of mulch is a somewhat tricky point. In the case of a shallow-rooted plant such as a dogwood or an azalea the mulch is there to maintain the soil's surface in an evenly moist condition and to keep it a few degrees warmer so that extreme cold does not injure the roots. But most plants should not be mulched until after the ground freezes, often as late as Christmas. By keeping the soil frozen, the mulch will prevent the plant from being heaved out of the soil by alternate thaws and freezes. Not only does this heaving expose the roots to air, drying them out and thereby killing them, the thawing and freezing also injures the roots directly by breaking down their cell structure. Areas that have a good snow cover on the ground all winter suffer less from these problems; in warmer areas you can use the boughs of discarded Christmas trees to trap whatever snow you get and keep it from melting. Salt hay (a grass native to seaside marshes) is also a good winter mulch, because it does not mat and contains no seeds that will sprout in garden soil.

Southern gardeners, while they can grow most plants that are grown in the North and many more besides, sometimes have to contend with extreme heat and drought. Here again, choosing the right species or varieties is important. Thorough watering and the choice of a site that receives shade at midday will often help a cold-climate plant to succeed in a southern garden.

MAKING A GARDEN
Design

In this book I have provided plans for you to work from. But since you may want to alter my schemes to suit your own needs, or to try an original garden based on a theme of your choosing, I will explain some of the principles

I tried to keep in mind when I designed these gardens.

Throughout the world—and throughout history—there have been many gardening conventions, and this book works within several. The one I have used most often, and the one most familiar to us, is the English flower border (we usually say "flower bed"). This is a particularly useful convention to master, for it teaches you how to combine many plants in a way that maintains harmony.

In a flower border there is actually not just one harmony but several. You must keep different flower and foliage colors, textures and heights in play at once, as well as to maintain a succession of bloom that keeps the whole thing a pleasing picture from spring through fall. In a sense you are creating, with more control and regularity, what nature creates in sunny meadows where, as the months pass, one combination of wild flowers gives way to another. Visualizing such a border is hard work; you must think in four dimensions at once—height, width, depth and time.

You need a few tricks that help keep a border in constant bloom, since it is a rare perennial that blooms all season; most of them last only a few weeks. Annuals are a great help in filling in gaps, especially since they start to make their finest show just as the August lull is approaching (after phlox and before chrysanthemums and asters) and continue blooming until frost. Keep some potted up, then plant them by burying the pots in the garden in spaces where color is needed. Foliage plants are useful as accents. Small shrubs can also be effective in the middle or back of the bed, for either their flowers, their foliage, their shape or their autumn color.

Such a garden works well only if it is thought out at the beginning. Some perennials are not easy to move, so parts of your scheme will always be fixed. How large do you want your bed to be? How much time will you have to take care of it? Which site will best satisfy the plants' needs?

You might also give some thought to how crowded you want your garden. Close planting will discourage weeds, look abundant sooner and enable plant groups to give one another physical support without staking. It can also lead to a tangled mess, with many plant losses, unless care is taken in the management of the garden. In the gardens in this book I have steered a middle course, but you can add to or subtract from the number of plants I suggest for each group.

Somehow a flower border frequently seems to have too little of this, too much of that. The spreaders and sprawlers try to overwhelm the more contained plants and the slow starters, unless you control them by dividing them and by staking. It is a rare garden that can simply be planted and forgotten, though there are some individual plants such as peonies and poppies that you can leave pretty much alone. The way to have a fine perennial garden is by dividing clumps and replanting the divisions (see box, p.24) in order to give them vigor, and to perform maintenance tasks such as weeding to keep the picture tidy and the plants in good health. The semipermanent nature of the bed is an asset; it means that the soil is always being cultivated as plants are moved and divided.

In choosing plants for the bed, I try to keep in mind the idea of habitats. You can compose a garden of woodland plants that like moist, shady places; you might do another that is sunny and dry like an upland meadow. Others might be moist and sunny, or shady and dry. The average garden, aims to accommodate sun-loving plants, and provides a soil that is average enough in moisture content, fertility, structure and pH that it will offend as few as possible. To plan this kind of garden, you generally begin with mainstay plants for each season, such as peonies for late spring, day lilies for midsummer, phlox for late summer and chrysanthemums for fall. Then you fill in around them, playing with form and color.

For the gardens in this book I have included a blend of colors for the background, middle ground and foreground, avoiding any large gaps. Some plants must be planted in clusters: a flax plant might look quite lonely all by itself; a heliopsis, on the other hand, will make a show even if you plant just one. Gaps will be less visible if you plant long, horizontal overlapping drifts rather than round clumps. Another design trick is to repeat plants several times in the garden, to give it a unity of design.

Preparing the Bed

Once the site is chosen, the size decided upon, and any necessary grading done, you should stake the bed out. This is done by making lines, circles and arcs with pointed sticks tied with string; use them just as if they were pencils, rulers and compasses. Informal curves can be made by laying down a garden hose or stout rope in the desired shape. When you have the lines you want, make a good sharp edging (see box, p. 197). The sod within the bed should be shaken out, to return precious topsoil to the garden, then placed on the compost heap.

Dig the bed at least a foot deep, removing rocks that are bigger than a jumbo-size egg. What about very large rocks? My rule of thumb used to be: if it wiggles at all when you nudge it with a crowbar, remove it. I once spent three months removing such boulders from a large garden, placing them around the sides. The result was a walled, sunken garden, not worth the labor. I now leave the largest boulders in the ground, adding topsoil and humus on top of them evenly to raise the soil level.

Incorporating organic matter, fertilizer and lime into a new bed is best done in fall in most areas. This gives the soil a chance to settle naturally, filling in air pockets and giving the added materials a chance to go to work on the soil. If you do these things in spring you may have to wait a long time before the ground is dry enough to work without compacting it and ruining the texture, and you will want to have the ground ready early in order to plant container-grown perennials and hardy annuals that you are growing from seed outdoors.

The Plants

There are several ways to obtain your plant material. You can grow plants from seed, buy them at a nursery or order them by mail. You can often get free plants from friends who are dividing their perennials, or who have bought more annuals than they know what to do with. Each method has its virtues. Growing from seed is the least costly. Plants potted at a nursery can be set out right away, and you can see what you are buying; look for the largest number of shoots, not the tall-est growth, or flowers in bloom. Mail order plants give you a wide range of choice, and are less expensive than plants potted in a nursery. They generally arrive dormant (without leaves) and bare-root (without soil). I like to pot them up and keep them in a sheltered location until they are hardened off (i.e., used to the outdoor world). Plants that arrive with tender green growth should not be put suddenly into a cold spring climate unless you can cover them with salt hay or plastic at night when a frost is expected, or with netting to shield them from burning sun. Potting them in compost will give you a pocket of rich soil you can add to the hole when planting.

Planting

How you put your plants in the ground will, of course, depend on what kind of plants they are.

Perennials: Before you begin, have everything ready: plants, fertilizer, tools and water. I usually set all my pots in the places I am going to plant them. If your plants are bare-root, however, you must never lay them

Ill. 1. To "heel in" bare-root plants, dig a trench deep enough to accommodate the roots, and lay the plants close together in the trench at a slant. Then fill the trench with moist soil, mounding it around the stems.

on the ground where sun and wind can dry them. Cover them with wet burlap or straw, or else heel them in (see above) until the moment you are ready to plant them.

To plant perennials, dig a generous hole with a trowel or spade, depending on the size of the plant. Sprinkle in a tablespoonful of superphosphate or a small handful of bone meal and work it well into the soil. Plant as shown on opposite page.

Annuals: Buying nursery-grown annuals saves a lot of time and is often worth the added cost. When planting annuals from flats or little plastic boxes, moisten them first

PLANTING PERENNIALS

Fig. 1

To plant a typical fibrous-rooted perennial, dig a hole in loose, well-prepared soil. Suspend the plant so that the crown (the place where stems and roots join) is level with the soil surface. Fill the hole with soil, tamping as you go to get rid of air pockets.

Fig. 2

To plant bearded iris, hold plant against the side of the hole, with roots level with the top of the soil, or slightly above it. If drainage is less than perfect, mound soil slightly.

Fig. 3

To plant oriental poppies, dig a hole deep enough to accommodate the taproot, with the crown 1 to 2 inches below the soil surface. Fill the hole with soil and tamp firmly but gently.

Fig. 4

To plant peonies, dig a large hole and fill the bottom with compost or humus, mixing this into the soil at the bottom of the hole. Stamp on the mixture to compact it firmly, and bring it to a level where the peony root can sit on the bottom of the hole with its pink "eyes" (buds) 1 to 2 inches below the soil surface. Then fill the hole very gently with soil, tamping with your fingers to remove all air pockets.

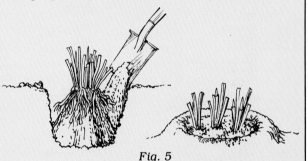

Fig. 5

To plant day lilies, dig a large hole with a cone-shaped mound of compost or enriched soil in the center. Spread roots over the sides of the mound, keeping the plant's crown level with the soil surface. Several divisions may be planted at once, by spreading roots on different sides of the mound. Fill hole with soil and tamp firmly. A saucerlike ring of earth around the clump will help to retain moisture. Mulch if planted in fall, to prevent heaving.

so that the soil ball around the roots comes out intact. If they are in peat pots, bury the pot completely so that the rim does not act like a wick, drawing moisture away from the plant. Many annuals such as alyssum, larkspur, California poppies, mignonette and sweet peas can be sown outdoors as soon as the ground has thawed. These are called "hardy annuals." "Tender annuals" such as zinnias, marigolds, petunias, ageratum, cosmos and nicotiana are usually better if started indoors or sown outdoors after danger of frost has passed. Some annuals, such as bachelor's buttons and love-in-a-mist, can be sown in fall for spring bloom, and in zones 8–10 you can sow annuals in fall that will bloom in midwinter.

Biennials: The seeds of biennials can be sown during the growing season (usually midsummer) to bloom the following year. Some common examples are Canterbury bells, foxgloves and pansies. Biennials can be handled in several ways. Sowing directly in the spot where they are to bloom leaves a gap until the following season and doesn't provide the young seedlings with much light. Most gardeners grow them in a separate little nursery bed, in a row in the vegetable garden or in a cold frame. A small plot such as this is a handy thing to have anyway, for propagating, for keeping extra plants on hand or for trying out new varieties. Biennials can also be purchased as started plants and set out in the spring. They will often self-sow near the original clump, and you can keep them going there continuously.

Bulbs: Spring-blooming bulbs are planted early in the fall, to ensure good root development. If you have just dug a new border in fall and the plan calls for bulbs, it would be best to plant them the following fall, after the border has settled and the other plants in it have become established. You can then find appropriate spaces to put the bulbs, making small clusters or drifts between clumps of perennials. I try to place them next to plants whose foliage will hide that of the bulbs, for bulb leaves must, alas, be left to die a natural death. If you cut them back too soon there will not be enough nourishment for the bulb. Most summer- or fall-blooming bulbs are planted in spring along with the rest of your garden.

Planting depth for bulbs varies with the type of bulb. I plant tulips and daffodils with a spade, making a hole wide enough to set three to six bulbs about three or four inches apart. I work about a tablespoonful of superphosphate or a handful of bone meal very thoroughly into the bottom of the hole, set the bulbs in it, and replace the soil, tamping firmly. (This measurement for superphosphate is approximate, since commercial preparations vary in their degree of concentration.) Be sure you plant all bulbs and tubers right side up. This is sometimes a confusing matter, but you can usually see some roots, live or withered, on the bottom side.

Shrubs and Trees

There is an expression: "Give a ten-dollar shrub a fifty-dollar hole." How you provide it with these luxurious accommodations will depend partly on whether the plant is balled-and-burlapped, container-grown or bare-root as shown at right. With all of them, however, the idea is to give the shrub or tree a pocket of good soil, easily penetrated by roots but without air spaces, and enriched with organic matter and fertilizer. The fewer nutrients and less organic matter you have in your soil, and the more compacted it is, the bigger your hole should be. With a large shrub or tree, part of the pocket will be at subsoil level, and you will need to provide plenty of enrichment in the bottom of the hole. Use sod clumps compost, rotted manure or wet peat moss. Make sure you have allowed enough depth so that the top of the root ball is level with the soil surface. (To check lay a

tool handle or long stake across the hole, then measure from the center of the handle to the bottom.) Set the plant carefully in the hole, checking the depth and adding more soil and organic matter around the ball, tamping firmly as you fill the hole to get rid of air pockets.

PLANTING SHRUBS AND TREES

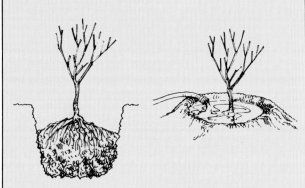

To plant a bare-root shrub, dig a hole several inches deeper than needed to accommodate the roots. To determine proper planting depth, hold the plant so that the soil surface is at the same point it was in the nursery where the plant was grown. Fill the bottom of the hole with topsoil mixed with organic matter. Cover the roots with enriched soil, tamping with your foot as you go, and making sure there are no air pockets. Water thoroughly. After the water has settled into the soil, fill in the rest of the hole, tamping soil. Then build a saucerlike ring around the plant, several inches high, firming the ring. Fill the "saucer" with water.

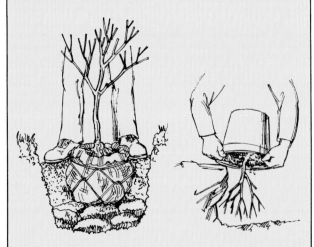

Plant balled-and-burlapped trees and shrubs as shown, with clumps of sod upside down in the bottom of the hole. To free a plant from its pot, turn it upside down and rap the rim of the pot on a hard object. Grasp the stem near the base and gently pull out the plant, keeping the earth around it as intact as possible.

Always handle a root ball very carefully so that it does not break apart. Unless the cloth and ties around the ball are made of plastic or other material that will not rot, leave them be. They will soon disintegrate. You may, however, peel back the burlap a little around the base of the stem or trunk, burying the loose pieces well in the soil so that they do not draw moisture from the root ball into the air. When the hole is about three-fourths full, add water with a hose, poking the hose into the bottom of the hole. After all the water has sunk in, fill the rest of the hole, making a saucer around the trunk as shown. Subsoil you have removed from the bottom of the hole is useful for this purpose.

A pot-grown shrub sometimes shows a hard tangle of matted roots when you remove it from the pot. Poke at these with a knife until you have loosened them up. Bare-root shrubs must be kept moist until planting. To give them a real boost, the roots can be "puddled in." To do this, mix soil and water in a bucket until they have formed a thick soup; swish the roots in this mixture for a few minutes until they are well coated.

To plant a very large balled shrub or tree single-handedly, roll it carefully on its side until it is next to the spot where you want to plant it. Dig a hole about four inches deeper than the ball and lay clumps of sod in the bottom. Roll the ball into the hole and adjust its height, also correcting any tilt, by adding and removing sod clumps. You can do this with one hand while you tilt the trunk with your other hand or with your foot.

MAINTENANCE CHORES

When a garden is new you want it to fill up quickly. Perennial gardens, especially, tend to be sparse the first year. You wait eagerly for your new plants to get bushy, for the bare earth to disappear, for the spots of color to turn into masses. In subsequent years you are more concerned with holding the garden back. The phlox has leaped out of control. The oenothera has established an empire. The bee balm is dispatching underground shoots like guerrilla bands through the jungles of five-foot-tall asters. Instead of building your garden, you seem to be forever taking things out of it.

Weeding

The most important thing to remove from a garden is the weeds. Weeds compete for light, water, nutrients, air—everything that a plant needs to make it grow well.

Flower gardens need to be weeded on hands and knees to get in under the clumps of foliage. Pull the weeds out, grasping the stems at or below soil level. Keep a pointed trowel in one hand, or nearby, to urge out any that threaten to break off, because some roots left in the soil will keep growing. Weeding bare-handed is easier, because you can feel underground roots. For grassy, carpet-like weeds, grab them like a fistful of hair and scalp them by running a trowel just under the surface and shaking out the clump. Always leave as much of the garden soil behind as possible. For taprooted demons such as dandelions, the best solution is to get them while they are still small and can be yanked out whole. Those long forked diggers are fine if you stick them in at just the right angle, but it is easy to go wrong. I find it is sometimes better to loosen the soil around them with a trowel, then try yanking.

The hardest time to weed is in early spring when everything is tiny and you cannot tell what is what. Usually you can recognize an established perennial because it is a clump, with hard little "eyes," or buds, visible just at soil surface level, and a root system that offers strong resistance if you go after it by accident. Self-sown plants are a different matter, and you just have to learn to recognize them by trial and error. Train yourself to look at foliage all year long, not just the flowers.

Deadheading

Deadheading refers to the practice of removing flowers after they have passed their prime (see Ill. 2, p. 22). Seed heads that have formed are removed too, but the goal is to remove the flower head before it has set its seed. Not only does it make the garden look tidy, it also keeps the plant from putting its energy into making seeds—energy you want it to spend on root growth. Deadheading will also often trick the plant into blooming repeatedly; if it has been denied the chance to set seed it may try again by producing more flowers. Another benefit of deadheading is that it keeps the plant from self-sowing when you don't want it to. Seedlings will revert to their original prehybrid forms, and they may be forms you do not like, such as magenta phlox, or muddy yellow-brown iris.

A good rule of thumb in gardening is: if it's dead, remove it. Dead plant matter invites disease. Sometimes you will want to leave attractive seed heads on plants in the fall and winter, but even these should be harvested or discarded eventually, to make a fresh start in spring.

How do you tell whether a plant is dead? With a herbaceous plant, there are no little buds, or "eyes," poking up from the roots in

Ill. 2. Deadheading: remove spent blooms as shown.

spring, and the clump lifts out without resistance. With woody plants, scratch the bark of a stem with a knife or your fingernail; if it is green underneath, that stem is alive.

Pruning and Pinching

Pruning applies to shrubs and trees, and is too large a subject to cover adequately here, though an art well worth learning. But here are a few simple guidelines to remember:

1. Remove dead matter.

2. When pruning a shrub or tree, try to keep the shape the way the plant normally grows, unless you are creating topiary or for some other reason want a formal shape. If it is a weeping plant, let it weep. Most shrubs appreciate an occasional thinning out from the inside, removing several large branches from the base.

3. The time of year you choose to prune will also depend on what kind of plant you are dealing with. In general, you should prune flowering shrubs just after they have bloomed, before new buds have formed. If you cut off the buds there will be fewer blossoms next year. Thus you would prune spring-blooming

shrubs in late spring or early summer; summer-blooming in late summer, fall or early spring.

Ill. 3. Pinching back: when planting branches pinch back each new shoot.

Pinching is a technique applied to some annuals and late-blooming perennials to encourage branching and more bloom. When the plants are about six inches tall, the tip of the central shoot is pinched off. Branches that are then formed are pinched when they in turn are six inches long. Some plants that respond well to pinching are chrysanthemums and asters. Stop pinching them in mid-July so that flower buds can form.

Staking

This practice is largely a matter of personal preference. I would rather look at a floppy plant than a green stake with plastic ribbons around it. I try to plant gardens in sheltered locations, or contrive unobtrusive means of staking (see facing page). Place a stake behind a plant when it is so tall that the next storm might knock it over. Use soft green twine, and hide it in the leaves. Brush and other natural materials can also be used. Break off a twiggy branch of a tree or shrub and "plant" it in the ground next to a newly-planted perennial.

Another nice trick is to peg down a tall plant—such as an aster—before the shoots are more than a foot or two high, using small metal hoops that look like little croquet wickets. The stems can then grow straight up from the point at which they are pegged, and will look shorter.

Mulching

As I explained above, mulch will protect plants from cold and heaving in winter. But mulch has other uses as well. It forms a barrier that keeps weed seeds from sprouting, it conserves moisture, and it keeps roots cool in

STAKING PERENNIALS

Staking with brush: twiggy sections of woody shrubs are "planted" in the ground before the plants to be staked have attained their full growth. By the time the flowers are blooming, the foliage will hide the brush.

Using stakes: green bamboo stakes can be purchased in many sizes, or you may use stakes and dowels purchased at a lumberyard. Attach the plants with loops of soft string tied loosely in a figure 8 so that the stems are not injured.

Staking peonies: A special three-legged wire ring can be purchased and placed around the plant before it blooms in spring. The foliage will soon hide the ring, which will keep the flowers from flopping onto the ground.

hot weather. It gives the garden a tidy, cared-for appearance. Mulch also has its drawbacks. It attracts slugs and rodents. It can keep the crowns of perennials too damp—especially in late winter and early spring—so that they rot. While weeds that seed themselves in mulch are easier to pull up than weeds rooted in soil, the weeds that come up from roots under the soil are hard to pull up without disturbing the mulch and depositing soil on top of it where more weeds can grow. It is also hard to rearrange and divide plants without messing up the mulch.

The way to deal with this in a perennial bed is not to think of the mulch as a permanent cover (as for a shrub planting), but as a seasonal one. As soon as your perennials are large enough to be recognizable, give the garden its first serious spring poke-around, being careful of late starters such as butterfly weed and platycodon. Pull out the first weeds, clean up any leftover debris and apply fertilizer and lime. Then apply a new mulch about two inches deep, but shallower close to the bases of the clumps, leaving spaces where you will be seeding in annuals.

Mulch is a man-made reconstruction of a forest floor, which has its own natural mulch of leaves, the leaf mold under them and the even finer layer under that called duff. To imitate this luxurious carpet use a light material such as buckwheat hulls, compost, salt hay, rotted manure, composted peat moss, pine needles or "root mulch" (ground-up roots). Actual leaf mold is the best of all, but should not be taken from the woods in large amounts, because there it is needed by the trees and other growth. Make your own by composting leaves or putting them through a shredder.

The beauty of all these materials is that they add organic matter to the soil when you turn them under. Most of them are quite acid, however, and you should add lime to the soil if you use them.

Propagation

Most garden perennials are propagated by division. This simple method takes advantage of the way the plant reproduces most vigorously in nature. In the fall, most perennials make side shoots at the edges of the original clump, which remain dormant through the winter. Removing and replanting these shoots not only makes new plants but rejuvenates the clump as well. How large you make each division depends on whether you want many new plants or a few that will bloom very freely the first season. In cold climates it is best to wait until spring, or to plant fall divisions in a cold frame.

Most taprooted plants such as Oriental poppies, unless absolutely necessary, should be neither moved nor divided, but propagated by stem or root cuttings. Cuttings are

DIVIDING PERENNIALS

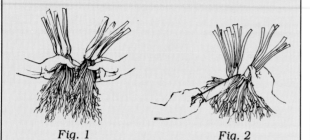

Fig. 1   Fig. 2

Many perennials, such as the hosta shown, can be pulled apart easily with the fingers (Fig. 1). Often a sharp knife is helpful in prying apart tough masses of roots, and even cutting them, as with the day lily shown (Fig. 2).

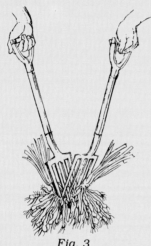

Fig. 3

Very large clumps may be pried apart with two digging forks intertwined back to back.

Fig. 4

A number of perennials, such as asters, heliopsis and chrysanthemums (shown), are divided by removing side shoots and replanting them. Discard the dead, woody center.

a good method of propagation if you have a greenhouse or even a cold frame and want to produce plants in large numbers.

Pests and Diseases

Recent knowledge of the harmful effects of insecticides and other pest killers has made gardeners more cautious about the use of poisons, but there are still gardeners who see a few bugs and spray everything in sight.

They do not know what "bug" they are trying to control, whether it is at a stage of its life where a spray can kill it. They use a beetle spray to attack mites, or they will attack insects when a disease is really the trouble.

You do not want to let serious problems get out of control. Occasionally plants that you buy are infested with pests that can threaten your whole garden; these should be burned immediately. One such mass destroyer is cyclamen mite, which lives in the crowns of plants, causing odd distortions in the leaves and central shoots. Another dangerous pest is the root nematode, a wirelike "worm" that attacks the roots of plants and causes stunted, distorted growth. Let an expert such as your Cooperative Extension agent identify a sample of the problem plant and advise you on treatment.

Most pests that attack flower gardens are not dangerous and are easy to control with mechanical means. Japanese beetles can be dropped in a jar of kerosene; traps which use sex hormones as a lure, are also very effective. Soapsuds can be sprayed on aphids. Slugs can be discouraged with cinders that hurt their feet. Leaf miner on columbine leaves is ugly, but seldom kills the plant; pick off infested leaves if they annoy you.

Often a stretch of muggy midsummer weather will bring a depressing collection of fungus diseases with it, such as leaf spot, powdery mildew and botrytis. I treat with a systemic fungicide. Keep the garden free of dead plant matter and the plants thinned to permit good circulation of air.

Do not use chemical poisons if there is a safer way to solve the problem, and never use them indiscriminately. If you use poisons, follow the instruction on the label to the letter. Do not spray on windy days, and try very hard not to get chemical sprays on flowers. Any flowering plant is being visited by insects that are beneficial to the plant and to the ecology in general. Store and dispose of chemicals safely, and if your area does not have approved disposal centers for toxic products, do not buy them. Wear rubber gloves when handling chemicals; avoid inhaling them or in any way contaminating people, pets, livestock, wild animals, and the water they drink.

A Fragrance Garden

The scents of plants are like unseen ghosts. They sneak up on you as you round a turn in the garden, before you can see the plants from which they came. Aromas float into a house through open doors and windows, intruding on the business of the indoor world. They hide in overgrown gardens, where the weeder's hand might suddenly stir up the freshness of mint or thyme.

Scents call up memories of the past, and transform an ordinary present into a romantic idyll, for they are not only invisible spirits but powerful ones. Perhaps this is because the chemistry of many

plant odors is tied to the plants' reproductive functions and that of the insects that fertilize them. They seem to touch something in the human sexual chemistry as well.

The ancient world was ever respectful of the mysteries of scent. Some odors were even considered holy. The ancient Egyptians buried their dead among treasured vials of perfume; the ancient Greeks and Romans sent incense and other sacred

© PAMELA HARPER

This garden at Mill House, a private garden in Oxfordshire, England, bursts with fragrance. Wallflowers bloom in the foreground with Chinese wisteria at left. In the background, white lilacs are planted next to red Clematis montana.

odors heavenward to reach their deities, as some worshipers still do today. In the Middle Ages, perfumes, which were thought to purify foul air, were considered such potent weapons against plagues that perfume-sellers were thought to be immune to disease just by handling them. As today's profusion of perfume advertising testifies, our own age sets great store by the romantic power of flower fragrances.

Oddly enough, modern gardens have become more and more scentless. Bigger, hardier, more bepetaled flowers are the goal of the hybridizers, and while the new plants are often superior in many ways to old favorites, they are rarely more fragrant. Scent is a ghost you find in old gardens, or in plantings of old-fashioned varieties. It is also found aplenty in gardens for the blind, who are particularly attuned to scent, and in herb beds where the subtle scents of foliage are treasured.

A garden planted for fragrance is thus an unusual creation, and a welcome one. By its very nature it is idiosyncratic and personal, just as everyone's body chemistry is personal. Not only do different people like different odors, but they perceive them differently. Sweet alyssum, for instance, may or

may not smell like new-mown hay to your nose. You may also have strong ideas about how scents should be mixed together, an art even more difficult than the mixing of color. It is nearly impossible to describe a scent without comparing it to something else; you must say that it is "like lemon" or "like violets" or some such. All you are really saying is that the essential oils found in one plant are chemically similar to ones found in something that is better known. Among that remarkable group of plants, the scented geraniums, for example, are varieties that are said to smell like apples, coconut, chocolate, pine, cinnamon and orange, to name only a few. There are even scents shared, because of similar chemistry, by plants and animals, such as the smell of skunk and skunk cabbage.

For many of these subtleties you must train your nose by paying more attention to scents, by fingering leaves and tracking down odd aromas when the wind brings them to you. Do your sniffing on days that are a bit damp and not too windy, not too hot and not too cold. Look for the most luscious fragrance in flowers that are white and naturally double, not made so by hybridization. Find scent in all the parts—petals, leaves, stems, roots, bark, seeds, resins—of growing things. Some are fragrant only at certain times of day—or night. Certain flowers, such as honeysuckle, send their fragrance far across the yard; for others, such as peonies, you must bury your nose in their petals.

There are different ways to arrange a fragrance garden. Gardens for the blind, for example, are often set in raised beds, so that the plants are at nose level; you may want to adopt this idea. Some people prefer to have their scents set apart from one another, with scentless plants in between, so that the fragrances do not mingle. One way to achieve this would be to plan your garden along a meandering path, so that you come upon individual scents one by one. Another way would be to plant around the periphery of a large lawn. On the other hand, you may want to mingle aromas deliberately, concentrating them all in a "scent pocket" where there is always fragrant air.

My garden here uses the last approach. It is small and partly enclosed by shrubs, all of which bear fragrant flowers. It is designed to be planted near a window, so that the trapped fragrance can enter the house. In addition to shrubs, there are fragrant annuals, perennials, bulbs and herbs. In some plants it is the flowers that are fragrant; in others it is the leaves. Furthermore, the blooming season lasts from spring until the end of summer, so different odors predominate at different times.

Once properly established, it is a very easy garden to maintain. The shrubs need almost no pruning, the flower beds are small, and there is no lawn to mow, just ground covers that can spread to their heart's content. It is a garden for someone who, quite literally, likes to sit back, enjoy life and take the time to smell the flowers.

PLAN OF THE GARDEN

The focal point of this garden is a window. On its sill grow a number of different scented geraniums, as well as rosemary and any other tender herbs that must be protected in winter. In mild weather, place these plants either inside or outside your window screen, depending on whether you want to pick them from indoors or outdoors. Below the win-

dowsill are other "nose herbs," as they were once called; plants with fragrant foliage used more for "strewing" and sweetening musty indoor corners than for cooking or curing ills. The window is surrounded by a good sturdy trellis to support fragrant climbing plants: sweet peas, roses and the subtly sweet autumn clematis. The trellis enables these plants to climb and frame the window without injuring the house. (The trellis on p. 154 can be adapted to this garden.) They will not be visible from indoors, but their fragrance will waft into the house.

Seen from the outside, the window is surrounded by flowers in different pastel shades mixed with white. Some of the nose herbs have grayish or white leaves—lavender cotton, and *Artemisia stellerana*, sometimes called dusty miller or old woman. The hues of the sweet peas and stocks are soft, not gaudy. Mixed in with the fragrant annual stocks are some of the night-scented kind—*Matthiola bicornis*—whose flowers are drab to the eye, but whose fragrance will drift into the house on warm summer nights. The rose

This walk at Hidcote Manor, one of the loveliest gardens in England, is lined with sweet-scented mock orange bushes and lavender.

THE FRAGRANCE GARDEN

PLAN OF THE FRAGRANCE GARDEN (MIDSUMMER) ³/₈″ = 1′

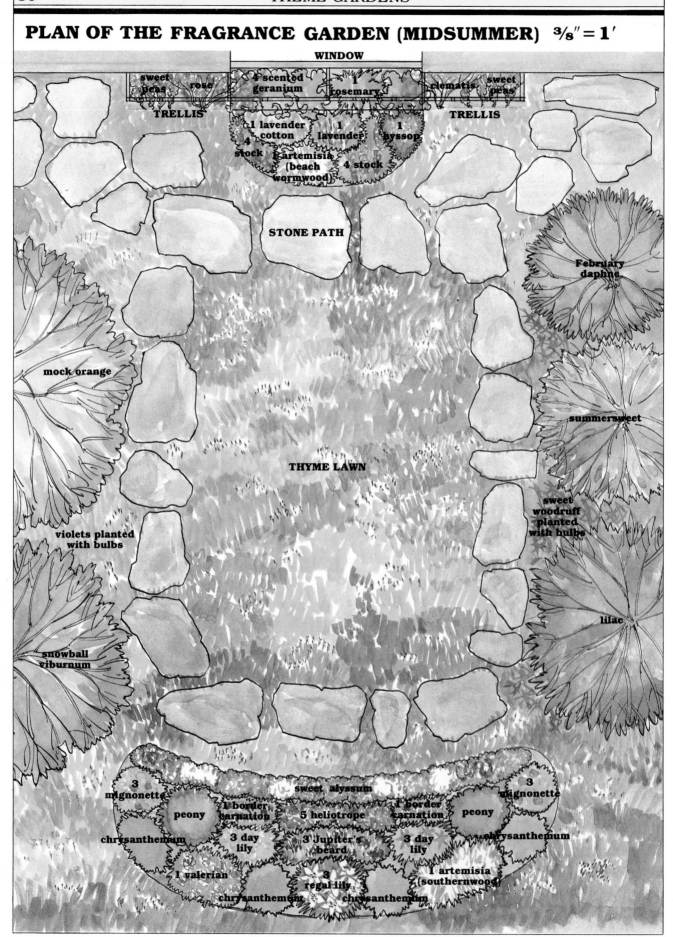

WINDOW

sweet peas

rose

4 scented geranium

1 rosemary

clematis

sweet peas

TRELLIS

TRELLIS

1 lavender cotton

1 lavender

1 hyssop

4 stock

1 artemisia (beach wormwood)

4 stock

STONE PATH

February daphne

mock orange

summersweet

THYME LAWN

sweet woodruff planted with bulbs

violets planted with bulbs

lilac

snowball viburnum

sweet alyssum

3 mignonette

3 mignonette

peony

1 border carnation

5 heliotrope

1 border carnation

peony

chrysanthemum

3 day lily

3 Jupiter's beard

3 day lily

chrysanthemum

1 valerian

3 regal lily

1 artemisia (southernwood)

chrysanthemum

chrysanthemum

THE GARDEN IN SPRING

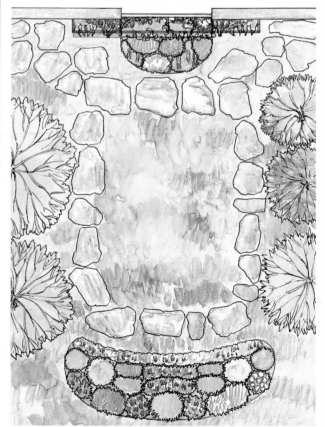

THE GARDEN IN FALL

could be any fragrant climber, but a pink or coral shade would look nicest, if you can find one that does well in your region. The most unusual plants in the group are the scented geraniums, of which there are several hundred known varieties, each giving off a different scent when the leaves are rubbed. Nurseries that specialize in them carry many different varieties. Most scented geraniums bear bright pink blossoms, some more showy than others.

The shrub plantings provide spring fragrance and color, except for summersweet, of course, which blooms in late July and August. The first shrub to bloom is *Daphne mezereum*, often called February daphne because it will bloom that early in mild climates and/or sheltered locations, though it may bloom as late as early April where it is colder. The lilacs and snowball viburnum provide rich, sweet smells in May, followed quickly by the equally heady mock orange. The shrub groupings are underplanted with two fragrant ground covers, violets and sweet woodruff. Both appreciate the shade cast by the shrubs in summer. In spring you can have fragrant bulbs come up through this cover—the ones here are snowflakes, poet's narcissus and hyacinths.

From indoors, there should be a focal point for the eye, and so a small flower garden is placed in this line of vision. It is a mixture of annuals and perennials, most with fragrant flowers, some with fragrant foliage. Unlike the windowsill garden, the flowers here are bright and showy, so that they can be appreciated at a distance. It is primarily a summer border, beginning in June with peonies, followed by border carnations, regal lilies, day lilies, Jupiter's-beard and valerian, along with the annuals—sweet alyssum, mignonette and heliotrope. But there will still be many blooms when fall comes—the annuals, Jupiter's-beard and the October-blooming chrysanthemums. The white southernwood has pungent leaves, and the carnations have a spicy fragrance in both their leaves and their flowers.

The center of the garden is a thyme lawn. (Paths are simply stones set in the earth; natural flat ones would look best, but cut flagstones would also be appropriate. The latter ought to be set in sand for stability, but natural ones can take some winter frost heaving without looking lopsided.) Plant as many different varieties of thyme as you can find (see Plant List, p. 35). Nurseries that specialize in herbs often sell dozens. Plant them no more than a foot apart. All have foliage that releases a pleasant scent when walked on, but each is a different color (green, white, gold, gray, variegated) and the blossoms are varying shades of pink, red and purple, blooming at different times. Mixing them will give a rich tapestry effect, and you can keep adding new varieties as you come across them. The thyme should be allowed to creep naturally around the stones, stopping only at the herb and flower beds, which should be edged neatly with a square shovel, or with a permanent edging material such as bricks or metal edging strips (see box, p. 197). The violets and woodruff, can grow into the thyme.

SITE

Pick a good sunny window, one that you will sit next to often. Ideally it will be a window that is attractive from the outside as well. It could even be a set of French doors, with the herbs and the geraniums set off to either side. A sheltered exposure is best, for you want the air to be fairly still. A gentle breeze will bring lovely smells into the house with it, but a strong wind will simply dispel them. The shrubs will provide some protection.

Choose a site with good drainage. The herbs, especially, like well-drained soil a little on the sandy side. If rain pours off your eaves where you want your fragrance garden, either channel it away with gutters on the roof or plant so that nothing grows directly beneath the drip line.

SACHETS, SWEET BAGS AND POTPOURRIS

If you are growing scented plants, you may want to try your hand at preserving some. It is not difficult. Pick leaves just before the plant blooms, when essential oils are strongest; pick petals and whole blossoms when they are at the peak of perfection. All should be harvested on a sunny morning when everything is perfectly dry. As you collect them, place them on screens for better air circulation (Fig. 1) in a spot where it is dry and still, stirring them often until they are crisp. You could also use the sand method for drying flowers described in the Gray Garden (see p. 134). Store in airtight jars out of the sunlight. Your mixtures will keep their scent longer if you add a fixative such as gum benzoin, or orris root (the dried root of Iris germanica florentina; grind it with a mortar and pestle). Mix about 1½ teaspoons of fixative into each cup of leaves and petals, leaving it to cure in the jar for several weeks or longer.

Fig. 1

For decorative potpourris, leave some of the flowers whole, especially rosebuds. Place in open bowls when dried and cured. For sachets, crush the dried mixture, cure it and stitch it up into squares of taffeta or some other slightly porous fabric, tying the corners with ribbons if you wish. For sweet bags, do the same, but gather one side of the square and tie it tightly with a ribbon. Hang the bags over the arms of chairs, in closets or any other place where you want fragrance (Fig. 2).

Fig. 2

Most of the recipes one sees for these mixtures rely heavily on roses and lavender. Lemon verbena (Aloysia triphylla) is another old favorite, prized for its fragrant leaves. Any of the fragrant leaves or petals in this garden might be combined, especially the flowers of stock, lilac, border carnations and valerian, or the leaves of thyme, rosemary and sage. The herbs and flowers may be kept separate or used together. You might also mix them with spices from your kitchen, such as nutmeg and cinnamon, or add the citrus scents of dried orange and lemon rind. Make a strong concoction, with tansy and wormwood, to keep moths away. A superb collection of old recipes for all of these, and other potions such as "sweet waters," may be found in a book written fifty years ago: Eleanour Sinclair Rohde's The Scented Garden. In those days scent-craft was practiced in earnest ("Take a thousand Damask Roses . . ."). But you may find that you like your own personal recipes best of all.

GROWING INSTRUCTIONS

The more care you take in planting this garden, the less work you will have to do later on. Give the rose and the herbs good drainage, installing a layer of gravel beneath the topsoil if necessary. Use lime when you plant the clematis, and plenty of fertilizer when you plant the sweet peas. Make the trellis sturdy. Mulch the flower border with shredded bark, buckwheat hulls or leaf mold, about two inches deep. (Bark and buckwheat hulls can be bought in plastic bags, an economical method when the garden is this small.) Add a little more mulch in May each year, just as the weeds are getting serious, and you will not have many of them. The thyme, woodruff and violets, once established, will suppress most weeds, but until this happens, you will need to pull out weeds and grass, being careful not to dislodge the roots of the thyme.

Care for the tender herbs much as you would any houseplants, taking them in before a freeze, cutting them back when leggy and fertilizing only occasionally during winter when they are "resting." Spring planting is preferable for just about all these plants, except for the spring bulbs. The annuals can all be grown from seed sown directly in the garden in spring.

ADDITIONS AND SUBSTITUTIONS

To make this garden smaller you could eliminate a shrub or two. You could also combine the herb bed with the flower border, though it might be wise to put some distance between the heliotrope and the night-scented stock. Both have a very strong aroma in the evening, and should enrapture only one part of the garden at a time. If you do not want to go to the trouble of starting a thyme lawn, plant ordinary grass or fragrant white clover.

To expand the garden, make the beds larger and add more fragrant plants—until your nose tells you to stop. You could try more night-scented flowers such as nicotiana, tuberoses, dame's rocket (Hesperis matronalis) and bouncing bet (Saponaria officinalis). More lilacs could be added; they will help shelter the garden, and can be chosen to provide early, middle and late bloom, so that you can have the lilac scent for a long time. More Dianthus species, both annual

The fragrance garden at Hatfield House in England, planted by Lady Salisbury, has plants in a raised bed: catmint, violas, nicotiana, santolina and roses.

and perennial, may be planted, except for sweet william (D. barbatus), which does not smell. Fragrant roses can be added indefinitely, as well as honeysuckles, both the shrub and vine forms. There are many bulb-grown plants, such as hyacinths and some tulips, that have a fragrance. Lily of the valley could grow along with the sweet woodruff and the violets.

In warm climates you will not have much luck with sweet woodruff, but you can grow many special fragrant plants that northern gardeners cannot. Try star jasmine (Trachelospermum jasminoides) or the true jasmines (Jasminum species), and more of the Daphne genus, especially D. odora. Grow passionflower (Passiflora), Stephanotis floribunda, gardenias, Pittosporum species, especially P. floribundum and P. viridiflorum, citrus fruits, box and sweet bay. In cold areas (zones 2 to 4) you may not be able to grow lavender or santolina outdoors, even in a sheltered bed. Grow them as house plants that you move outdoors in summer, setting the pots either in or on the ground. In dry climates you will probably concentrate more on the fragrant-leafed herbs that do so well there, but there are many fragrant flowers that do well in low-moisture areas: lilies, pinks, sweet peas, freesias, hyacinths, roses and dame's rocket among them.

PLANT LIST FOR FRAGRANCE GARDEN

ANNUALS AND TENDER PERENNIALS

ALYSSUM, SWEET. *Lobularia maritima.* White, purple, pink or mixed shades. Grows 4–6 inches tall and blooms from late spring to frost. Tiny, fragrant blossoms make a carpet. Easily grown from seed.

GERANIUM, SCENTED. *Pelargonium* species, hybrids and varieties. Perennial in zones 9–10. These include *P. graveolens* (rose-scented leaves, lavender flowers), *P. tomentosum* (peppermint scent, large fuzzy leaves), *P. crispum* (lemon scent, small leaves, ruffled pink flowers), *P. 'Clorinda'* (eucalyptus scent, showy pink flowers), *P. 'Mrs. Kingsley'* (mint scent, showy pink flowers), *P. denticulatum* (pine scent, finely cut foliage, pink flowers), *P. fragrans* 'Showy Nutmeg' (nutmeg scent) and many, many more. Geraniums like full sun. Let soil almost dry out between waterings. Lower leaves will yellow if plant is too dry. Use good potting soil and fertilize often in summer (up to once every two weeks) and less often in winter (as little as once every two months). Cut back if leggy.

HELIOTROPE, COMMON. *Heliotropium arborescens.* Grows 1–2 feet tall, with huge clusters of small, richly fragrant flowers, usually purple. Likes rich soil and full sun. Sow seeds indoors in the winter for spring planting, or buy

started plants and set out after last frost.

LAVENDER COTTON. *Santolina chamaecyparissus.* Perennial as far north as zone 7, sometimes zone 6 with protection. In colder zones, winter indoors. Shrublike, it grows up to 2 feet tall and more in warm climates, 1 foot in cool ones. Aromatic, lacy silver-gray leaves. Prune the plant severely several times a year to keep it from getting too woody. Likes sun and light, sandy soil, not too much moisture.

MIGNONETTE, COMMON. *Reseda odorata.* Grows about 1 foot tall, with extremely fragrant, short, thick spikes of yellowish flowers. Likes rich, cool soil. Sow seeds in the ground after danger of frost, or indoors in flats. Successive sowings will prolong blooming season.

ROSEMARY. *Rosmarinus officinalis.* Hardy in zones 8–10, and up to zone 6 with protection. Otherwise winter indoors. Shrublike, growing up

to 2 feet tall in cool climates, much larger in warm ones. Likes sun, well-drained soil, lime. Indoors, grow like geraniums, above. Has narrow, pungent-scented leaves and small lavender-blue flowers in winter or early spring.

STOCK, COMMON. *Matthiola incana,* 'Annua' hybrids. Plant trysomic strain in hot climates, others in cooler regions. Common stocks grow 1–3 feet tall and bear showy spikes of usually double flowers, in shades of pink, purple, red and white.

STOCK, NIGHT-SCENTED (EVENING). *Matthiola bicornis.* Grows 1–1½ feet tall and bears small lavender flowers that usually close during the day but release a strong, delightful fragrance at night. Note the "two-horned" seedpods that give it the name *bicornis.* Both stocks are annuals and prefer sun, fairly rich soil and ample moisture. Sow seeds in the ground in March or April; thin out the weaker (usually single-flowered) seedlings so that plants are 10–12 inches apart. Plant in fall in warm climates for winter and spring bloom.

SWEET PEA. *Lathyrus odoratus.* Climbs 5–10 feet high by means of tendrils. Bears flowers in shades of pink, red, blue, coral, violet and white. Large, showy hybrids are apt to be less fragrant than the smaller, old-fashioned varieties. Choose heat-resistant strains for hot, arid regions. Sow in ground in early spring, 3 inches apart, in fertile soil,

soaking seeds first. Mulch to keep roots cool. Pinch to encourage branching, and remove spent flowers. Do not let pods form or bloom will cease.

BULBS

HYACINTH. *Hyacinthus orientalis.* Zones 4–10. Any variety, since all are fragrant. Plant in fall, 6 inches apart and 5 inches deep, in informal groups. Division not necessary.

LILY, REGAL. *Lilium regale,* improved strain. Zones 4–9. Grows about 4 feet tall and blooms early (June-July). Plant in spring or fall, 6 inches deep, in very well-drained soil. Stake just before blooming, if necessary. May not attain full height the first year.

NARCISSUS, POET'S. *Narcissus poeticus,* zones 4–10. Tazetta narcissus, *N. tazetta,* zones 8–10. *N. poetaz* (a cross between *N. poeticus* and *N. tazetta*), zones 4–10. All these are fragrant, usually white with a brightly colored center. 'Cheerfulness,' a *poetaz* narcissus, is a good double white or yellow variety. 'Thalia,' a miniature, about 10 inches tall, is charming and very fragrant. All bloom a bit late in the narcissus season. In hot

climates, grow the tazettas. Plant in early fall about 10–12 inches deep, fertilizing with bone meal.

SNOWFLAKE, SPRING. *Leucojum vernum.* Zones 4–8. Tiny white bell-like flowers, tipped with green dots. Grows 6–9 inches tall. Blooms early in spring. Likes sun or light shade. Plant early in fall, 4 inches apart and 3–4 inches deep, fertilizing with bone meal.

PERENNIALS AND GROUND COVERS

ARTEMISIA (SOUTHERN-WOOD, OLD MAN). *Artemisia abrotanum.* Zones 6–9. Grows to 3–4 feet, shrublike, and evergreen in warm climates. Has aromatic, gray-green foliage and yellow-white flowers. Needs good drainage. Cut back dead wood in early spring before new growth starts. Responds to division and replanting every few years.

ARTEMISIA (BEACH WORMWOOD, OLD WOMAN, DUSTY MILLER). *Artemisia stellerana.* Zones 4–

9. Grows 1–2 feet and sprawls widely. Has deeply toothed aromatic white foliage. Pinch the terminal shoot when the plant reaches a height of 6 inches to encourage branching. Cut off flowers in midsummer and any straggling foliage. Prefers light, sandy soil with good drainage.

CARNATION, BORDER. *Dianthus caryophyllus.* Zones 6–7, farther north with winter protection. Grayish foliage, grows 1–3 feet high. Clove-scented flowers in many shades bloom all summer.

CHRYSANTHEMUM. *Chrysanthemum morifolium.* Zones 4–10. Any tall variety. Blooms from August to October. Likes sun and rich, well-drained soil lightened with humus and cultivation. Pinch the terminal shoots until mid-July to encourage branching. Some gardeners winter their chrysanthemums in a cold frame and start new plants in early spring by removing stolons with new growth on them and replanting. With pinching, mulching and good care, you can keep them going for several years.

DAY LILY. *Hemerocallis.* Zones 3–9. Fragrant variety such as 'Hyperion,' or the lemon lily *H. lilioasphodelus.* 'Hyperion' is yellow and blooms during July and August.

Lemon lily blooms in late spring. Day lilies are among the easiest plants to grow, but

the clumps will become dense and must be divided about every 4 years.

HYSSOP. *Hyssopus officinalis.* Zones 3–8. Shrublike plant about 2 feet tall with dark green, narrow leaves. Flowers are usually blue, sometimes pink or white, and appear from June throughout the summer. Seeds are best sown in very early spring, though nursery-grown plants can also be used. Plant in well-drained soil. Cut mature plants back to the ground in early spring to prevent the plants from becoming too woody.

JUPITER'S-BEARD (RED VALERIAN). *Centranthus ruber.* Zones 4–10. Grows 2–3 feet tall and bears red blooms from early summer to fall. Cut often for rebloom, and fragrant indoor bouquets. Plant 12–15 inches apart and divide every few years when crowded.

LAVENDER. *Lavandula angustifolia angustifolia (L. officinalis).* Or use any species, variety. Zones 6–9. Usually grows about 2–3 feet tall with flowers that give the color its name, and blooms from June or July onward. Winter in-

doors in cold climates. Grow in well-drained soil (wet will kill it faster than cold) and prune back to just above the previous year's growth in early spring.

PEONY. *Paeonia lactiflora.* Zones 3–8. Choose fragrant varieties, most of which are white or pale pink, and double. Prefers cool nights, well-drained soil, humus. Plant in early fall as follows: dig a hole 1½ feet wide and equally deep. Place 1–2 shovelfuls of compost in the bottom along with a handful of bone meal and mix with the soil in the bottom of the hole. Tamp with your foot, leaving just enough room to set the peony root carefully in the hole with most of the eyes 1–2 inches below soil level, facing upward. Carefully fill hole with soil. Planting any deeper will prevent flowering. Plant may not bloom first year. Division not necessary.

THYME. *Thymus vulgaris* and some of the many thyme varieties such as *T. v. citriodorus* (lemon-scented, light green foliage, lavender flowers), *T. v. aureus* (creeping golden thyme—yellow leaves, lavender flowers), *T. lanuginosus* (woolly thyme—gray leaves and lilac flowers), *T. serpyllum album* (white wild thyme—white flowers), *T. s. lanuginosus* 'Splendens' (scarlet thyme—dark green foliage, red flowers), and others. Zones 4–10. All prefer sun and light, well-drained soil. Slow to grow from seed, but you can sow in spring between established clumps. Best propagated by division. Fertilize with bone meal but not a fertilizer high in nitrogen. Trim taller varieties in early May. In very cold climates use a mulch such as salt hay in winter.

VALERIAN. *Valeriana officinalis.* Zones 3–10. Old-fashioned plant with pale pink flowers in midsummer, fern-like foliage. Grows 3–4 feet tall in sun or shade. Tolerates moist soil. Plant 15–18 inches apart and divide as needed.

VIOLET, SWEET. *Viola odorata.* Zones 6–10. Fragrant, usually purple flowers in late spring. Obtain plants from a nursery or from a friend. Prefers light shade and moist soil rich in organic material.

WOODRUFF, SWEET. *Galium odoratum (Asperula odorata).* Zones 4–8. Ground cover, native to woodland with light shade. Grows 6 inches tall. Prefers moist, acid soil (pH 4.5–5.5). Fragrant star-shaped leaves used in making May wine. Tiny foamy white flower clusters in May and June. Plant in spring or early fall 10–12 inches apart; divide in early spring or fall.

SHRUBS AND VINES

CLEMATIS, AUTUMN. *Clematis paniculata.* To zone 6, zone 5 with winter protection. Vigorous woody vine, growing up to 30 feet high. Bears small, white, fragrant, star-shaped blossoms in August-September, then beautiful fuzzy seed heads in fall. Less prone to disease than most clematis species. Plant with a cupful of lime in fertile soil. Mulch to protect roots from summer heat and winter cold. Do not disturb roots. Replenish the lime and mulch each year. Prune only if too rampant.

DAPHNE, FEBRUARY. *Daphne mezereum.* Zones 4–9. Grows 3 feet tall. Bears small, fragrant, lilac-colored flowers in early spring, before leaves appear. Likes sun, moisture, lime and a light, well-drained soil. Keep roots cool in summer with mulch. Transplant only young plants, and don't disturb the roots around them.

LILAC, COMMON. *Syringa vulgaris.* Zones 2–7. Intensely fragrant flowers in mid-May (in zone 6) in shades of "lilac" or white (more variation in hybrids). Prune out a third of the old wood each year

after flowering to keep plant compact and flowering, and spray with dormant oil spray before plants leaf out in spring to prevent lilac scale. Control borers by cutting out infested growth and burning it.

MOCK ORANGE. *Philadelphus* species. There are a number of species and varieties to choose from. The Lemoine hybrids such as 'Avalanche,' which grows 4 feet high and bears single white flowers, will do well in zones 5–9; *P. virginalis* grows up to 9 feet high and does well within the same range, but it is leggy and should be planted behind a lower shrub; *P. coronarius,* an old-fashioned tall mock orange with single white blossoms, is hardy to zone 4 and will tolerate dry places better than most. In very cold climates plant 'Frosty Morn,' which grows 4 feet tall.

ROSE. *Rosa* species. Not all of the climbing roses are fragrant, and in this case the modern hybrids are more apt to have fragrance than the old ones. Some pastel varieties that would look good in this garden are 'Mrs. Sam McGredy,' a hardy double salmon-pink that blooms all season, 'Dr. W. Van Fleet,' which has large double pink flowers and blooms once in early summer, or 'America' (shown). In mild climates you could plant 'New Dawn,' a lovely double pale pink, or 'Gloire de Dijon,' an old-fashioned climbing tea rose with yellow-pink-apricot blossoms. There are a number of

fragrant red climbers such as 'Chrysler Imperial' and, in mild climates, 'Don Juan.' You could also grow eglantine (*Rosa eglanteria*) for its apple-scented leaves. Climbing roses usually bloom on second-year wood. Do not prune the first year; in subsequent years remove several old, woody canes and train some canes parallel to the ground. Cut off spent blooms as far as the first group of 3–4 leaves. Grow in moderately rich soil with good drainage.

SNOWBALL VIBURNUM (FRAGRANT SNOWBALL). *Viburnum carlcephalum.* Zones 5–9. This shrub grows up to 9 feet tall, with flowers like white fragrant snowballs in May, followed by red and black berries in summer. Other good choices would be *V. carlesii,* a shorter and very fragrant plant, or *V. burkwoodii,* which is similar. In the South, *V. odoratissimum* (sweet viburnum) is a good choice. Easy to grow. Likes sun or light shade and rarely needs pruning.

SUMMERSWEET. *Clethra alnifolia.* Zones 3–10. Usually grows to about 5 feet but may grow as tall as 9. Spreads sideways by stolons. Bears small spikes of white or pink flowers in late July or August, gold foliage in fall. Likes moist soil and can even stand in water. Appreciates humus and an acid pH. Should need no pruning, but if you want to cut it back, do so in very early spring before new growth appears.

A Colonial Garden

People often say to me, "I have an old Colonial house. What kind of garden should I plant around it?"

They have lovingly rescued the old structure from dry rot and furnished it with Early American antiques. They have scraped off layers of Victorian wallpaper, exposing plaster and wood paneling. They have found the perfect Williamsburg color with which to paint the outside trim. Now they want to create a nostalgic garden, full of old herbs and traditional flowers with such names as meet-her-in-the-entry-kiss-her-in-the-buttery or welcome-home-husband-however-drunk (the plant we know today as hen-and-chickens) and other plants that will look right with the house.

This part of the restoration is not a simple one. Old gardens have not lasted the way old houses have; the plants the settlers tended have long since perished.

Luckily we know something about what grew in those gardens, however, and can re-create them, if not with precise fidelity, at least in spirit.

There are good reasons to do this, quite apart from historical authenticity. A Colonial garden was a pleasant spot, and even a modern house would be enhanced by one—a place near the kitchen door for herb-snipping, a plot of cottage-garden flowers for color, and a wooden bench under a fruit tree for sitting and doing the chores.

There was no "typical" kind of Colonial garden. For the first settlers at Plymouth and other early towns, gardens were mostly a matter of survival. Hungry and homesick, these new arrivals planted familiar herbs, fruits and vegetables from home, together with new ones recommended by the Indians or discovered in the wild. There were even a few flowers grown from slips and seeds lovingly carried in the holds of ships, and wild ones gathered from the New World's woods and meadows. The garden's main function was to provide food, medicines and other household aids, and some spots of color to remind them of the homes they had left behind. They were sometimes weedy gardens, not laid out with an eye to artistic design. In the early days there was too much else to do.

The gardens of later Colonial years tell a different story, particularly those planted by well-to-do landowners and merchants. These men and women built and landscaped estates to rival those of England. They were much influenced by the romantic style of gardening then in vogue among the English gentry: broad, sweeping lawns, well-kept woods, serpentine paths and walls, artificial "mounts" within the garden and grand vistas in the distance. The spaciousness of the New World gave them room to create these "landscapes".

Between the two extremes lay the diverse styles of different localities and nationalities: the tidy kitchen gardens and flower beds bright with bulbs that the Dutch planted; the lush orchards of the Spanish colonies; the flower-filled dooryards of New England towns; the "parlor gardens" planted by housewives next to prosperous farmhouses; the formal yards behind brick homes in the coastal cities. These colonial gardeners all had one thing in common: their gardens flourished.

The colonists carried on a prodigious exchange of plants and horticultural information with the homeland. Most of what we know

The Whipple House in Ipswich, Massachusetts, has a typical dooryard garden combining flowers and herbs for household use.

about Colonial plants comes from this correspondence. European growers were always eager for new American plants—exotic things like black-eyed Susan, milkweed and wild columbine—that were soon all the rage in England and on the Continent. Of the hundreds of plants sent to America from Europe, many escaped into the wild, like yarrow, Solomon's seal and bouncing bet, and are now thoroughly naturalized.

Garden design in the colonies had its paradoxes. England in the eighteenth century was busy discarding the formal concepts of Renaissance gardening. The rustic beauty of woods and farms had thoroughly captured the Romantic imagination. Meanwhile, the New World was carving a civilization out of the wilderness in the old geometrical style. The colonists were busy staking out gardens with rigidly laid-out walks and beds and planting neat little hedges around them. After all, that formality had its practical advantages, just as it had in the old cloister gardens. Those small squares and tidy paths made the gardens easy to work.

Most people nowadays would call a Colonial housewife's garden an herb garden, but "herb" did not mean the same thing that it does today. Though botanically speaking an herb, or herbaceous plant, is simply a soft-stemmed plant as opposed to a woody one, we think of an herb as a garden plant appreciated chiefly for its usefulness. The colonists did not make a distinction between medicinal herbs, seasoning herbs or herbs used as greens in salads. The word "salad"— or "sallet," as the colonists called it—has also changed meaning. A Colonial sallet could be eaten raw, as ours are, but more often than not it was cooked, and contained some plants we now grow chiefly as flowers, such as calendulas (also called pot marigolds) and nasturtiums (called Indian cress). Only occasionally were garden flowers used to decorate the house.

The art of drying flowers for winter bouquets was practiced more then, and there were customs, now largely lost, such as that of making tussie-mussies. The tussie-mussie probably originated as a fistful of aromatic foliage or flowers—possibly chosen for their astringency rather than their sweet soporific scents—to be sniffed in church to keep the very young or very old awake during long Puritan sermons. But they evolved into something more stylized and decorative—small dainty bouquets, surrounded with lace, to be held in the hand. It was a joy and a challenge to see what you could put together from the plants currently blooming.

PLAN OF THE GARDEN

The oddest thing about a true Colonial garden, if we were to see one today, would be the total disregard of the type of organization that we take for granted. Flowers, herbs, vegetables and even fruits were all grown together. Vegetables might have their own section, and a wife might put her "best" flowers in a special place near the house for show and safekeeping, but by and large you could find anything anywhere. In my garden here, flowers, herbs and a few salad greens are combined. It is a dooryard garden, small enough to fit into a town or city yard, but it would also be appropriate for a house in the country. It is designed to be practical, but with a bit of the formality of a town garden.

There is a series of small plots with gravel paths between them, and a picket fence surrounding the whole area. Field vegetables such as corn, beans and pumpkins ("pompions") would naturally need more space, and would be in larger beds farther from the house; but even these plots might be a strange mixture of crops, and arranged in patches rather than rows, with herbs and flowers tucked in among them. Most of the fruit trees, too, would be in an orchard some distance from the house, but it would not be unusual to have one or two right in the yard for fruit and shade. There is a quince in this one.

The backyard of a Colonial house was an area where outdoor work was done, especially in the country. Clothes were washed; wood was split; drying, tanning and other domestic crafts were carried on there. Of course, today people work and play in the yards, and there should be a space in your

This Colonial garden features gray-leafed herbs, a brick walk, a sundial and a picket fence.

THE COLONIAL GARDEN

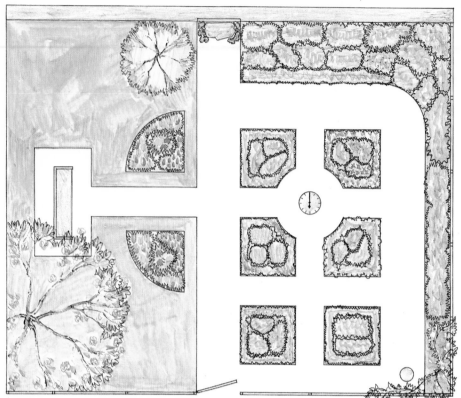

THE GARDEN IN SPRING

THE GARDEN IN FALL

GRASS

BENCH

quince

PLAN OF THE COLONIAL GARDEN (SUMMER) ³⁄₈″ = 1′

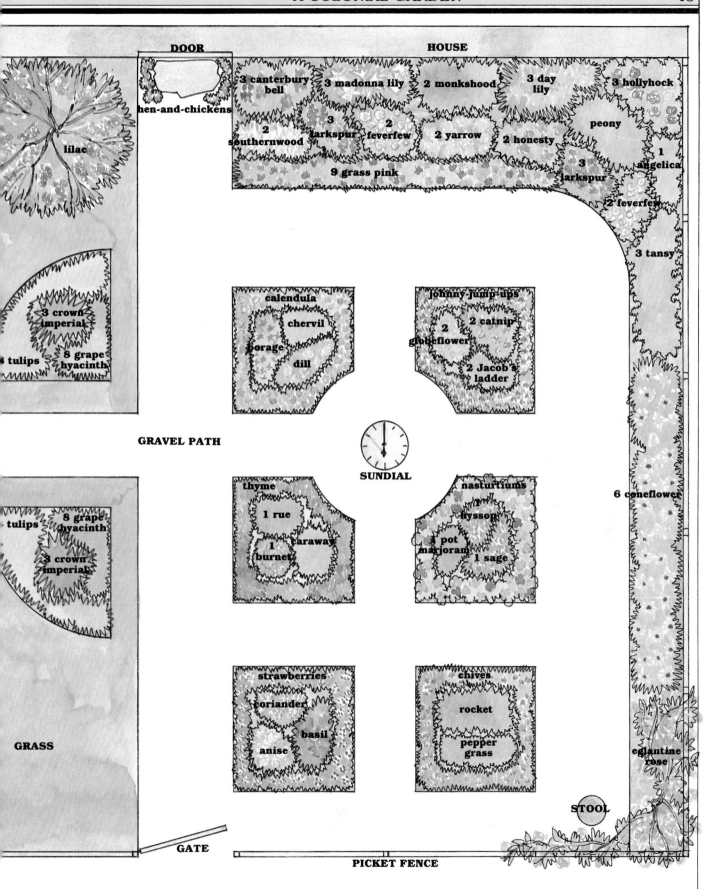

DOOR

HOUSE

hen-and-chickens

3 canterbury bell

3 madonna lily

2 monkshood

3 day lily

3 hollyhock

lilac

2 southernwood

3 larkspur

2 feverfew

2 yarrow

2 honesty

peony

9 grass pink

3 larkspur

1 angelica

2 feverfew

3 tansy

3 crown imperial

tulips

8 grape hyacinth

calendula

chervil

borage

dill

johnny-jump-ups

2 globeflower

2 catnip

2 Jacob's ladder

GRAVEL PATH

SUNDIAL

6 coneflower

tulips

8 grape hyacinth

3 crown imperial

thyme

1 rue

1 burnet

caraway

nasturtiums

1 hyssop

1 pot marjoram

1 sage

GRASS

strawberries

coriander

basil

anise

chives

rocket

pepper grass

eglantine rose

STOOL

GATE

PICKET FENCE

garden for these activities. In this garden it is between the quince tree and the lilac bush, with a little bench and two small tidy parterres of spring bulbs. (If you need more open space than this, plant the tree and bulbs farther away.) A Colonial garden would have grass in this space, though it would not look like a modern close-cropped lawn. Hand-mow it with a grass scythe for accuracy.

The fence should be made of wood, though living hedges were sometimes used as well. Palings tied together vertically might have been used to provide a complete barrier, especially in the earliest gardens, but a picket fence is probably the most typical kind of Colonial fence, and it is practical, too. It lets air circulate while keeping animals out. Even the pointed pickets have a purpose—they discourage roosting fowl. Wooden gates of a style consistent with the fence can be placed as needed. Along the fence is a good place to plant rudbeckia and tansy, or any other garden plant that is vigorous and spreading. I've also suggested an old-fashioned climbing rose, eglantine (sweetbrier).

Ornamental shrubs were not much cultivated or sold for their own sakes in the early Colonial days, though mock orange, viburnum, azaleas, lilacs and many others soon became popular, including the native *Franklinia*, named for Benjamin Franklin. Lilacs certainly bloomed in dooryards, as Walt Whitman reminds us, and there may have been a boxwood bush on either side of the front door.

The question of boxwood is a controversial one. Many people think of box-edged knots and borders as an indispensable Colonial feature. Certainly these did exist before the Revolution, but box edging was more widely used in the first half of the nineteenth century (which is sometimes considered part of the Colonial period for purposes of style), and only in fairly warm parts of the country.

As I've suggested here, I think it would be more fun to give each of the beds a different edging: pinks, calendulas, johnny-jump-ups, thyme, nasturtiums, woodland strawberries and chives. There are tidier, more conventional edgings you can use, such as lavender cotton (*Santolina chamaecyparissus*), thrift (*Armeria maritima*) and germander (*Teucrium chamaedrys*). But the

This contemporary rose-covered arch is the type that might well have led to the side entrance of a home in the mid-eighteenth century.

ones in my plan can, with a little effort, be kept in line, and all are extremely colorful at one time or another.

The plants in the various plots have been grouped together according to how they grow, as well as how they look together. Alongside the house is a typical cottage garden border; it is filled with old-fashioned flowers such as Canterbury bells, hollyhocks and honesty, together with some of the taller herbs such as southernwood, angelica and tansy. Annual larkspur and the prolific feverfew fill in any gaps, and a border of grass pinks gives the bed definition. It is a summer border, the blooms beginning with peonies and lemon lilies and ending with autumn monkshood. The tansy, the yarrow and the seedpods produced by honesty can all be dried for fall or winter decoration.

The six square beds are primarily of herbs, with some garden flowers tucked in here and there. Most of the herbs also have fine blooms—the lavender spikes of catnip, the intense blue whorls of borage, the lacy varicolored umbels of anise, coriander and dill. (You can make bouquets of them.) Some can be eaten in salads—calendula, nasturtium, peppergrass, rocket, burnet, borage, even the tiny leaves of the johnny-jump-ups. You should plant a large lettuce patch somewhere, so that you will have plenty of blander fare as a base for these piquant additions. You can add some dashes of color to your salads if you also toss in some flowers, as the colonists did. In spring you can eat the flowers of lemon lilies, johnny-jump-ups and chives. Later on, try yellow calendulas, red nasturtiums and blue borage. These can turn a green salad into a dazzling bowlful. Use snippings of basil, chervil, coriander, dill, chives, pot marjoram, sage and thyme to season your cooking, and gather bunches of "strewing" herbs from hyssop, rue, sage, feverfew, southernwood and tansy. Store the dried seeds of coriander, anise and dill for your winter larder. Make tea from the catnip. Don't expect a large crop from your woodland strawberries, just small handfuls occasionally to sprinkle on hand-churned ice cream or a whipped cream-topped pie.

The plants in these six beds have been grouped not only for color harmony but also for moisture and soil preferences, and whether they are annuals or perennials. This way you can treat everything in a bed the same way (though perennial edgings sometimes surround annual herbs and vice versa). Here are the six, referred to by their edgings:

1. The calendula bed is composed of annuals that like a fairly rich soil. The blue flowers of borage will look good with the yellow and orange calendulas.

2. The johnny-jump-up bed has perennials that like rich soil. It is full of color: purple johnny-jump-ups, yellow globeflower and blue Jacob's ladder in spring, followed by lavender catnip in summer.

3. The plants in the thyme-edged bed are all perennials that like average soil. Rosy burnet blooms in late summer at the same time as white caraway. Earlier, the red thyme flowers look nice with the bluish leaves of rue.

4. The nasturtiums surround perennials. All the plants, including the nasturtiums, like dry soil that is low in nitrogen. The warm reds and yellows of the nasturtiums contrast with the cooler pinks of hyssop and pot marjoram, and the blue or purple of the salvia.

5. The strawberry bed contains annuals that like a fairly rich soil. The flowers have a misty look.

6. The chive bed is like a miniature vegetable garden, all of whose occupants like rich soil. The chives bear handsome purple flowers in spring that attract many butterflies.

The bulb beds have an overlapping succession of bloom in brilliant colors—first the blue grape hyacinths, then the showy red and yellow crown imperials and bright tulips.

Plant some hen-and-chickens around the doorstep to welcome home a drunk husband—or to rub on burns to ease the sting. If you wish, lay more flat stones to make a path to the door, and plant thyme and pot marjoram where they will creep around them. Both plants are aromatic if they are disturbed, as when stepped on.

Your outdoor furniture should be simple in style and made of wood that has been treated to resist moisture. An appropriate sundial in the center of the herb area would be an effective (and useful) touch. But in choosing garden ornaments, remember that the concept behind a Colonial garden is to put things to good use, not just decorate with them. Do not set out a wooden wheelbarrow and plant petunias in it. Use it.

SITE

I have imagined this garden at the back of a house, but your own domestic geography will

BUILDING RAISED BEDS

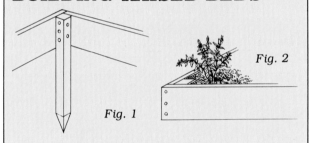

Fig. 2

Fig. 1

Make a box with 2-by-8-inch boards, nailed together with 3-inch nails. Cut 4 stakes, 2 by 2 by 18 inches, and point them at one end with a hatchet. Nail stakes to the inside corners of the box. Pound corners to sink stakes, making sure that box is level. Then fill with soil and plants.

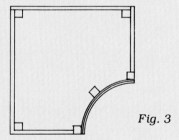

Fig. 3

To make curve, build two short sides, ending them with 2-by-2-inch stakes, just as for corners. Position box, then drive another stake in the ground in the desired position for curve. Take 2 strips of ¼-inch plywood, 8 inches wide, and nail them to the stakes at each end. For the middle stake, drive screws through the plywood and then into the stake. All wood used for these beds should be either a rot-resistant type or treated with a preservative.

probably determine where you lay it out. A Colonial dooryard garden might be in front of the house, if large trees do not cast shade there, or in a side yard. You should weigh several factors: What entrance do you use? Is it handy to the kitchen? Where are windows located, and what do you want to see when you look out? If you live in an old house, you may be able to figure out logically where an old garden might have been. But be sure there is enough sunlight; there may be trees there now that were not there two hundred years ago, and most herbs, especially, need full sun—at least six hours a day. If there is a shady corner of this garden (from the quince tree, perhaps), plant the things there that will tolerate shade, such as Jacob's ladder, globeflower, johnny-jump-up, chervil, peonies and angelica; and add others such as the mints.

GROWING INSTRUCTIONS

The flower bed next to the house can be dug in summer or fall. Add some organic matter and whatever other soil improvements seem necessary. Plant the annuals and perennials in spring, except in climates warm enough for fall plantings. Sow the biennials in fall, noting the Plant List for details. There are two biennials in this garden—Canterbury bells and honesty—as well as three things that often act that way—hollyhocks, feverfew and angelica. This number warrants the use of a cold frame so that you can grow the seedlings one summer to transplant into the flower bed the following spring. You can use the cold frame to grow lettuce and other greens for winter salads, too.

Plant the madonna lilies and peonies in late summer or early fall. At the same time, get the bulb beds ready. Edge them with a square shovel and add organic matter if the soil is at all sandy or clay. But don't add much fertilizer, just incorporate some bone meal or superphosphate into the whole bed when you plant the bulbs.

The small square beds and the paths should be staked out carefully, all at once. Use a long string with a pointed stake at each end as your ruler and compass. All herbs appreciate good drainage, and many demand it. The best way to make this garden a suc-

cess is to raise the beds, which is exactly what Colonial gardeners would have done. The earliest settlers used logs notched at the corners to make a frame to contain the soil. Then, as sawed boards became readily available, these were used, nailed to stakes at the corners. You could follow this practice, or you could use hewn beams or even the railroad ties that are available to gardeners today.

Once you have built the boundaries of these beds (see p. 45) you can dig the topsoil out of what will become the paths and fill the beds with it. Whether you use gravel, brick or stone for the paths, removing the topsoil will provide a stable base, and why not put this good soil to use? Refill the paths with the gravel (if you use another paving material, follow the instructions for a brick terrace, on page 165) so that they are again at the original soil level. The beds themselves should be anywhere from six inches to two feet high, so you might need more topsoil.

When finished, you will have small growing areas, all parts of which you can tend without ever having to step inside. This technique is no different from what we now call the French intensive method, and it dates back at least as far as the Middle Ages.

Prepare the soil for each bed according to what is in it:

1. In the calendula bed, apply one or two inches of compost or well-rotted manure, and turn it under in the fall before you plant. The plants in this bed are self-sowers, so the following fall you will probably just want to take away the debris and sprinkle on a little more compost or manure, cultivating it into the soil in the spring only after the small volunteers have sprouted and identified themselves.

2. The johnny-jump-up bed should also have a two-inch application of fertile humus—your best stuff. Dig up nothing in the fall. These perennial clumps will grow larger, especially the catnip, which might best be grown inside a bottomless bucket sunk in the soil, to keep it from taking over. The johnny-jump-ups will self-sow.

3. The perennials in the thyme bed like average soil, so an inch of compost will do, unless your soil is poor to start with. These, too, are permanent clumps.

This dooryard garden in Craftsbury, Vermont, is bursting with color.

4. The nasturtium bed would benefit by adding an inch of sand and an inch of peat moss to lighten the soil—more if your soil is very heavy. But add no fertile material such as manure or compost unless your soil is very deficient in nutrients. Otherwise the nasturtiums will be bunches of huge leaves and hidden flowers and the aggressive perennials will go for a walk down your nice tidy paths. Plant all three perennials in buckets or tubs; divide them often, too.

5. The strawberry bed will take a fairly rich soil; add two inches of compost. Divide the strawberries every year or so and replant to keep the edging evenly distributed. The rest of the bed contains annuals and can be dug up in fall, unless you are trying to get the coriander to self-sow.

6. The chive edging is permanent too, and can be evened out just the way you do the strawberry edging, bringing little clumps indoors for winter growing. All the plants in this bed like rich soil, so add at least two inches of compost. Dig up the bed inside the edging and resow the rocket and peppergrass each spring.

How you take care of your herbs depends on what you are going to use them for. If you want plenty of fresh young foliage for snipping, then keep snipping and more will come, especially if you snip the central stems to keep flowers from forming. If, on the other hand, you do want flowers, let them bloom. If you want to use the seeds for seasoning, or to save them for planting the following year, shake them into a paper bag when ripe but not yet fallen. If you want large quantities of an herb for drying (see photo, p. 135), harvest it just before it flowers, when the essential oils are most potent. You may want to bring some of your herbs indoors for the winter; chervil, basil, borage, sage, thyme and chives all grow well in pots on a sunny windowsill. Bear in mind that this whole garden will look tidier if you keep cutting the plants back.

ADDITIONS AND SUBSTITUTIONS

There are many other flowering plants that you could include in your Colonial border, among them dame's rocket (*Hesperis matronalis*), perennial flax (*Linum perenne*), bouncing bet or soapwort (*Saponaria officinalis*), false dragonhead (*Physostegia virginiana*), elecampane (*Inula helenium*), peach-leafed bellflower (*Campanula persificola*), pearly everlasting (*Anaphalis margaritacea*), any of the lavenders (*Lavandula* species) or various columbines, including the native *Aquilegia canadensis*. The Turk's-cap lily, *Lilium martagon* was popular, though you would probably not want to grow the original species, but one of the many modern hybrids—which are showier and less prone to disease—with a Turk's-cap shape. Colonial gardeners grew many kinds of phlox, too, including our common garden phlox (*Phlox paniculata*), Carolina phlox (*P. carolina*) and blue-flowered *Phlox divaricata*. Other spring bulbs might include crocus (*Crocus vernus*), hoop-petticoat daffodils (*Narcissus bulbocodium*) or the common daffodil (*N. pseudonarcissus*), which early folk called daff-a-down-dillies.

There are also countless herbs you could add to the selection here, such as tarragon (*Artemisia dracunculus*), winter savory (*Satureia montana*), fennel, lovage, camomile (*Anthemis nobilis*), any of the mints (*Mentha* species) and clary (*Salvia sclarea*), a species of sage reputed to keep the eyes healthy. Any of the herb plots could include more vegetables that do not require a great deal of space: lettuce, spinach, garlic (*Allium sativum*) and chicory (*Cichorium intybus*), which was used as a salad green but also bears lovely blue flowers, the same ones you see along country roads in summer. Horseradish (*Armorica rusticana*) would be a good addition too, but it is a spreader and needs to be contained.

The fence around your Colonial garden might also be put to more use than just as a fence. In addition to eglantine, you could grow other roses that were Colonial favorites: cinnamon rose (*Rosa cinnamomea*), with long, arching stems and deep pink flowers, a species probably introduced from Europe and naturalized in the colonies; scotch rose (*R. spinosissima*), which is prickly, with white flowers, and will ramble luxuriantly over a fence if given rich soil; the old damask roses, with long, arching canes and very fragrant red double flowers; or the moss roses, which are shorter (up to five feet) with pink, globe-shaped flowers and fuzzy "moss" on the sepals, calyxes and stems. Another good fence plant would be an old-fashioned honeysuckle, such as the yellow *Lonicera flava*. Early gardens might also have had a row of berries growing next to a fence—raspberries, blueberries, gooseberries (*Ribes hirtellum*) or currants (*Ribes rubrum* or *R. nigrum*). The last two are prohibited in some areas, how-

ever, because they are alternate hosts for white pine blister rust; so check first with your county Cooperative Extension Service before you plant them. Grapes or strawberries might also be grown and, space permitting, other fruit trees—old-time pears with names like 'Bon Chretien' (now known in the United States as 'Bartlett') or 'Lady's Buttock,' old apples such as 'Seek-no-Further' and 'Sops-in-Wine.' These are not always easy to find, but some are being rediscovered and there are specialty nurseries that can supply you with them.

PLANT LIST FOR COLONIAL GARDEN

ANNUALS

CALENDULA (POT MARIGOLD). *Calendula officinalis.* Grows 1–1½ feet tall with single or double blooms in shades of orange, yellow, near-white or cream. The single orange ones would be especially nice in this garden. Sow seeds as soon as the ground thaws in spring; set plants 1 foot apart. An easy plant to grow, it can be sown in succession through the season, especially in warm climates where winter bloom is desired.

LARKSPUR. *Consolida ambigua (Delphinium ajacis).* Most varieties grow 3–5 feet tall and come in shades of blue, lavender, purple, pink and white; any would look good here. Plant seeds outdoors in fall or early spring. Do not transplant, but thin to 1–1½ feet apart.

NASTURTIUM. *Tropaeolum majus.* Choose one of the dwarf varieties, which grow about 1 foot tall, in mixed shades: these range from very dark red to red, orange, yellow and almost white. Sow seeds indoors in early spring, or outdoors after danger of frost is past, thinning plants to 6–8 inches apart. Nasturtiums do best in soil that is dryish, sandy and rather poor in nitrogen.

BULBS

CROWN IMPERIAL. *Fritillaria imperialis.* Zones 6–10. A member of the lily family, this bulb produces a truly regal head of bright flowers on a 3-foot stalk in April and May. The flowers are red, yellow or orange. This plant prefers gravelly, well-drained soil. Plant 6–8 inches deep in early fall and divide every few years.

GRAPE HYACINTH. *Muscari botryoides.* Zones 2–10. Grows about 8 inches tall and bears little spikes of flowers, usually bright blue, in early spring. Very easy to grow. New leaves appear in fall and should be left undisturbed until they wither after blooming in early summer. The bulbs do not need to be divided and will often spread by seeding themselves in new places. Plant in late summer or early fall, 3 inches apart and 3 inches deep.

LILY, MADONNA. *Lilium candidum.* Zones 3–10. Grows 3–4 feet tall and bears large snow-white flowers in June and July. Plant by covering the bulbs with only 1 inch of soil in late summer. Set them 1–1½ feet apart. Keep the soil damp but not wet. These lilies like lime and gravelly soil. The bulbs develop some leaves in the fall.

TULIP. *Tulipa* hybrids. Most varieties are zones 4–7. Choose the old egg-shaped cottage tulips, or one of the 'Bizarres'—yellow splashed with red—that were sometimes planted in Colonial times. Most tulips grow about 2 feet tall and bloom in May. Plant about 6 inches apart in late fall, storing the bulbs below 70° until ready for planting. Deep planting (10–12 inches) will prolong years of bloom, since

they will multiply more slowly, and multiplication produces smaller bulbs and smaller flowers. It will also discourage rodents from eating the bulbs. But plant deeply only if the soil is enriched to that depth, and you will still need to replace tulips from time to time. Add bone meal or superphosphate when planting.

FRUITS

QUINCE. *Cydonia oblonga.* To zone 6, sometimes 5. J.I. Rodale accurately describes this old-fashioned fruit as "something like a lumpy, woolly pear." It has reddish flesh inside the yellow-green skin and is not very good to eat raw. Cooked, however, it makes an excellent jelly. Quince trees have a twisted, scraggly shape, often quite picturesque, but improved by pruning in late winter or early spring. Remove suckers and any thick, tangled growth. Buy 2-year-old stock and set out in early spring. Heavy fertilization is not necessary unless the soil is poor. Since quinces are shallow-rooted, it is helpful to mulch them unless there is grass growing around the tree, as in this garden. They prefer a heavy but well-drained soil. Fruit may be picked after the first frost and stored for several months in a damp, cool place.

STRAWBERRY, WILD (WOODLAND STRAWBERRY, *FRAISES DES BOIS*). *Fragaria vesca.* Zones 4–10. Several hybrid varieties are available, such as 'Baron Solemacher' or 'Charles V.' These bear small white flowers and tiny sweet red berries from June to fall. They prefer sun and a rather dry location. Easily divided in spring to extend or fill in an edging. Initial planting should be about a foot apart.

HERBS (ANNUAL)

ANISE. *Pimpinella anisum.* Grows up to 2 feet tall, with rounded lower leaves and feathery dill-like leaves on the upper part of the stalks. Flowers are flat and white, somewhat like those of Queen Anne's lace. Sow seeds in the ground early in the spring in warm climates; in cool ones, start indoors in peat pots and put out when the weather becomes warm. Harvest seeds when ripe and dry well before storing.

BASIL, SWEET. *Ocimum basilicum.* Grows up to 3 feet tall with bright green leaves. There is a dark purple form also used for seasoning and especially handsome in gardens. Basil is vigorous and easy to grow. It is usually sown in the ground after danger of frost, thinned to 10–12 inches apart. The leaves are cut for flavoring as soon as they are large enough. Use the top leaves first, and pinch off the

---

blossoms to encourage branching. Some watering may be necessary in very hot, dry weather. Harvest leaves for drying or for making pesto, that delicious Italian seasoning, before the first frost. You can also sow some in pots, or root some cuttings, for winter use.

BORAGE. *Borago officinalis.* Sprawling herb about 2 feet tall. Easy to grow, with hairy leaves and stems, bright blue flowers from late spring through midsummer. Seeds may be sown directly in the garden in early spring, then thinned to at least a foot apart. Likes a rather dry, sandy soil, though rich soil will produce a more abundant bloom. Self-sows very easily and can be sown in fall for next year's crop.

CHERVIL. *Anthriscus cerefolium.* Grows about a foot tall, with light yellow-green parsleylike leaves and tiny white flowers in spring. Grows easily from seed; best sown in early spring or late fall. Will self-sow readily if allowed to bloom, especially in light, rich soil. Harvest leaves often for seasoning and to promote new growth. Appreciates some shade: if exposed to hot sun, keep the soil moist, or plant next to something that will shield it from the afternoon sun.

CORIANDER (CILANTRO, CHINESE PARSLEY). *Coriandrum sativum.* Grows about 2 feet tall, with leaves much like those of anise. Flowers are small umbels, pinkish lavender or white. Sow seeds in the garden in early spring or any time thereafter. Keep soil rather moist if possible. Coriander self-sows in the garden but does not transplant well. Harvest the fresh leaves for seasoning as you would parsley. Dry the mature seeds and split open the large round pods to get at the flavorful kernel.

DILL. *Anethum graveolens.* Usually 2½ feet tall with threadlike, bluish leaves and umbel-shaped yellow flowers that bloom all summer. Sow outdoors in early spring or throughout the summer, thinning to 10 inches. Snipping before bloom will produce more foliage for seasoning, but let the aromatic seeds form if you want to use those too. Dill likes a fairly rich, moist soil and self-sows easily. Do not transplant.

PEPPERGRASS (GARDEN CRESS, PEPPER CRESS). *Lepidium sativum.* Featheryleafed herb with a sharp, biting flavor, used in salads. Peppergrass germinates quickly. Sow the seeds in the garden

early in spring and start snipping it when the plants are just several inches tall. Repeat sowings throughout spring, summer and fall for a continuous supply of fresh foliage.

ROCKET (ROQUETTE, ARUGULA). *Eruca sativa.* Grows up to 3 feet tall and sprawling, with narrow, toothed leaves and purple or white flowers. The strong peppery flavor is good in salads. Sow the seeds in cool weather (usually early spring), thinning to 6 inches. Water in drought.

HERBS (PERENNIAL)

ANGELICA. *Angelica archangelica.* Zones 3–6 (farther south with partial shade and sufficient moisture). A very tall herb (up to 7 feet) which bears umbels of greenish white flowers in July. It was much prized by Colonial gardeners for its many culinary and medicinal

uses. Though perennial, it is often short-lived, and is sometimes grown as a biennial from very fresh seeds sown in midsummer. Stalks should be harvested the second year. Angelica often self-sows, and if cut the second year will send up shoots from the base of the plant. It can be perpetuated by either of these means in the garden. Appreciates slightly acid soil that is moist and rich in humus. Also likes some shade during the hottest part of the day.

BURNET, SALAD. *Poterium sanguisorba (Sanguisorba minor).* Zones 3–9. Easily grown herb; usually 1½–2 feet tall. Bears fuzzy rose-tipped flowers in late spring and early summer. May go to seed if flowers are not cut. Sow seeds directly in the garden in early spring or in fall, thinning to a foot apart. Harvest leaves to keep the growth fresh and young for salads.

CARAWAY. *Carum carvi.* Zones 3–9. Biennial herb grown for its flavorful seeds, which are produced in the second year. Grows up to 2½ feet tall with threadlike foliage and small white flowers in late summer. Sow in early spring or in fall and thin to 6–10 inches apart. Harvest seeds when brown and scald before drying, to kill insects that may hide in the seeds and eat them.

CATNIP. *Nepeta cataria.* Zones 3–8. Grows up to 3 feet tall. Gray-green hairy leaves, white or lavender flowers all

summer. Begin harvesting leaves to dry for teas or cat toys when flowering starts, then successively through the summer. Catnip can be easily grown from either seed or division.

CHIVES. *Allium schoenoprasum.* Zones 3–10. Tufts of slender tubelike leaves up to a foot tall, with onion flavor; purple cloverlike blooms in May and June. Usually grown from started clumps, easily divided and planted in early spring. (Also easily started from seed.) Chives benefit from frequent division, and a large clump can be taken apart to make a border, spacing each division a foot apart. The foliage often stays green all winter and can be snipped for seasoning even when blanketed with snow. The seeds are also edible.

HYSSOP. *Hyssopus officinalis.* Zones 3–8. Shrublike plant that generally grows to about 2 feet tall, with narrow dark green leaves. Flowers are blue, sometimes pink or white, and bloom all summer. Seeds are best sown in the garden in very early spring, though nursery-grown plants can also be used. Prefers well-drained soil. Cut mature plants back in spring. Harvest branches in late summer for "strewing" or hanging in closets.

MARJORAM, POT (WILD MARJORAM, OREGANO). *Origanum vulgare.* Zones 3–10. Grows up to 2½ feet tall, with aromatic leaves and attractive pink flowers in late summer and fall. Prefers a light, well-drained soil. Can be grown either from seed sown in spring or from divisions. Self-sows and spreads by runners. Thin it out whenever it becomes overcrowded.

RUE. *Ruta graveolens.* Zones 4–9. Used as a "strewing" herb, not for consumption; rue also looks lovely in the garden. Its dainty bluish foliage is attractive long after other plants have withered in fall. It grows about 2 feet tall. Easily grown from seeds sown in early spring or late summer. Thin to 1 foot apart, and cut back mature plants to encourage bushiness.

SAGE. *Salvia officinalis.* Zones 3–10. Grows at least 2 feet tall and sprawls widely. It has aromatic, wrinkled gray-green foliage and small spikes of blue flowers in midsummer. Salvia prefers sun and requires well-drained soil. Ob-

tain a started plant. After a few years if it is large and straggly, propagate new plants by cutting or layering. Dry the leaves thoroughly and store whole. Try other sages such as pineapple sage *(Salvia elegans)* and clary sage *(S. sclarea).*

THYME (COMMON THYME). *Thymus vulgaris.* Zones 4–10. (Plant either the broad-leafed English or the narrow-leafed French variety.) Common thyme is a shrubby 10-inch plant that bears rosy flowers in June. Harvest leafy shoots just before the plant blooms, for drying. This will encourage new growth, which can be snipped at the tips throughout the season. Requires well-drained, slightly limy soil and may need a winter mulch in cold climates.

PERENNIALS AND BIENNIALS

CANTERBURY BELLS. *Campanula medium.* Zones 4–10. Biennial. Either the single, the cup-and-saucer or the hose-in-hose variety would look good in this garden. Hose-in-hose has one ring of petals inside another; cup-and-saucer is similar but more open. Most Canterbury bells are blue, but some are white or pink. They grow up to 4 feet tall. Sow seeds in early summer to bloom the following summer.

FEVERFEW. *Chrysanthemum parthenium.* Zones 6–10. This bushy 2–3-foot perennial often acts like a biennial in cold zones. It self-sows plentifully and must sometimes be weeded out of the garden here and there. You can grow it like an annual and sow seeds in early spring for mid or late summer bloom the same

season. The foliage is pleasantly aromatic.

GLOBEFLOWER. *Trollius europaeus.* Zones 3–9. This lovely plant is native to moist, semishaded places but will thrive in a sunny garden if the soil is moist and enriched with humus. Grows about 1½ feet tall. The leaves are dark green, the flowers golden orbs that fill with sunlight like enlarged buttercups (to which they are related). They bloom in late spring, but will recur throughout the summer if cut. Plant 12–15 inches apart.

HEN-AND-CHICKENS. *Sempervivum tectorum* and hybrid varieties. Zones 3–9. These plants are prickly rosettes in green and other foliage shades that make "babies" next to them and bear flowers, generally pink in midsummer. Their foliage keeps its color in winter. They like dry, sandy soil. Plant 6 inches apart.

HOLLYHOCK. *Alcea rosea (Althaea rosea).* Zones 3–10. Plant the old-fashioned single varieties if you can find them. Hollyhock clumps persist for years in some gardens; in others they act like biennials, self-sowing in fall to bloom the following summer. They bloom from midsummer through fall.

Plant 2 feet apart and stake with sturdy poles or tie them to the house to keep them from being blown over.

HONESTY (MONEY PLANT, WHITE SATIN). *Lunaria annua.* Zones 5–10. Sometimes grown as an annual, honesty produces better flowers as a biennial. It was treasured in old gardens for its fragrant purple flowers in May and June; its seedpods with thin, silvery-white, disklike center dividers are attractive in dried bouquets. Grows 1½–2½ feet tall. Sow seeds in midsummer and thin to 15 inches apart.

JACOB'S LADDER (CHARITY). *Polemonium caeruleum.* Zones 2–8. Grows 2–3 feet tall with attractive ladder-like leaves that give the plant its name, and sky-blue flowers in May. Its requirements are similar to globeflower's. Plant 1½ feet apart and divide as needed.

JOHNNY-JUMP-UP (MEET-HER-IN-THE-ENTRY-KISS-HER - IN - THE - BUTTERY, HEARTSEASE). *Viola tricolor.* Perennial in zones 6–8, but will self-sow freely in much colder zones. Grow from seed sown in early spring or fall, buy a few started plants or find a friend whose garden is crowded with these little spreaders. Prefers light shade, but will prosper in sun if the soil is moist and rich in humus.

LEMON LILY. *Hemerocallis lilioasphodelus (H. flava).* Zones 4–10. These day lilies grow 3 feet tall. The flowers are slightly smaller and bloom earlier than most hybrid day lilies. They are light yellow, with a sweet fragrance. Like other day lilies, they are easy to grow. Plant in a group of 3 plants, spreading out the roots over a cone of earth and compost. Divide the clumps every 4–5 years or as needed.

LILAC, COMMON. *Syringa vulgaris.* Zones 2–7. Intensely fragrant flowers in mid-May in shades of "lilac" or white. The old common lilac is more authentic in a Colonial garden than the hybrids, but be sure to prune it to keep it from getting too leggy, or you

will see flowers only from your upstairs windows. After flowering, remove faded blooms and cut off several stems near the base of the plant. Spraying with dormant oil before the plant leafs out in spring will prevent lilac scale, and any stems with borers should be cut out and burned.

MONKSHOOD. *Aconitum henryi (A. autumnale).* Zones 3–8. This monkshood grows 3–5 feet tall and provides bright blue color for the garden in late summer and fall. It likes rich, moist soil, and a mulch in winter. Do not move or divide.

PEONY. *Paeonia lactiflora.* Zones 3–8. Bright red peonies were popular in old gardens. A variety like 'Kansas' would be a good choice. Mature peonies grow in a mound about 3 feet high and as broad, with huge flowers in late May and June. They prefer cool nights, well-drained soil, humus. Plant according to instructions in the box on page 19, leaving just enough room in the hole to set the peony root carefully with most of the eyes (buds) 1–2 inches below soil level, facing upward. Carefully fill the hole with soil. Planting any deeper will prevent flowering. Plants may not bloom the first year. Division is not necessary.

PINK, GRASS (SCOTCH PINK, COTTAGE PINK, BORDER PINK). *Dianthus*

plumarius 'Semperflorens.' Zones 4–7 as a perennial, 8–10 as a biennial. This variety grows about a foot tall and bears pink and red flowers all summer. The foliage forms a blue-gray mat. It likes full sun, dry soil.

ROSE, EGLANTINE (SWEET BRIER). *Rosa eglanteria.* To zone 4. This rose was brought over from England by the early settlers. It grows at least 6 feet tall and could ramble beautifully over a picket fence. It bears single, pale pink flowers in June, and red or orange hips in fall. The foliage has an applelike scent after rain. There are no special requirements except adequate drainage.

RUDBECKIA (BLACK-EYED SUSAN, CONEFLOWER). *Rudbeckia fulgida.* Zones 3–10. There are many native American rudbeckias. This one is a perennial. Hybrid varieties include the 2½-foot 'Goldsturm,' which blooms all summer and into fall. Plant 1½ feet apart in an area where they can self-sow without disturbing other plants.

SOUTHERNWOOD (ARTE-MISIA, OLD MAN, LAD'S LOVE, MAIDEN'S RUIN). *Artemisia abrotanum.* Zones 6–9. If your climate is too cold

to grow this successfully, plant another artemisia such as common wormwood *(A. absinthum).* Southernwood grows 4 feet tall with aromatic grayish leaves and inconspicuous yellow-white flowers. Prefers a dry, sandy soil. Like most artemisias it is shrublike. Cut it back hard in early spring and whenever it looks scraggly.

TANSY. *Tanacetum vulgare.* Zones 2–10. Tansy grows up to 5 feet tall, with very aromatic fernlike leaves and clusters of button-shaped yellow flowers in late summer. Plant a few divisions 2 feet apart and you will soon have a thick bed of tansy. Not for consumption, but a good strewing herb, and handsome in dried bouquets.

YARROW. *Achillea millefolium* or *A. filipendulina.* Zones 3–10. These yarrows grow 1½–3 feet tall, with flowers in shades of yellow and sometimes red, all summer long. They are good for dried bouquets. The foliage is fernlike and aromatic but not as strong as that of tansy's. Easy to grow, but prefers dry, sandy soil. Plant 1½ feet apart.

A Butterfly Garden

One of the joys of having a garden is seeing the butterflies come. On a sunny June or July morning, when the garden bloom is at its height, they hover over the flowers like flowers in motion—bright spots of orange, red, yellow, blue, purple. Color brings more color.

You may have noticed that some gardens attract more butterflies than others. This is usually because some gardens contain more flowers that are rich in the nectar that butterflies drink. But it may also mean that there are more plants in the area for butterfly caterpillars to feed on. You can plant a garden whose sole purpose is to attract *Lepidoptera* (butterflies). By choosing the right plants, you can lure many different species and your garden will be all the more

beautiful. You may also find that you have begun a fascinating project that will change forever your attitude toward insects in the garden.

If you watch your butterflies you may learn surprising things about them. Did you know that they are extremely aggressive and will try to drive off intruders, even human ones? Did you know that the males of certain species will form "drinking clubs" in which dozens of them drink by the hour at small pools of water? (No one knows why.) Have you ever seen a butterfly emerge from its chrysalis, dry its wings in the sun and fly away? If you observe

The caterpillar of the Spicebush Swallowtail (Pter-ourus troilus).

these insects in all phases of their life cycle, you will gain a greater understanding of how a creature fits into its total environment—in this case your garden.

People often have strange immigration policies toward the insects on their property. There are either good bugs or bad ones. A list of bad bugs might include aphids, stinging red ants and all caterpillars, since they "eat everything up." Bees, on the other hand, are generally regarded as good insects—workers who earn their keep. And butterflies are always good. Most people would like to have as many as possible for the sheer beauty of them, not realizing that the insect they so admire in this phase of its life might send them running for the malathion were they to see it in another stage. You have to take into consideration the needs of the caterpillars as well as the butterflies they will become.

What are their needs? If you were able to ask your local butterflies what they would most like to find in your yard, you might be a bit discouraged. "We'd like an untidy mess," they would say. "The grass should never be cut. The most common weeds should overrun the garden and lawn. We would prefer that logs, dead plants and any other rubbish be left around to rot. Muddy puddles of stagnant water are important to us, especially if filled with manure, urine, dead animals and decaying fruit. Even some tobacco smoke might be pleasant."

Fortunately, butterflies have other enthusiasms that are easier for us to share with them; namely fragrant, nectar-filled flowers,

in all the major garden categories: annuals, perennials, shrubs, trees, grasses, herbs, vines. The food plants that the caterpillars eat, while less apt to be obvious garden choices, also include many plants that are pleasant to grow. Not surprisingly, wild plants are the best, since those are the ones the insects find in their natural environments, and wild plants can be an addition to—or even the mainstay of—a flower garden, with fine results. Since butterflies do like a more natural, unmanicured garden, you may be glad to have an excuse not to do as much tidying as you normally would. On the other hand, it is possible to construct a butterfly garden that is civilized—even elegant—and one that you will enjoy as much as they will.

To plan an environment where butterflies can thrive you need to understand something about their life cycle. This cycle has four stages: egg, larva, pupa and adult. The adult female butterfly lays eggs from which the larvae (caterpillars) hatch. These feed ravenously on plant foliage, growing larger and shedding layers of skin as they outgrow them. (These shedding phases are called molts.) When full grown they form pupae—dormant forms in which they are covered with a shell or chrysalis. They rest in this form until it is time to turn into butterflies and emerge from the chrysalis. As adult butterflies they mate and feed on the nectar of flowers until it is time to lay eggs. Specific species generally lay their eggs on the particular plants or groups of plants that their caterpillars will want to eat when they hatch.

The caterpillar of the Monarch (Danaus plexippus) feeds on milkweed (Asclepias species).

The garden at Drum Manor, County Tyrone, Northern Ireland, planted exclusively to attract butterflies.

The length of time it takes to complete this cycle, and the time of year at which different stages happen, varies from species to species. In some it takes a year or more; in others there may be several broods in a single summer. Furthermore, a butterfly might spend the winter in any of the four stages—egg, larva, pupa or adult—depending on its species and geographic location. Some species migrate south for the winter, breeding along the way and sending each successive brood farther along. In most species of the temperate zone, however, the creature overwinters as a pupa, so that it is ready to burst forth as an adult butterfly in the spring. You must be ready to attract them with an array of early, nectar-bearing flowers. When the newly emerged adult lays eggs, they usually hatch quickly, so you must also have a supply of early foliage plants for the hungry, young caterpillars to feed on. (They are not likely to consume so much that they will ruin the look of your garden.)

If you want to try butterfly gardening, you should decide how much effort you will be able to put into it. If you just want to attract a few more butterflies than you have in past years, it is sufficient simply to plant more of the nectar flowers commonly visited by adults. But if you want to attract many different species, you will have to plant things that will provide a variety of food for their caterpillars as well, especially if you live in an urban or suburban area where there are few pastures or woodlands. This is a more chal-

lenging project, since most caterpillar foods are wild plants, and it is not always easy to duplicate the natural conditions under which wild plants grow. Nor is it easy to provide the total habitat that the butterfly is accustomed to in the wild. But it can be done, and it is very satisfying when it works. Butterfly gardening can be so engrossing that you may want to try your hand at rearing some of your favorite butterflies from caterpillars you have found. Some of the books listed on page 217 will show you how to begin.

The garden presented here is for a gardener who wants to attract adult butterflies and also provide some caterpillar food plants. What are butterflies' basic needs? They need nectar for energy, and though they will flutter all about the neighborhood, they will always return to an attractive nectar source. The nectar plants I have included here would be effective in any part of the country. Butterflies also need water. They need shelter from wind, because it is difficult for them to fly if they are buffeted about. And they need sun to warm their wings for flight, and to orient themselves.

Since species in local butterfly populations vary enormously across the country, it is impossible to suggest larval foods that will suit every region. The ones here are planned for western Connecticut. But by doing a bit of research you can adapt the plan to your area. Using the chart of larval foods on pages 60 and 61, a good butterfly guide, your own observations and perhaps a call to a wildlife

THE BUTTERFLY GARDEN

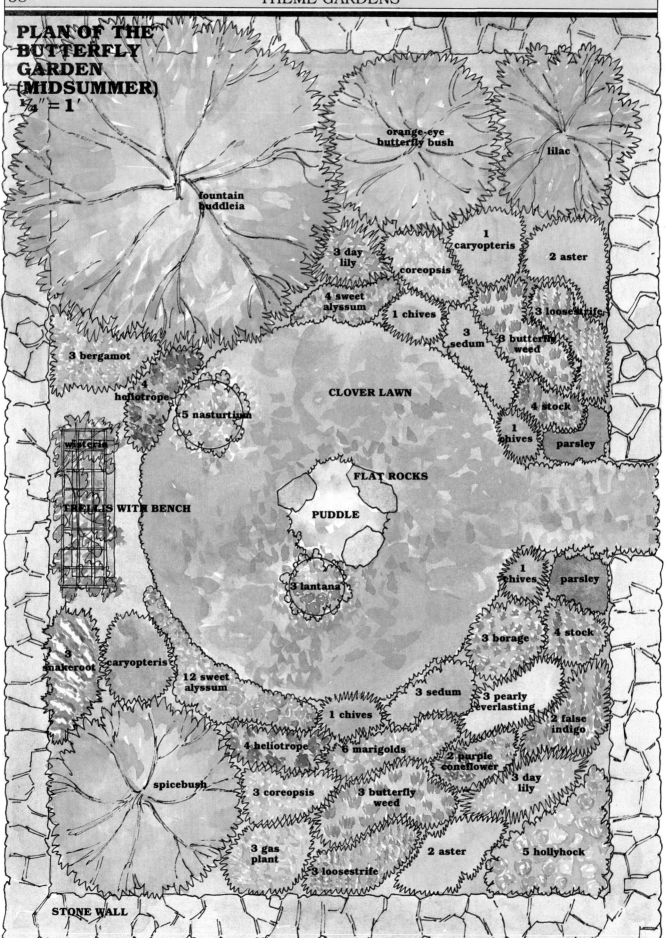

PLAN OF THE BUTTERFLY GARDEN (MIDSUMMER)
¼" = 1'

orange-eye butterfly bush

lilac

fountain buddleia

3 day lily

coreopsis

1 caryopteris

2 aster

4 sweet alyssum

1 chives

3 loosestrife

3 sedum

3 butterfly weed

3 bergamot

4 heliotrope

5 nasturtium

4 stock

1 chives

parsley

CLOVER LAWN

wisteria

FLAT ROCKS

TRELLIS WITH BENCH

PUDDLE

3 lantana

1 chives

parsley

3 snakeroot

caryopteris

12 sweet alyssum

3 borage

4 stock

3 sedum

3 pearly everlasting

1 chives

2 false indigo

4 heliotrope

6 marigolds

2 purple coneflower

3 day lily

spicebush

3 coreopsis

3 butterfly weed

3 gas plant

2 aster

5 hollyhock

3 loosestrife

STONE WALL

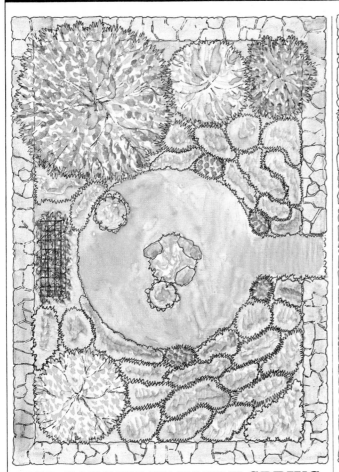

THE GARDEN IN EARLY SPRING

THE GARDEN IN LATE SUMMER

sanctuary or research station in your state, you can identify the species you are likely to attract and the major food plants for their caterpillars. This is worth doing, because it will encourage a butterfly to carry out its whole life cycle in or near your garden.

The perfect butterfly garden would be at least several acres in size and have enough different microenvironments to attract all the different butterflies native to your region. There would be a meadowful of wild flowers, grasses and common weeds, and a nettle bed where the Red Admiral can breed. There would be many kinds of native trees and shrubs. There would be a wet spot where moisture-loving plants could grow and some puddles of water would collect. There would be some woods, with low-growing native plants growing in soil rich in leaf mold. There would be an orchard or stand of old apple trees where the fallen fruit could be left to ferment and rot. And best of all, there would be a sunken place—an old foundation perhaps, or small

valley—sheltered from the wind but not the sun in which to grow your flowers.

If you do have large areas like this on your property I recommend that you leave them as wild as possible, except where you would like to have a lawn or want to grow cultivated flowers. If there is a part of your present lawn that you can leave unmowed, or mow only occasionally, so much the better. Let it fill up with dandelions and tick trefoil, a relative of clover. Introduce as many wild plants as possible—ones that butterflies are known to need for caterpillar foods. Buy a wild flower seed mixture and plant it in a strip between meadow and lawn. You might not want plants like crabgrass, ragweed and burdock near the house, but let them grow somewhere. Above all, start paying attention to the butterflies you see in the wild, and find out which plants they lay eggs on and which ones the caterpillars eat. Transplant these, if you can do so without trespassing or taking an endangered plant. Better yet, take the

SOME PLANTS THAT BUTTERFLY CATERPILLARS FEED ON

Plant	Butterfly
AGAVE, DESERT (*Agave deserti*).	Giant Skipper (*Agathymus stephensi*), southern California.
ASTER (*Aster* species).	Pearly Crescentspot (*Phyciodes tharos*), most of U.S.; other Crescentspots and Checkerspots.
BLUEBERRY (*Vaccinium*).	Blueberry Sulphur (*Colias pelidne*), Rocky Mountains; Brown Elfin (*Incisalia augustinus*), much of U.S.; also the less common Henry's Elfin (*Incisalia henrici*).
BORAGE SPECIES (*Boraginaceae*).	Anicia Checkerspot (*Occidryas anicia*), western states; Painted Lady (*Vanessa cardui*), throughout U.S.
CEANOTHUS SPECIES (*Ceanothus*).	California Hairstreak (*Satyrium californica*), West Coast, Rocky Mountains; Spring Azure (*Celastrina ladon*), throughout U.S.; Hedgerow Hairstreak (*Satyrium saepium*), West Coast, Southwest, Rockies.
CHERRY (*Prunus*).	Tiger Swallowtail (*Pterourus glaucus*), east of Rockies; Two-tailed Swallowtail (*Pterourus multicaudatus*), western states; Red-spotted Purple (*Basilarchia astyanax*), most of U.S. except West Coast.

Plant	Butterfly
CHICKWEED (*Stellaria media*).	Dwarf Yellow (*Nathalis iole*), most of Southwest and Midwest.
CLOVER, WHITE (*Trifolium repens*); other clovers.	Orange Sulphur (*Colias eurytheme*), most of U.S.; other Sulphurs.
CORN, INDIAN (*Zea mays*).	Clouded Skipper (*Lerema accius*), mostly the South, Southeast.
CRABGRASS (*Digitaria sanguinalis*).	Mottled Roadside Skipper, (*Amblyscirtes nysa*), Midwest and Southwest.
DOGWOOD (*Cornus*).	Spring Azure (*Celastrina ladon*), throughout U.S.
HOLLYHOCK (*Alcea*).	Painted Lady (*Vanessa cardui*), throughout U.S.; West Coast Lady (*Vanessa annabella*), West Coast; some Skippers.
HOP VINE (*Humulus*).	Question Mark (*Polygonia interrogationis*), east of Rocky Mountains; Comma, also called Hop Merchant (*Polygonia comma*), East and Midwest; Red Admiral (*Vanessa atalanta*), throughout U.S.
INDIAN PAINTBRUSH (*Castilleja* species).	Paintbrush Checkerspot (*Occidryas anicia*), Northern Checkerspot (*Charidryas palla*) and other Checkerspots, chiefly the West.
LUPINE SPECIES (*Lupinus*).	Northern Blue (*Lycaeides argyrognomon*), mostly Northwest; Common Blue (*Icariciau icaroides*), the West; other Blues.
MALLOWS (*Malvaceae*).	Same as for Hollyhock.

seeds when mature and plant them. Seeds and plants of wild species can also be ordered from the many nurseries that specialize in them (see Where to Order Plants, p. 215).

PLAN OF THE GARDEN
The garden in this chapter is designed for the person who wants to provide a good butterfly environment in a small space. Such a garden would be feasible in a town or even a city lot. Or on a larger piece of property, it could be a small gemlike garden near the house, augmented by wilder butterfly habitats in outlying areas.

The garden pictured here is surrounded by a stone wall. Any kind of wall would do; the garden could even be planted in the cellar of an old house of which only the foundation is standing. If you have a spot like this it would make a wonderful butterfly garden, because it would provide excellent shelter from the wind. There are many other ways of providing this, however. You could also plant it within the "L" of house that shields the area from the prevailing winds. A living hedge of a shrub such as blueberry or lilac would be an excellent enclosure.

This garden is a mixture of annuals, perennials and shrubs. They surround a circle of lawn, so that someone sitting there is surrounded by flowers—and butterflies. When you lay out the garden you should grade the

Plant	Butterfly	Plant	Butterfly
MARIGOLD (*Tagetes*).	Dwarf Yellow (*Nathalis iole*), most of Southwest and Midwest.	**SENNA** (*Cassia*).	Sulphurs.
MILKWEED species (*Asclepias*).	Monarch (*Danaus plexippus*), most of U.S.	**SNAKEROOT, BLACK** (*Cimicifuga racemosa*).	Spring Azure (*Celastrina ladon*), throughout U.S.
NASTURTIUM (*Tropaeolaceae*).	Cabbage white (*Artogeia rapae*), throughout U.S.	**SPICEBUSH** (*Lindera benzoin*).	Spicebush Swallowtail (*Pterourus troilus*), mostly eastern U.S.
NETTLE, STINGING (*Urtica*).	Red Admiral (*Vanessa atalanta*), throughout U.S.; Question Mark (*Polygonia interrogationis*), east of Rockies; Comma (*Polygonia comma*); Satyr Anglewing (*Polygonia satyrus*), the West; Milbert's Tortoiseshell (*Aglais milberti*), northern mountains.	**THISTLE** (*Circium*).	Painted Lady (*Vanessa cardui*), throughout U.S.; Viceroy (*Basilarchia archippus*), throughout U.S.; some Crescentspots.
		TREFOIL, TICK (*Desmodium*).	Eastern Tailed Blue (*Everes comyntas*), east of Rockies; Hoary Edge (*Achalarus lyciades*), east of Mississippi River.
PARSLEY (*Petroselinum*).	Eastern Black Swallowtail (*Papilio polyxenes*), most of U.S.	**TURTLEHEAD** (*Chelone glabra*).	Baltimore (*Euphydryas phaeton*), East Coast, parts of Midwest.
PASSIONFLOWER (*Passiflora*).	Gulf Fritillary (*Agraulis vanillae*), the South, migrates to parts of the North; Variegated Fritillary (*Euptoieta claudia*), mostly the South.	**VIOLET** (*Viola*).	All the Fritillaries, feeding at night.
PEARLY EVERLASTING (*Anaphalis margaritacea*).	American Painted Lady (*Vanessa virginiensis*), most of the East.	**WILLOW** (*Salix*).	Gray Hairstreak (*Strymon melinus*), most of U.S.; Tiger Swallowtail (*Pterourus glaucus*), east of Rockies; Western Tiger Swallowtail (*Pterourus rutulus*), west of Rockies; Viceroy (*Basilarchia archippus*), most of U.S.; Red-spotted Purple (*Basilarchia astyanax*), east of Rockies but not far north; Mourning Cloak (*Nymphalis antiopa*), throughout U.S.; various Sulphurs, Hairstreaks, Fritillaries and Duskywings.
PLUMBAGO SPECIES (*Plumbago*).	Cassius Blue (*Leptotes cassius*), the South; Marine Blue (*Leptotes marina*), mainly the Southwest.		
QUEEN ANNE'S LACE (*Daucus carota*).	Eastern Black Swallowtail (*Papilio polyxenes*), the East, Midwest.		
RAGWEED (*Ambrosia trifida*).	Gorgone Crescentspot (*Charidryas gorgone*), the Midwest.	**WISTERIA** (*Wisteria*).	Silver-spotted Skipper (*Epargyreus clarus*), most of U.S.

beds so that they are slightly higher along all four edges, sloping gradually down to a low point in the center of the lawn. This slope, combined with the graduation in heights of the plants, from high in the rear to low in front, will give you the feeling of being inside a bowl of color, some of it fixed and some of it hovering in flight. It will also create an area of deliberately poor drainage in the center for butterflies to drink from. Treat this as a tiny seasonal pond. Place some large flat stones in it and next to it and smear them with beer or sugar water from time to time. The butterflies will perch on them. Let rainwater collect there, and fill it with a hose when dry. But keep it shallow; it should be more of a puddle than a pond. It may never be as enticing to butterflies as is barnyard muck, or the after-rain mud puddles in a country road, but some species will sip there. You might even play host to a "male drinking club."

The shrubs I have suggested bloom at various times, from the spicebush in April (the larval food of the Spicebush Swallowtail) to the lilacs and fountain buddleia in late May, to the late-summer orange-eye butterfly bush and caryopteris. A trellis covered with a purple wisteria vine will also lure butterflies in May, and a seat under it will provide a fine spot for butterfly watching.

The annuals and perennials here are a combination of nectar plants and larval foods.

Most of them are both. Some of them are wild flowers, or hybrid forms of native plants, and the garden has the feel of a wild flower garden, as if meadow flowers had sprung up within the enclosure. If you have a choice between using the wild form of a plant and the cultivated one, use the wild species for this garden. (Though there are exceptions to this rule: the Black Swallowtail butterfly, for example, prefers garden carrot tops to the wild carrot—Queen Anne's lace.) As a group, many of these flowers do not have large, showy heads, but are daisylike, or have feathery spikes or umbels. Their blooming season extends from spring flowers (spicebush, chives) to early summer ones (false indigo, gas plant, coreopsis) and midsummer ones (butterfly weed, hollyhock, borage, coneflower, loosestrife, snakeroot) and ends with sedum and aster. Annuals are there mainly for nectar and continuous bloom, but the nasturtiums and alyssum are also larval foods. Parsley is planted to feed the Black Swallowtail caterpillar as well as humans. The lawn is white clover, both a larval food and a nectar plant. So are the dandelions which should be encouraged to grow in it.

The color scheme here corresponds to the butterflies' own choice. Of all colors, they love purple best, with yellow their second preference. So the garden is a display of royal purple and gold, with touches of pink, blue and orange. It is a bright garden with some vibrant juxtapositions—the orange of butterfly weed next to the purple-pink of loosestrife, for example. You will find that butterflies make daring contrasts in these color mixtures. Disregarding all thoughts of camouflage, lavender-gray Hairstreaks will perch on the orange butterfly weed, for example, and bright orange Fritillaries will light on the loosestrife. There are probably scientific ways to explain this behavior; butterflies see in the ultraviolet range for one thing. But looking at all those mingling and moving colors, it seems part of a larger well-orchestrated harmony that is quite beyond our range of understanding. It is something to marvel at.

The center of the circle, where the "puddle" is, can be brightened with some pots of nasturtium and lantana. Lantana is a good pot plant because you can prune it back in fall, keep it in a pot indoors in winter in areas where there are freezing temperatures and grow it outdoors again the following year. Nasturtium works well in a pot because it looks pretty spilling over the sides, and because potting it is sometimes the only way to give it the kind of soil it needs—sandy and rather poor in nutrients. Most gardens are too rich for it, so it grows big leaves that hide the flowers.

SITE

A sunny site is essential, both for the plants and for the butterflies. Besides being out of the wind, the plants should be in good soil with adequate drainage. If you do not want to enclose the garden in the ways suggested, you could let the recommended shrubs do the enclosing. Add some more lilacs, for example, choosing varieties that bloom at different times. Place them behind the flower borders where they will block the wind.

GROWING INSTRUCTIONS

In this garden, some of the finer points of gardening will have to be abandoned. Cutting back plants to encourage continuous bloom or a fall reblooming is apt to deprive caterpillars of their food, or wipe out the site of newly laid egg masses. Unless a plant is a nectar plant only, it is better to sacrifice a few blooms. While weediness is considered a good thing in butterfly gardens, I would not leave this one totally unweeded, but would proceed thus: when a new "wild" plant appears, identify it and find out if it is a larval food for butterflies of your region, using a butterfly guide. Notice whether butterflies visit

Tiger Swallowtail sips nectar from lilac.

© JO BREWER

its flowers. If it is interesting on either of these counts, let it stay; make a proper place for it with the understanding that it is not to take over.

The beds should be staked out accurately. A tidy shape, well edged, is especially important because of the informality of some of the plant material. Scribe a circle with an eight-foot radius for the central lawn. It would be a good idea to edge the beds with bricks placed vertically in a sand-filled trench.

The garden should be tilled and fertilized at the beginning, as for any permanent border. Most of these plants like soil of average fertility and a neutral pH. Moist clay, sandy or dry soil should be avoided. Lighten the soil in the shrub areas with humus and mulch with leaf mold.

Several of the plants, like butterfly weed and false indigo, are slow starters, but be patient and in a few years you will have plenty. Some should not be disturbed once planted, such as gas plant and butterfly weed. Others must be divided from time to time, such as aster, day lily and chive. Coreopsis and bergamot will need to be policed so that they don't spread too vigorously. A collar of metal flashing around the bergamot will make this job easier.

All these plants can be obtained already started from nurseries, but you may want to start some of them from seed, especially the annuals and wild flowers. If you are raising plants from seed, or want to encourage self-sowing, avoid using a mulch except in the shrub sections.

You will, of course, get some nonlepidopteral insect visitors that you will want to get rid of. Do not use any chemical insecticides, fungicides, herbicides or rodenticides. Pick off Japanese beetles and large insects or use a pheromone trap. Smother aphids with liquid soap, then flush them away. Any chemical poison you use could kill the caterpillars on that or any other plant in the garden. You may find that even your neighbors' use of these products is keeping butterflies away. Tell them what you are doing, and ask them to watch for new species of butterflies and their larva. They too might start to look at garden insects in a different light.

Gray Hairstreak (Strymon melinus) *on coreopsis.*

ADDITIONS AND SUBSTITUTIONS

As I have noted, the best way to design your own butterfly garden would be to find out what butterflies you might realistically be able to attract in your region, and discover which foods their larvae feed on. And you may want to choose several habitats on your property suitable for specific groups of plants and butterflies. For example, a sunny, moist section might include turtlehead (*Chelone glabra* and *C. lyonii*) and forget-me-not (*Myosotis*). In shady, woodsy places plant wild ginger (*Asarum*) and violets. You should grow some bothersome but important weeds, such as nettles (*Urtica*), thistle (*Cirsium*) and burdock (*Arctium lappa*). Many trees feed the larvae of *Lepidoptera*. Some that attract many different species are the willows, the poplars and wild cherry. Meadow grasses are important too, for Wood Nymphs and Satyrs.

Here are some flowering plants that you could add to this particular garden: snapdragons, goldenrod (*Solidago* species), sunflower (*Helianthus* species), valerian (*Valeriana* species), dame's rocket (*Hesperis matronalis*), phlox (*Phlox* species), lupine (*Lupinus* species), lavender (*Lavandula* species), Queen Anne's lace (*Daucus carota*), catnip (*Nepeta cataria*), scabiosa (*Scabiosa caucasica*), fleabane (*Erigeron* species), honesty (*Lunaria annua*), red clover (*Trifolium pratense*), sage (*Salvia* species), petunia and candytuft (*Iberis sempervirens*).

Gardeners in warm climates should certainly grow passionflower (*Passiflora*), the larval plant for all of the heliconian species. Lantana can be grown as a perennial in frost-free regions. The *Ceanothus* species are a good nectar plant for the West Coast, and New Jersey tea (*Ceanothus americanus*) will thrive as far north as zone 5. *Buddleia globosa*, the yellow-flowered butterfly bush, requires a fairly mild climate, but a northern butterfly gardener I know grows it in pots on her terrace. A good butterfly shrub for Florida and other very warm places is flame-of-the-woods (*Ixora coccinea*). California gardeners grow fennel for the Anise Swallowtail, lots of senna for the Sleepy Orange and the Cloudless Sulphur, and cape plumbago for the Marine Blue.

PLANT LIST FOR BUTTERFLY GARDEN

ANNUALS AND TENDER PERENNIALS

ALYSSUM, SWEET. *Lobularia maritima.* A purple variety would be best for this garden. Grows 4–6 inches tall and blooms from late spring to frost; the tiny fragrant blossoms make a carpet. Easily grown from seeds sown in the ground in early spring or started indoors. Transplant clumps to fill gaps in the border. Cut back for lush, recurrent bloom. Often self-sows.

BORAGE. *Borago officinalis.* Sprawling herb about 2 feet tall. Easy to grow, it has hairy leaves and stems and bright blue flowers from late spring through midsummer. Sow seeds directly in the garden in early spring and thin to at least a foot apart. Borage will often self-sow; you may also sow some seeds yourself in fall to produce a crop the following year. It will grow well in rather dry sandy soil, but a rich soil will produce more abundant bloom.

HELIOTROPE, COMMON. *Heliotropium arborescens.* Grows 1–2 feet tall, with huge clusters of small, richly fragrant flowers. Choose a purple shade. Likes rich soil and full sun. Sow seeds indoors in the winter for spring planting, or buy started plants and set out after the last frost.

LANTANA, COMMON. *Lantana camara.* Or trailing lantana (*L. montevidensis,* also called *L. sellowiana*). Common lantana is an evergreen shrub in zones 8–10; in colder climates it is grown as an annual or pot plant and is anywhere from 1 to 3 feet tall. It stands erect and bears flowers in various shades, usually red or yellow, or mixtures of these colors. Trailing lantana, hardy only in tropical and subtropical climates, is a prostrate creeper with pinkish lavender flowers that is especially good in pots or hanging planters. For this garden, grow either species from started plants that you winter indoors, cutting back hard in fall and watering sparingly afterward. Obtain new plants from rooted cuttings.

MARIGOLD. *Tagetes erecta* and other species. Any marigolds would look good in this garden, especially the showy yellow African marigolds, which grow as high as 3 feet. Sow seeds indoors, or in the garden after danger of frost; or buy started plants, setting about 1 foot apart.

NASTURTIUM. *Tropaeolum majus.* Choose a yellow variety such as 'Golden Gleam.' Sow seeds indoors in early spring or outdoors after danger of frost, thinning plants to 6–8 inches apart. Fill pots with soil that is dryish, sandy and rather poor in nitrogen.

PARSLEY. *Petroselinum hortense.* Plant any variety you prefer. Sow seeds directly in the garden as soon as the ground can be worked; they germinate slowly and only when the ground is fairly cool. The plants like moist, rich soil and will often self-sow, acting as biennials.

STOCK, COMMON. *Matthiola incana* 'Annua' hybrids. Plant the trysomic strain in hot climates, others in cooler regions. Common stocks grow 1–3 feet tall and bear showy spikes of usually double flowers in shades of pink, red and white. They prefer sun, fairly rich soil and plenty of moisture. Sow seeds in the ground in March or April; thin out the weaker (usually single-flowered) seedlings so that the plants are 10–12 inches apart. Plant in fall in regions of mild (essentially frost-free) winters for winter and spring bloom.

PERENNIALS

ASTER, NEW ENGLAND (*Aster novae-angliae*) **OR NEW YORK** (*A. novae-belgii*). Zones 5–9. Choose tall purple or blue shades of horticultural varieties or the native species. Most varieties grow 3–4 feet tall; stake as needed. Asters like plenty of sun and moisture. Bloom is in late summer and fall. To keep the clumps vigorous, divide in early spring, discarding the center of the clump and replanting the young shoots at the edges.

BERGAMOT, WILD. *Monarda fistulosa*. To zone 3. This plant is similar to bee balm (*M. didyma*), but prefers a dry rather than a moist site and its flowers are lavender. It grows 3–4 feet tall and blooms in July and August. Collect seeds at the end of summer and plant immediately, or grow from clumps of roots, divided in spring. Bergamot spreads vigorously and sometimes needs to be contained by an underground barrier.

BUTTERFLY WEED. *Asclepias tuberosa*. Zones 3-9. Grows 2 feet tall and bears flat red-orange flower clusters from mid to late summer. Prefers slightly dry, sandy soil that is low in nitrogen. It is taprooted and, except when quite young, is extremely difficult to transplant. You may grow butterfly weed from seed, but it takes 4–5 years to produce plants mature enough to bloom. Even nursery-grown plants are slow to become bushy clumps. However, once established, with good drainage, they will grow large, last a long time and even self-sow, making them well worth the wait. New growth is slow to appear in the spring, so watch for it and don't dig the plants up by mistake.

CHIVES. *Allium schoenoprasum*. Zones 3–10. Chives grow a foot tall, with purple cloverlike heads of flowers in May and June, much visited by butterflies. Usually grown from started clumps, easily divided and planted in spring,

they benefit from division and their foliage often stays green all winter.

CLOVER, WHITE (DUTCH CLOVER). *Trifolium repens*. To zone 3. This common creeping clover forms a thick matlike lawn that does not need mowing. Flowers have a sweet fragrance. Sow seed in early spring or early fall, water as needed. Heavy fertilization should not be necessary. If the soil is acid apply a dressing of lime.

CONEFLOWER, PURPLE. *Echinacea purpurea*. Zones 3–10. Grows to 3 feet tall and bears flowers similar to those of black-eyed Susan (*Rudbeckia*), but are a striking purple with red-orange centers. July to September bloom. Plant 1½ feet apart and divide when crowded.

COREOPSIS (TICKSEED). *Coreopsis grandiflora* or *C.*

lanceolata. Zones 4–10. Grows to 2½ feet tall. Blooms bright yellow. Likes sun and well-drained soil. Spreads and self-sows readily. Divide in spring or fall.

DAY LILY. *Hemerocallis*. Zones 3–9. Day lilies come in shades of orange, yellow, red, pink, peach and maroon; any of these would look good in this garden. Heights range from 1½ feet up, with the flower stalks sometimes reaching 4 feet and taller. Blooming period varies according to the variety, from June to September. The plants are very easy to grow, but the clumps will become dense and require division every 4 years or so.

FALSE INDIGO. *Baptisia australis*. Zones 3–10. Grows 3–5 feet tall and bears bright blue flowers in June. Likes sun in cool climates, but prefers a little shade in warm ones. Starts off slowly, but establishes vigorous taproots and should not be moved. Can be grown from seeds or from young plants set out in spring.

GAS PLANT. *Dictamnus albus* (*D. fraxinella*). Zones 3–8. Grows 3 feet tall and bears flower spikes, usually rosy purple, in early summer. Like some other plants with unpleasant-smelling foliage, insects do not bother it, but butterflies will visit the fragrant

flowers. The flowers are said to produce a gas that can be ignited with a match on still evenings in hot weather. (The cut roots give off gas, too). Gas plant likes fairly rich soil and is best grown from nursery clumps. Give it 3–4 feet to spread, and leave it in place indefinitely.

HOLLYHOCK. *Alcea rosea* (*Althaea rosea*). Zones 3–10. The old-fashioned single varieties open themselves more invitingly to butterflies; I also simply prefer them, though they are less commonly available than the double or powderpuff varieties. Set out started plants 2 feet apart, and stake against summer storms. Easily grown from seed, they will often self-sow in your garden, though as perennials they are sometimes short-lived.

LOOSESTRIFE. *Lythrum salicaria*. Zones 3–9. The wild

form of this tall, spiky, purple-pink flower can be seen in marshes in summer in many parts of the United States. Cultivars range from 18 inches tall to 4–5 feet and are vigorous garden plants. They will often bloom from July to September. Set plants 1½ feet apart.

PEARLY EVERLASTING. *Anaphalis margaritacea.* Zones 3–6. Pearly everlasting is a common North American wild flower. Like many plants that prefer a rather dry location, it has hairy leaves and stems to help it conserve moisture; this gives it a gray-white appearance. Its white flowers with yellow centers in summer are easily dried for winter bouquets. Set divisions about 1½ feet apart in well-drained soil. Plants or seeds can be obtained from some wild flower or perennial nurseries. Otherwise transplant from the wild in early spring, or grow from collected seeds sown in late summer.

SEDUM (STONECROP). *Sedum spectabile.* To zone 3. Any of the showy sedums would look good here. This one bears large clusters of small pink flowers in August and September, has light green foliage and grows 2 feet tall. The red, late-blooming *S. telephium* 'Autumn Joy' would also be a good choice. Sedums have no stringent require-

ments, though they appreciate a well-drained soil. They do not need to be divided.

SNAKEROOT. *Cimicifuga racemosa.* Zones 3–9. In July and August, bears long, white fuzzy flower spikes that are gracefully curving. Usually grows to 6 feet tall. Prefers moist, rich, humus-filled soil. Plant 1½ feet apart; division rarely needed.

SHRUBS AND VINES

BUDDLEIA, FOUNTAIN. *Buddleia alternifolia* 'Argentea.' Zones 5–10. This shrub can grow as tall as 12 feet, with an even greater spread. It is covered with long lavender spikes of bloom in late spring. It likes fairly rich soil and needs room for the branches to arch out. Prune only just after bloom, to encourage more flowers the following year.

BUTTERFLY BUSH, OR-ANGE-EYE. *Buddleia davidii.* Zones 5-10. There are a number of species of *Buddleia,* many of them called butterfly bush, but in common parlance the name usually applies to varieties of *B. davidii,* a large shrub when grown in warm climates, but smaller in cool ones, where it often dies back in winter. Unlike *B. alternifolia,* it blooms on new wood in August in

shades of lavender, purple or pink, and should be cut back in early spring before blooming to encourage vigorous new growth.

CARYOPTERIS. *Caryopteris clandonensis.* Zones 5–9. 'Heavenly Blue' and 'Blue Mist' are common varieties. A small shrub, about 3 feet tall, it bears misty bright blue flowers in late summer. It dies back in winter in cold climates, with no harm to the plant—in fact pruning out the dead wood in early spring will encourage bushiness and profuse flowering.

LILAC, COMMON. *Syringa vulgaris.* Zones 2–7. Any of the French hybrids would do as well as the common lilac here. Prune after flowering to keep the plant from becoming too leggy, removing several crowded stems from near their bases and cutting off spent blooms. Dormant oil spray applied before the plant leafs out will combat lilac scale, and stems with borers should be

removed. But, as with this garden as a whole, it should not be sprayed with insecticides.

SPICEBUSH. *Lindera benzoin.* Zones 4–9. This shrub, native to the eastern United States, is easy to grow and bears small, fragrant yellow flowers in early spring, before the plant leafs out. In fall its foliage changes to bright yellow. It has red berries. It can grow to 15 feet (usually 8 feet or so) and can be kept within bounds by pruning after blooming. Spicebush prefers moist woodsy soil rich in humus.

WISTERIA, JAPANESE. *Wisteria floribunda.* To zone 4. This is the hardiest wisteria and the most fragrant. It is a twining vine with long, elegant, dangling flower clusters in May, in shades of lavender and sometimes pink or white. Failure to bloom can often be cured by root pruning (making vertical cuts with a square spade in a circle a few feet from the base of the plant) and by pruning the ends of the plant after bloom, when bloom occurs. Fertilizing, especially with a fertilizer rich in phosphate, may also help.

A Moon Garden

A garden planted with only white flowers is by day a pleasing and unusual picture. By night it is enchantment. In the daylight it has a feeling of coolness and refinement; the green foliage frames the white blossoms, which in turn provide a foil for the different greens of the leaves. In the moonlight the shapes of the flowers stand out as if they themselves were lights.

It is a picture full of movement, for night gardens have a life of their own. Fireflies twinkle through the swirling evening mists, and pale moths feed on the nectar of nocturnal blooms which open just to receive them.

There have been many moonlight gardens throughout history. In medieval Japan, such gardens were constructed with pale rocks or sand, white chrysanthemums and pools of water, all to catch the moon's light. In 1639, the Mogul emperor Jahan built a moonlight garden (the Mahtab Bagh) at the Red Fort in Delhi, India, with fragrant white flowers such as jasmine, narcissus, tuberoses and lilies. A nineteenth-century garden in Newburyport, Massachusetts, described by Alice Morse Earle in her book, *Old Time Gardens*, had white borders over seven hundred feet long, not to mention white oxen, cows, sheep, pigeons and poultry. Author Vita Sackville-West's gray and white garden at Sissinghurst in England is a moon garden, modeled, I expect, on those of India.

A moonlight garden does not have to be all white. Many pale pink, blue or yellow flowers will reflect the glow of the moon at night, though their colors will be muted. And many flowers that are night-blooming are colored, such as yellow evening primroses, or are night-scented, such as night-scented stock. The garden in this chapter is composed completely of white flowers and is meant to be seen by day or night. When I set out to design this garden I had no intention of giving it the shape of a crescent moon. I was trying to find a shape that would partly enclose a terrace, a pool or a patch of lawn. I wanted the viewer to be surrounded by white flowers and their fragrance. Unconsciously I drew a crescent, and a crescent —appropriately—it remained.

PLAN OF THE GARDEN

I have made this a small garden, because in many cases the owner will want to grow colored flowers somewhere else on the property and will not want to devote all of his or her labors to an all-white garden. So the garden in this chapter is an intimate one, whose interest lies in small details to be viewed at close range.

The main focal point is a lamppost set in the wide part of the crescent, just off center. This lamppost will provide soft light for viewing the garden on moonless nights. A cast iron one would be in keeping with the dignified formality of this garden, but a handsome wooden post would look good too. A moonflower vine climbs on the post, opening its large, fragrant, saucerlike blooms at night. Three deutzias provide a base of green shrubbery and a mass of frothy white flowers in spring. The rest of the garden is planted with herbaceous perennials and annuals, some flowering and some there for their foliage alone. Tall white flowers—cosmos, delphinium and phlox—are the background, while perennial candytuft and petunias edge the front of the border. The rest are arrayed in between.

Clumps of white trumpet daffodils start the season, followed quickly by the candytuft and deutzias in May. By the light of the June moon you can see white Japanese fan columbines with their exquisite spurred flowers and dainty fanlike leaves. These dwarf columbines grow only about a foot tall, but taller white ones such as 'Silver Queen' would look good too. These are followed by the lavish flowers of white Japanese iris. Under the midsummer moon the blooms of phlox, moonflower, annual nicotiana, petunias, baby's breath and cosmos appear. The harvest moon shines on white hosta, Japanese anemones, chrysanthemums, tuberoses and dwarf asters.

The white garden at Sissinghurst in England includes white wisteria, Pyrus salicifolia, *lamb's ears and artemisias.*

There is considerable contrast among the types of foliage in this garden. The columbines have blue-green leaves; the deutzias have small, dark green leaves that are attractive long after the flowers are gone. These are a good foil for the moonflower that winds up from them like a bottle genie, opening its blooms on days when it is a bit cloudy.

The candytuft also has dark green leaves, making it a good edging even without flowers. The narrow upright foliage of the Japanese iris is a vertical accent. The cosmos foliage is feathery. The hosta makes a mound of broad shiny leaves that are its main feature, though the dainty fragrant white flowers are also a nice detail in the garden. A lady fern provides a graceful mass of greenery, balancing the mass of the hosta on the opposite side of the lamppost.

Despite the showiness of some of these flowers, such as petunias, there is an airy quality to many of them—the columbines, the anemones, the deutzia and especially the baby's breath with its clouds of tiny flowers. The fact that only white is used causes the eye to focus on the difference between one flower shape and another: the cosmos floating on wiry stems in the night like little stars, next to the tall fat spires of the delphiniums.

Several of the plants are fragrant: tuberose, chrysanthemum, moonflower, hosta, phlox and nicotiana, which has a peculiar fragrance by day but is sweet at night. Petunias smell odd at any time, and if you are not fond of their scent, plant white sweet alyssum instead; it would make a perfect edging.

In this garden it is particularly important for the edge to be tidy, because the garden should have a strongly defined shape; it does not have a rustic, informal style. A row of flagstones around all the edges would be suitable (see Fig. 5, p. 197); so would brick or cobblestones.

SITE
The garden is meant to be viewed from inside the crescent, and the heights of the flowers are graded accordingly. You might want to place the garden where it could be seen from above, from an upstairs window for instance; the crescent moon shape would reveal itself

A white border at Bampton House, Oxford. In front of the bench are hebe, campanula and daisies (Matricaria); behind is gray-leafed senecio.

beautifully. As I have suggested, a terrace, lawn or pool could lie within the crescent. The terrace should be made of the same material as the edging of the garden. The pool might be an ornamental one with white night-blooming tropical lilies (Nymphaea) floating on it. (This garden would be a wonderful one to partially enclose a swimming pool, reflecting the white flowers and tempting swimmers with their fragrance.)

The garden will look best with a dark background. An evergreen hedge would set off the white flowers nicely. The hedge, however, should not be placed in such a way that it casts a deep shadow for a large part of the day; all the plants here are tolerant of full sun, and some of them require it. You could also plant a shady white garden—there are many lovely white-blooming plants that like partial shade, such as the fragrant woodruff, white violets and foam flower (Tiarella)—but remember that a site in partial sunlight will be in partial moonlight too, and the effect will be one of flickering light, not a blaze of night whiteness.

GROWING INSTRUCTIONS
Mark out the garden as shown in the diagram and edge it neatly with a square spade (see Figs. 1 and 2, p. 197). Lay your edging material, if you are putting in an edging, and install the lamppost (see p. 73). The ideal time to carry out all this preparation would be fall, enriching the soil at the same time and lightening it with humus. You would then wait until spring to set out the plants, except for the daffodils.

THE MOON
GARDEN

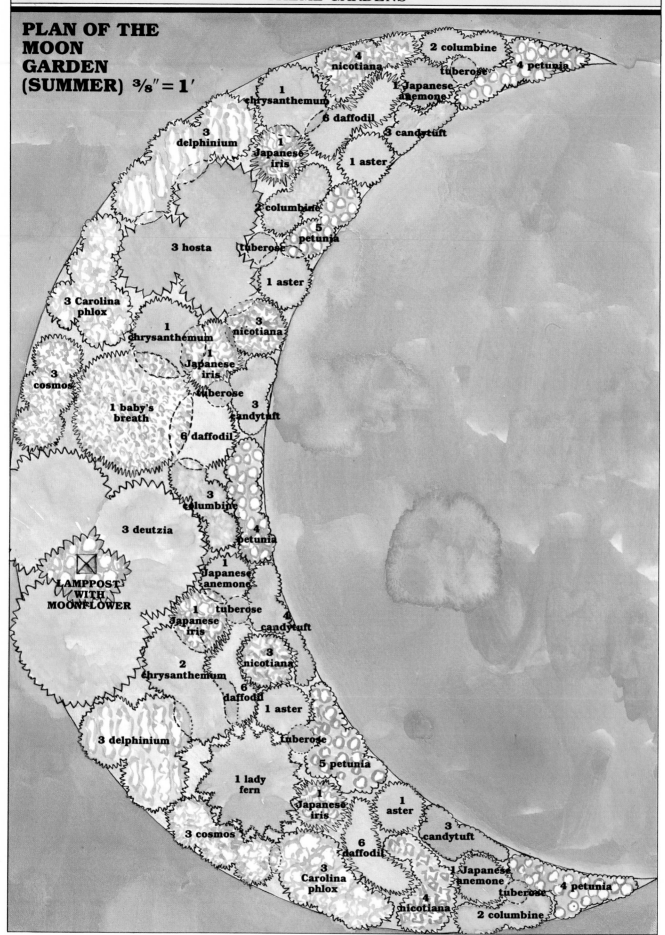

PLAN OF THE MOON GARDEN (SUMMER) ⅜″ = 1′

4 nicotiana

2 columbine

tuberose

4 petunia

1 chrysanthemum

1 Japanese anemone

6 daffodil

3 candytuft

3 delphinium

1 Japanese iris

1 aster

2 columbine

5 petunia

3 hosta

tuberose

1 aster

3 Carolina phlox

1 chrysanthemum

3 nicotiana

1 Japanese iris

3 cosmos

tuberose

1 baby's breath

3 candytuft

6 daffodil

3 columbine

3 deutzia

4 petunia

1 Japanese anemone

LAMPPOST WITH MOONFLOWER

1 tuberose

4 candytuft

1 Japanese iris

3 nicotiana

2 chrysanthemum

6 daffodil

1 aster

3 delphinium

tuberose

5 petunia

1 lady fern

1 Japanese iris

1 aster

3 candytuft

3 cosmos

6 daffodil

1 Japanese anemone

3 Carolina phlox

tuberose

4 petunia

4 nicotiana

2 columbine

THE GARDEN IN SPRING

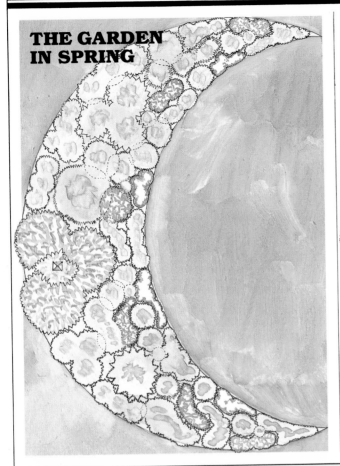

THE GARDEN IN FALL

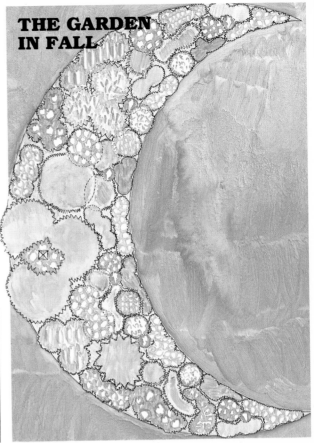

TWO WAYS TO WIRE A LAMPPOST

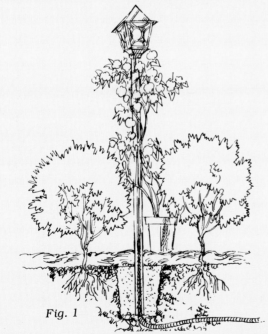

Fig. 1

Fig. 1. This prewired metal lamppost, with standard 120-volt current, is sunk in concrete (at least 2 feet) with the wiring encased in a metal conduit and buried at least 18 inches. Conduit leads to a power source.

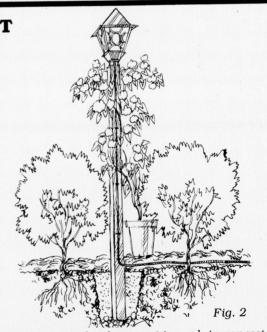

Fig. 2

Fig. 2. This wooden lamppost is sunk in concrete for stability, but the low-voltage wiring (12 volts) is simply stapled to the outside of the post and is run along the surface of the ground, under the mulch. Wire leads to a transformer which is connected to a standard-voltage power source. If the low-voltage wire will cross a lawn or other high-traffic area, it is a good idea to bury it.

The plants I have suggested vary in their requirements, so use a soil of average texture and fertility, with a neutral pH. They will benefit from a two-inch mulch, especially if next to a swimming pool, which reflects the sun's rays and generates a lot of heat. But weeds will not be a big problem, since the garden is small and closely planted. In the plan, several plants, in fact, almost overlap—these bloom at different times. When the withered foliage of the daffodils, iris and columbines is cut, other plants will fill up the space; chrysanthemums, for instance, start slowly but get very bushy by the end of summer if you pinch them industriously. It is especially wise to cut withered or brown foliage, as well as spent blooms, in a small, gemlike garden like this; any debris will be conspicuous.

Most of the plants here are easy to grow, though some have special requirements. Phlox needs thinning; delphiniums need to be cut back. In regions where the ground freezes, tuberoses are too tender to overwinter in the ground. Best to plant a few here and there in the spring, let them bloom, then dig them up before the first frost and store them for the winter. Or you may display them as pot-grown plants in or near the garden.

The annuals and the columbines may self-sow, but because such volunteers do not always land in good spots or breed true to color you may prefer to raise them afresh each year from purchased seed. Weeds will not show at night, but unstaked plants will. Sprawling phlox and bent-over delphiniums are quite undignified by moonlight.

A shady wild-flower garden near Center Bridge, Pennsylvania is carpeted with white Quaker ladies. Phlox divaricata is at right.

© DEREK FELL

ADDITIONS AND SUBSTITUTIONS

Since there are repeating patterns in this garden, you could make it smaller by simply planting one group of each plant and making a tiny crescent. You could also eliminate all need for construction by having no edging material, just firm cuts with the spade, and by using a simpler means of illumination, such as a torch you stick in the ground or paper lanterns strung on a wire instead of an electric lantern.

To make the garden larger, increase the size of the crescent and add more of the many white flowers there are to choose from: dahlias (a good substitute for chrysanthemums), shasta daisies and other white daisies, peonies, yucca, gladioluses, snapdragons, foxglove, veronica, regal or madonna lilies, Siberian or bearded iris, coral bells, spiderwort, woodland strawberries (fraises des bois), snakeroot (Cimicifuga species), tulips, snowdrops, crocuses, sedum, Silene alpestris, verbenas and several of the campanulas. If you want to plant trees and shrubs that produce white blossoms, you could choose star magnolia, flowering dogwood, rose of Sharon (Hibiscus syriacus), hydrangea, mock orange (Philadelphus species), lilac (Syringa species), Viburnum species, Spiraea species, Sargent crabapple, Japanese andromeda, azalea, sweet bay (Magnolia virginiana), rhododendron and roses, especially the old Blanc Double de Coubert, which is fragrant at night. You could approach this garden through a long pergola covered with climbing white roses, white wisteria, honeysuckle and white clematis, including the late-blooming Clematis paniculata. (You could also plant a white large-flowered summer-blooming clematis on the lamppost in place of the moonflower.) Another good vine for a pergola would be five-leafed akebia (Akebia quinata). Its flowers are not white but they are inconspicuous and night-scented; it is vigorous—give it room. If you have some shade in your garden, plant astilbes, Japanese primrose and lily of the valley.

If your major concern is to have a garden that is beautiful and fragrant at night, you might want to modify the white theme by including more kinds with night-scented or night-blooming flowers that are colored. Some of them are: dame's rocket *(Hesperis matronalis)*; gas plant *(Dictamnus albus)*; lady-of-the-night, also known as Franciscan nightshade *(Brunfelsia americana)*—a shrub with tube-shaped white flowers that are fragrant at night; fairy lily *(Cooperia pedunculata)* and evening star *(C. drummondii)*—both tender night-scented bulbous species from the Southwest; *Gladiolus tristis concolor*, a fragrant white night-blooming gladiolus; bouncing bet *(Saponaria officinalis)*, a spreading pink or white primarily night-blooming annual; evening primrose *(Oenothera* species), some of which are white. You might also plant some of the night-scented stock *(Matthiola bicornis)* suggested for the Fragrance Garden (see p. 25). Even in an all-white garden you could tuck its inconspicuous purplish flowers in somewhere and let them release their delicious scent by night.

One exotic addition might be spider lily *(Ismene calathina*, also called *Hymenocallis narcissiflora)*; it is a tender bulb you can grow the way you would tuberoses. Another is night-blooming cereus *(Hylocereus undatus)*, a tropical plant best left in a pot and brought indoors before frost. Gardeners in frost-free climates can grow them without worry, though, along with the richly fragrant jasmines *(Jasminum* species) and citrus trees with their fragrant white blossoms.

Another way to vary this garden would be to add plants with foliage in contrasting shades of white, gray and blue. The artemisias, lavender cotton *(Santolina chamaecyparissus)* and blue fescue would all blend well in a white garden.

PLANT LIST FOR MOON GARDEN

(see p. 25)

ANNUALS

COSMOS. *Cosmos bipinnatus.* 4–6 feet tall, sometimes taller. Choose a white variety.

The plant will bloom more profusely if the soil is sandy and not too rich. Pinching will keep the plant fairly low and also produce more bloom. Sow outdoors after danger of frost, or indoors in early spring. Set plants 12-18 inches apart.

NICOTIANA (FLOWERING TOBACCO). *Nicotiana alata grandiflora.* Try to find the old-fashioned white variety that grows about 3 feet tall and is especially fragrant—almost jasmine-scented—at night. Otherwise plant a white variety of the lower modern hybrids. Sow seeds in early

spring indoors or buy nursery-grown plants and set out after danger of frost, 10 inches apart.

PETUNIA. *Petunia hybrida multiflora.* Single white variety. Petunias like plenty of sun and water, and fairly fertile soil. Seeds are best sown in late winter or early spring indoors, to have plants to set out, 8–12 inches apart, after there is no longer danger of frost, or you may buy started plants.

BULBS AND TUBERS

DAFFODIL, TRUMPET. *Narcissus.* Zones 4–10. Plant the white trumpet variety or the fragrant white *N. poeticus* in early fall, 8–10 inches deep. Fertilize with bone meal. Do not cut the tops back until they turn brown.

TUBEROSE. *Polianthes tuberosa.* Winter-hardy only in the Deep South. Varieties range from 1½ to 4 feet tall. Plant the bulbs around June 1 in the garden, or start in pots indoors in early spring, then set out before the late summer blooming period, either in the ground or in the pots. Dig up before the first frost and store over the winter in dry peat moss, or purchase new bulbs each year.

PERENNIALS AND FOLIAGE PLANTS

ANEMONE, JAPANESE. *Anemone hupehensis japonica.* Zones 5–9. Grows about 2½ feet tall. The foliage is a low dark green mound. Flowers are single or double and are borne on tall slender stems from late summer to frost. They prefer light shade but will grow well in full sun with adequate moisture. Division is not necessary. In northern climates, protect with mulch in winter.

ASTER. *Aster* 'Snowball.' Zones 5–9. A dwarf variety that grows 8–10 inches tall, producing a mound of single white blooms in September.

BABY'S BREATH. *Gypsophila paniculata.* Zones 4–8. White double variety such as 'Bristol Fairy.' Grows 2–4 feet tall and blooms in June and July, repeating if cut. Prefers sun and needs water in dry weather. Work a cupful of lime into the soil surrounding the plant before planting and every few years thereafter. It has a sprawling habit and will look better in this garden if a "corset" is set in the ground around the plant when it is 1–2 feet tall. Stick 3-foot bamboo stakes firmly in the soil surrounding the plant and weave twine through the stakes to give support. Most varieties are grafted; plant with the graft just below soil level. Baby's breath is tap-rooted; do not transplant or divide.

CANDYTUFT. *Iberis semper-virens,* 'Autumn Snow.' Zones 3–9. This variety bears white flowers in spring and again, more sparingly, in fall if cut back just after blooming. It prefers rich, well-drained sandy soil and full sun. You can propagate it easily from cuttings. Plant 1 foot apart.

CHRYSANTHEMUM (HARDY CHRYSANTHEMUM). *Chrysanthemum morifolium.* Zones 4–10. Choose one of the white decorative varieties (the common large-flowered type). These grow 1½–3 feet tall and bloom from August to October. They like sun and rich, well-drained soil lightened with humus and cultivation. Pinch the terminal shoots until mid-July to encourage branching. Some gardeners winter their chrysanthemums in a cold frame and start new plants in early spring by removing stolons with new growth on them and replanting. Others—by pinching, mulching, and good care—keep their clumps going for several years before they lose their vigor.

COLUMBINE, JAPANESE FAN. *Aquilegia flabellata,* 'Nana Alba.' Zones 4–9. Grows about a foot tall, blooming in April and May. Plants will be more long-lived if spent blooms are pinched off to prevent them from setting seed.

DELPHINIUM. *Delphinium,* Pacific Coast hybrid, white variety. Zones 3–7. Grows 5–8 feet tall, with magnificent flower spikes in June-July, and again in fall if cut after blooming. Plant 2 feet apart and stake with a sturdy dowel or green bamboo pole to keep plants from being blown over. Not dependably perennial. The white form of garland, Chinese or Connecticut Yankee delphinium might be substituted, but remember that these are all shorter than the Pacific Coast strain.

FERN, LADY. *Athyrium felix-femina.* Zones 3–8. Grows 3 feet tall with lacy fronds that darken as the season progresses. The plants are variable in appearance. Tolerates full sun, but appreciates a mulch, or generous watering in dry weather. Prefers a slightly acid soil with some humus added.

HOSTA, FUNKIA, PLANTAIN LILY. *Hosta plantaginea.* Zones 4–9. Foliage is 1½ feet tall, flowers to 2 feet. Fragrant white flowers appear in August and September. In cold zones use a winter mulch the first year. Easily propagated by division.

IRIS, JAPANESE. *Iris kaempferi.* Zones 5–8. Choose a white variety. Blooms in early summer and grows 3–3½ feet tall. Prefers sun, slightly acid soil and moisture. Water in dry periods or provide a summer mulch. Plant 15–18 inches apart. Division not usually necessary. Generally planted in spring but can also be planted in summer or fall.

PHLOX, CAROLINA. *Phlox carolina (P. suffruticosa)* 'Miss Lingard.' Zones 3–9. Grows 2½–3 feet tall and bears loose white flower heads from June to September. Plant ½–2 feet apart in full sun or light shade. Likes moist, rich soil. Thin as needed, and cut spent blooms for more profuse bloom.

SHRUBS AND VINES

DEUTZIA, SLENDER. *Deutzia gracilis.* Zones 5–9. Dense, compact, low-growing shrub, usually about 3 feet tall. Bears a profusion of small white flowers in late May.

MOONFLOWER. *Calonyction aculeatum (Ipomoea alba).* Perennial in warm climates. Vigorous vine which may grow to 20 feet in rich soil. It has fragrant, trumpet-shaped flowers up to 6 inches across that open at night and on cloudy days, and large heart-shaped leaves. The plants need ample sun and moisture. Nick the seeds or soak them overnight to speed germination. Start indoors in early spring in peat pots, since seedlings do not transplant easily, then set in soil after danger of frost. In this garden you may want to transfer the peat pots to a larger container, filled with rich potting soil, and set it at the base of the lamppost among the deutzias, feeding several times during the season with liquid fertilizer. Do this when the plants are tall enough to reach above the shrubs, so they will have enough light. This method will also curb the growth of the plant's roots, which are invasive.

A Children's Garden

Gardening has a magical quality when you are a child. You plant little dry brown bulbs in the fall, and while they are sleeping through the winter you almost forget about them. But in the spring they remember to come up as bright yellow and purple crocuses.

You plant tiny radish seeds, and in just a few weeks they have turned into something you can eat. Or you cut off a piece of potato with an eye in it, and it grows a whole plant, with baby potatoes dangling from its roots. Some people, no matter how old they are, never get over the feeling that these things are magic. These

are often people who, as children, had a piece of the family garden to work themselves, or even a separate little plot they could call their own.

The garden I have outlined puts the idea of a children's garden on a slightly grander scale. What would children put inside a fence if they could grow anything they wanted? Only a child can answer this question, of course, but I have made some suggestions for things that might appeal. This isn't a huge garden, but there are twenty-eight different plants in it—
things that

are fun and easy to grow. It is a place where childen can have a world of their own. Inside that fence it is their garden.

This garden is ideally suited to a family with several children in it, or perhaps a group of neighbors or a small school group. It could also be one child's horticultural playground. But preparing and maintaining it would be a big task to fall on one small pair of shoulders without help from someone older. That older person might enjoy helping and teaching as much as the child liked being helped.

Above all, the garden should be fun. Its main purpose is not to teach horticulture, or to get a child to eat vegetables, although both these things might result. The garden's theme is "Always something to do," not just the weeding, but special things that keep happening all through the gardening season. Spring is the time for watching the bulbs come up, and planting new things. In summer you watch all the plants get big, and eat some of them. You watch butterflies visit your flowers, and pick bouquets for the people you like. In the late summer and fall you harvest your vegetables, and maybe even preserve some of them if you have a lot of extras. A good pumpkin crop might supply a roadside or streetside stand for Halloween. On cold winter days you can make dried arrangements and bouquets with some of the flowers you have grown, and enjoy popping the popcorn you grew yourself.

The key is variety. You are a farmer in one part of your plot, a flower grower in another, a frog raiser in another. And each year you can add something different: some new vegetables (spaghetti squash, for example), some new annuals or some new spring bulbs,

A garden for children at River Farm in Mount Vernon, Virginia, headquarters of the American Horticultural Society features a tepee planted with peas, squash and cucumbers.

which can be planted in the other flower areas without disturbing the plants that bloom later. Even though there are many plants, they can all fit together in a small space.

PLAN OF THE GARDEN

The garden is a fifteen-by-twenty-five-foot plot, enclosed by a stout fence made of good cedar or locust posts and heavy-gauge one-by-two-inch fencing, with a gate on one side (see p. 82). There are paths about one and a half to two feet wide for easy access to the plants, so that small feet can walk close to them without trampling them. These are covered with about four inches of shredded bark to keep weeds and mud away. There are also some small stools or benches here and there.

An important feature of the garden is a shallow pool about a foot or two feet deep and five feet in diameter (keep it on the shallow side if there are toddlers about). Highbush blueberries on the south side of the pool give some shade to that corner, as well as berries to pick and eat. Floating aquarium plants could provide hiding places for fish, while rocks along the pool's edge provide shelter for newts and frogs. These also hold down the pool's plastic lining and provide space for

With some help from adults, a garden can be a place where children have fun working together.

a tiny rock garden composed of portulaca and hen-and-chickens. A dwarf bleeding heart is planted in the semishade directly under the blueberries, but there is sunlight shining on the pool itself.

A vegetable area includes favorites such as popcorn, Halloween pumpkins, lettuce, cherry tomatoes and radishes, as well as sugar peas that grow up the fence and can be eaten pod and all. Tiny wild strawberries bear all summer and are good for nibbling. Gourds are a wonderful thing to grow. They come in all sizes, wild colors and a variety of odd shapes; some even twist themselves into a knot. You can also make boxes, bowls and castanets out of them or just have them to look at. Mint is there for nibbling and for cold drinks. Catnip is for cat toys. (Catnip may attract cats that will be a nuisance in the garden; if this happens, move the catnip outside the fence.)

There is also a space for annuals that are fun to grow: petunias, marigolds, snapdragons to snap and red salvia. For every adult who dislikes red salvia there is a child who loves this bright plant. A row of giant sunflowers along one side of the fence is an important part of the garden, not only as a source of birdseed, but just because it is fun to grow something that enormous. There are some very early spring bulbs—snowdrops and crocuses—for those who can hardly wait for spring to come, as well as a summer bulb: *Allium giganteum*. This member of the garlic family has huge, round purple flower heads that are not quite like anything else. The bulb patch is also a good place to plant pansies— the flower with a face. For winter drying, there are annual strawflowers, yarrow, little red Chinese lanterns and money plant, whose seed pods look like round white coins.

The little frog pond is designed to be as simple as possible. A year-round pond is difficult to build and maintain, but a young friend of mine in Vermont once had a pond like this one that worked beautifully. He refurbished it each spring, adding new creatures as he found them. It was just a shallow hole lined first with sand and then with heavy black plastic and filled from a hose whenever it needed water. There were plants and rocks for shelter for the fish and other small ani-

mals. Whenever he caught a new crayfish, polliwog or newt in a nearby stream it went into the pond—and stayed there. Even goldfish from the pet store could live there. The fish must be kept indoors over the winter, but the frogs can be left on their own; those of my Vermont friend always came back the following year. A few inches of soil at the bottom are necessary.

SITE

Any sunny well-drained site will be suitable for the garden as long as it is not full of big rocks. Make sure the sunflowers are on the north side so they do not cast shade across the other plants. It is worth taking the trouble to start this garden off properly, so that young people can take care of it easily. A group of children could spade it over by hand if there is no tractor or tiller to do the job. In either case, work in humus, fertilizer and lime if needed. A good fence is important if you have wild animals that will eat vegetables, or neighborhood dogs that will chase through the flowers. Corner posts should be

Lettuce is an easy crop for a young gardener to grow, especially if well fenced against rabbits and other visitors.

THE CHILDREN'S GARDEN

GARDEN FENCE AND GATE

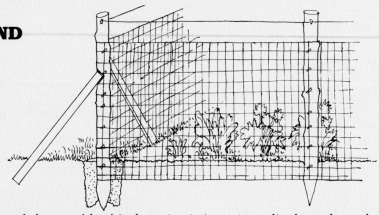

Fig. 1

For fence, use rough logs or 4-by-4-inch posts at least 8 feet long. They could be made of any rot-resistant wood such as cedar, locust or redwood, or any wood that has been treated with preservative. They should be sunk at least 2 feet in the ground, with the ones at the corners sunk in con-crete and/or braced, as shown. A fence of 1-by-2-inch heavy-gauge welded wire is the most durable. Bury it a foot below the soil surface and extend it 5 feet up the posts and it will keep out most creatures. A white laundry line strung across the top will keep deer from jumping over the fence.

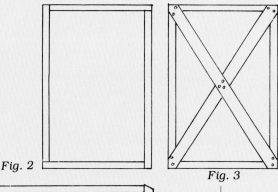

Fig. 2

Fig. 3

To build gate, make inner frame out of 2-by-4's nailed together (Fig. 2). Brace with 1-by-4's (Fig 3).

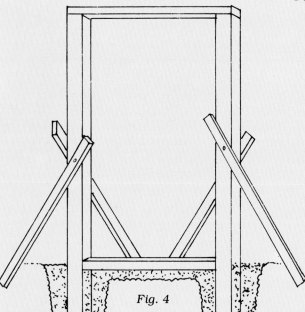

Fig. 4

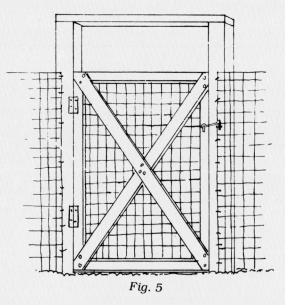

Fig. 5

For outer frame, sink 4-by-4-inch posts in the ground, in concrete, nailing on temporary braces, as shown, and using a level to keep the posts upright. At the same time, sink a 2-by-4 in concrete for the doorsill, keeping it flush with the surface of the ground. (Wood should be treated to resist rot.)

When concrete is dry, remove bracing lumber and attach inner frame to outer frame with hinges. Use a heavy metal hook and eye as a latch, and stretch a section of fence mesh across the gate, stapling it in place.

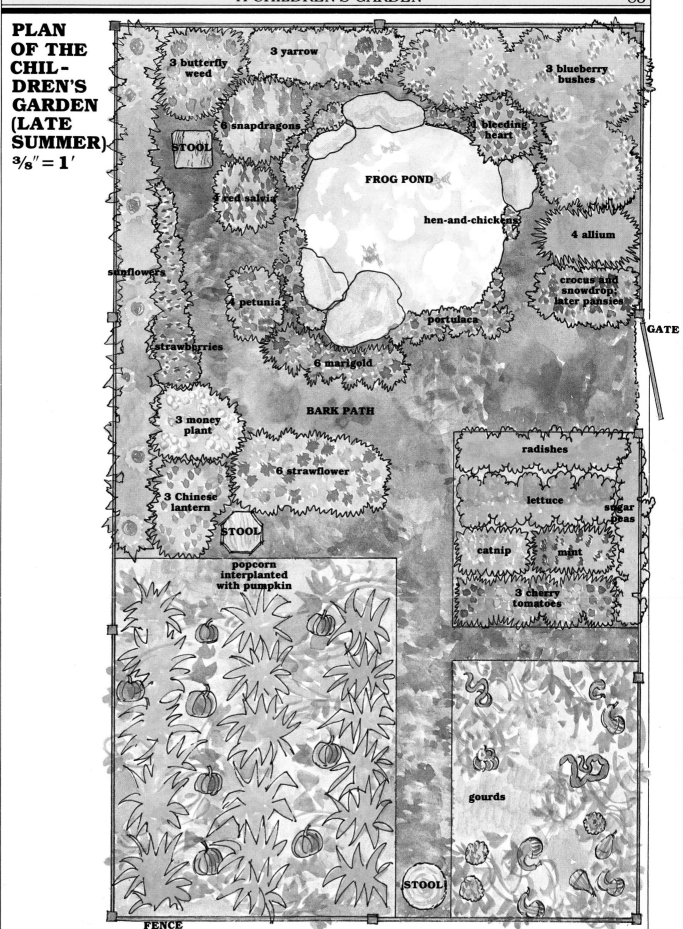

PLAN OF THE CHILDREN'S GARDEN (LATE SUMMER)
3/8" = 1'

3 butterfly weed

3 yarrow

3 blueberry bushes

6 snapdragons

1 bleeding heart

STOOL

FROG POND

4 red salvia

hen-and-chickens

4 allium

sunflowers

crocus and snowdrop; later pansies

4 petunia

portulaca

GATE

strawberries

6 marigold

BARK PATH

3 money plant

6 strawflower

radishes

lettuce

sugar peas

3 Chinese lantern

catnip

mint

STOOL

3 cherry tomatoes

popcorn interplanted with pumpkin

gourds

STOOL

FENCE

GROWING INSTRUCTIONS

This garden is composed of several distinct areas; if the garden belongs to a group, or even just two or three children, it might be a good idea to assign one to each child. Then she or he would have a little piece of it to call "mine." The habit of regular maintenance, especially weeding, is a good one to learn, but if it is too large an area it will turn a child off gardening forever. A mulch of bark or salt hay will make the job easier.

Build the fence, paths and pool first. Most of the garden can be planted in spring. To make fall bulb planting simple, all the bulbs are in one place. The annuals, for the most part, are also together, as are the vegetables. The perennials are in places where they are least likely to be disturbed and dug up by mistake by an eager seed sower. Nonetheless, some guidance will often be necessary. The tomatoes ought to be staked, especially in such a tiny tomato patch. The soil around the pool should have some sand added to it, an extension of the sand bed on which the pool's plastic lining is laid. This will make the soil better for hen-and-chickens and portulaca. When the growing season is over, give the garden a good cleanup, or till the debris under, adding some compost or well-rotted manure to settle in while the garden rests in winter.

ADDITIONS AND SUBSTITUTIONS

Any number of intriguing plants can be added if you have enough space for them. Watermelons, for example. You can grow other kinds of corn—sweet corn to eat, or colored corn such as 'Mexican Blue' or 'Strawberry.' Grow peanuts and roast them. Make a tepee from some tall stakes and grow a scarlet runner bean on it; you will have a secret hideaway when the plant grows up the stakes, and you can eat the beans too. Grow some dramatic flowers such as black tulips, and some other huge plants such as hollyhocks. Grow common vegetables in unusual colors: red lettuce, purple beans, purple cabbage, purple

broccoli. If you have a large and very sturdy fence, grow a bittersweet vine on it; bittersweet will add color to your winter bouquets. Grow dainty coral bells and lily of the valley, and some more annuals such as bachelor's buttons and nasturtiums. Baby's breath is another interesting plant, and good for drying.

If your family enjoys plants but doesn't have room in your garden for very many, you can have fun with wild plants, too. Make chains out of daisies, clover and dandelions, or make the dandelions into one huge yellow fuzzy ball by tying the stems together. You can also make an enormous ball by sticking together the round burrs from burdock plants in fall. You can pop the pods on jewelweed, blow the silk on milkweed (or the butterfly weed in your garden), or look for pitcher plants in bogs and wet places and jack-in-the-pulpits in the woods. Pull up a Queen Anne's lace plant and look at the root, which is really a little wild carrot. Find the one tiny purple flower that is always in the center of the white flower cluster. Then cut off the root, put the plant in a vase of water colored with food coloring, and watch the flower gradually change color.

You can find out a lot about how people have used plants, especially the Indians. Or discover new uses for them. For instance, if you are in a field and need a handkerchief, you can use a large fuzzy leaf like that of the mulleins. But these are just a few examples. Children find things to do with plants that no one ever heard of before, and you will surely come up with some of your own.

PLANT LIST FOR CHILDREN'S GARDEN

ANNUALS

MARIGOLD. *Tagetes erecta* (African), *T. patula* (French) or *T. tenuifolia* 'Pumila' (dwarf marigold). There are many varieties of marigold to choose from—singles and doubles, different heights, different colors. These three species all have low-growing compact forms; choose one about a foot tall for this garden. Sow indoors in flats for early bloom, transferring 3-inch seedlings to peat pots and setting 8 inches apart in the garden after danger of frost has passed. You can also buy a flat or two of started plants. Frequent cutting and removal of spent flowers will make the plants bushier.

PETUNIA. *Petunia* hybrids. Choose your favorite among the many types and colors available. Most grow about 1–1½ feet tall, but there are also dwarf varieties. Sow seeds indoors in late winter or early spring or buy a flat of started plants. Set out plants in the garden 8–10 inches apart after danger of frost has passed. Pinch off the tops when the plants are 6 inches tall to encourage branching, and snip off faded blooms to produce more flowers and keep the plants from becoming straggly.

PORTULACA. *Portulaca grandiflora.* Trailing plants 6–8 inches tall, with small narrow fleshy leaves and single or double flowers in brilliant shades of pink, red, orange, yellow, purple or white. Often used as a rock garden plant, portulaca likes a fairly dry soil and plenty of sun. Sow indoors in early spring, or outdoors after danger of frost has passed. Thin or transplant to 6 inches apart. Most varieties close up on dark days. They will often self-sow, so look for the young seedlings the following spring.

SALVIA, RED (SCARLET SAGE) *Salvia splendens.* Choose a dwarf red variety such as 'St. John's Fire,' which grows about a foot tall. This salvia is a shrubby perennial in tropical climates. Sow seeds outdoors in early spring or buy started plants and set out in the garden 10–12 inches apart, after danger of frost has passed. Do not overfertilize, or plants will be too leafy.

SNAPDRAGON. *Antirrhinum majus.* Choose a short variety, about 1–1½ feet tall, in any bright shades. Buy nursery-grown plants or start indoors and set out after danger of frost, 8–10 inches apart.

STRAWFLOWER. *Helichrysum bracteatum.* These yellow, red, lavender, orange or white flowers, which grow 2–3 feet tall, are popular for winter bouquets. When dried their petals become crisp and strawlike, but they keep their bright colors. Sow seeds in the garden after danger of frost has passed, then thin to 8–10 inches apart. Cut the flowers for drying before they open fully (they will continue to open while drying). Hang upside down in a dark, dry place.

SUNFLOWER. *Helianthus annuus.* Choose the giant varieties that grow up to 12 feet tall, with flowers up to a foot across. Birds love to peck at the seeds; you can save them indoors when they are ripe for winter bird food. Sow seeds right in the garden after dan-

ger of frost has passed, 2 feet apart.

BULBS

ALLIUM, GIANT. *Allium giganteum* (zones 6–10) or *A. albopilosum (A. christophii)* (zones 4–10). Both are called giant allium, and their flowers are big round balls made up of tiny purple flowers. But *A. albopilosum* is hardier in cold climates and its June-blooming flowers are as large as 10 inches across. *A. giganteum's* flowers bloom in July and are about 4 inches across. Both are fun to grow. Plant the bulbs in spring or fall, 5 inches deep. The bulbs smell so strongly of garlic, to which they are related, that mice won't touch them.

CROCUS (COMMON CROCUS, DUTCH CROCUS). *Crocus vernus.* Zones 3–10. Varieties come in yellow, pur-

ple, orange, lavender and white, and grow 4–8 inches tall. They will multiply by themselves. Plant them 3 inches apart, 4 inches deep.

SNOWDROP. *Galanthus nivalis.* Zones 3–9. Snowdrops have single white flowers and grasslike foliage that dies down after the flowers have bloomed. They grow 6–12 inches tall, will spread by themselves, and they like moist but well-drained soil. Plant 3 inches apart, 3 inches deep.

FRUITS

BLUEBERRY, HIGHBUSH. *Vaccinium corymbosum.* Zones 3–8. Blueberries not only bear luscious fruit for pies and nibbling, they are also an attractive 6–7-foot shrub with a graceful shape, small white flowers in late spring and bright red-orange leaves in fall. Different varieties are suitable for different localities. Consult your local Cooperative Extension Service or nurserymen for those that prosper best where you live. Plant 2 or 3 different varieties that bloom at the same time, so that they will cross-pollinate. Buy 2- or 3-year-old plants. Give them moist, light soil, to which an acid form of humus such as peat moss or rotted manure has been added. Mulch with an acid material such as pine needles, or the same shredded bark you use for the paths of this garden.

STRAWBERRY, WILD. *Fragaria vesca.* Zones 4–10. Several hybrid varieties are available. Fruits are tiny red ovals and flowers are white. Both recur all summer, especially if fruits are picked (a garden chore no one will ever complain about). They prefer lots of sun and a dry location. Easily divided in spring. Plant 1 foot apart.

HERBS

CATNIP. *Nepeta cataria.* Zones 3–8. A perennial herb that grows 2–3 feet tall, with fuzzy heart-shaped leaves and lavender or white flowers for most of the summer. Cats will roll in it mindlessly if the leaves are bruised; if you are concerned about the looks of the plant, and those next to it, handle it as little as possible. Be sure you plant *N. cataria.* Other ornamental species don't appeal to cats at all. Catnip likes moist soil. It can be grown either from divisions of clumps or from seeds sown in early spring (it will also self-sow). Harvest it just as the seeds are ripening for the best leaves for drying, and to keep the plant vigorous. It is a spreading plant, and should be divided and thinned if it starts to take over the garden, or contained within a barrier such as a large pot sunk in the gound, or a bucket with the bottom cut out.

PEPPERMINT. *Mentha piperita* or other mint species. Zones 3–9. This strong-tasting mint, good for nibbling, for seasoning or for tea, grows about 2–3 feet tall and bears lavender flowers in midsummer. Like catnip, mint likes moist soil, is a spreader and may take over. It is best, in a small garden, to contain it, like catnip. Mint is usually grown from divisions of started clumps planted in the spring, donated by a friend who has too much mint. It also roots easily in water.

PERENNIALS AND BIENNIALS

BLEEDING HEART, FRINGED. *Dicentra eximia.* Zones 4–9. You could also grow the larger *D. spectabilis,* but *eximia* is a compact 1–1½ feet tall and blooms over a much longer period, from early spring to long after the first frost, and the foliage lasts much longer too. It prefers a cool climate, some light shade and a well-drained soil rich in humus.

BUTTERFLY WEED. *Asclepias tuberosa.* Zones 3–9. This handsome plant, much visited by butterflies, grows 2 feet tall and bears red-orange flowers in mid to late summer. It prefers light, dry soil and does not need much fertilizer. It has a long taproot and cannot easily be moved once you have planted it unless the plants are very young. Best grown from purchased plants, since seed-grown plants take 4 or 5 years to flower. Even your new plant will make a slow start, but be patient. In a few years it will be large, almost indestructible, and will probably self-sow in unexpected places. New growth is late to appear in the spring, so watch for it and don't dig up the plants by mistake.

CHINESE LANTERN PLANT. *Physalis alkekengi.* Zones 3–10. This 2-foot plant bears red-orange fruits that are inflated like little Chinese lanterns, each with a little red seed inside it. The plant spreads very quickly, and you would do best to contain it the same way you do the peppermint and catnip, by planting it in a pot or bottomless bucket. When the lanterns turn red in fall, cut the stems on which they hang, and dry them in a cool dark place.

HEN-AND-CHICKENS. *Sempervivum tectorum,* and other kinds of *Sempervivum.* Zones 3–9. These prickly rosettes come in shades of green, red and purple. One kind, *S. arachnoides,* has little threads like spiderwebs among the prickles. The plant makes "babies" next to it and sends up stalks with usually pink flowers in summer. The foliage keeps its color all winter. These plants like dry, sandy soil, the same soil you need for the portulaca. Plant 6 inches apart.

MONEY PLANT (HONESTY). *Lunaria annua.* Zones 5–10. Sometimes grown as an annual, this plant produces better as a biennial. It bears fragrant purple flowers in May and June, then seedpods with thin, silvery-white, disklike center dividers that are attractive in dried bouquets. Grows 1½–2½ feet tall. Sow seeds in midsummer and thin plants to 15 inches apart.

PANSY. *Viola tricolor hortensis.* Zones 6–10. Most people are familiar with pansies, whose flowers come with innumerable color combinations and "facial expressions." They grow about 8 inches tall. You can raise them from seed started indoors in late winter, or sown in the ground in late summer, but the best way is to buy started plants.

YARROW. *Achillea millefolium* or *A. filipendulina.* Zones 3–10. Most of the garden yarrows would suit this garden, except for 'The Pearl,' whose clumps get very large. Varieties such as the yellow 'Coronation Gold' or the rosy 'Fire King' are good for drying. These grow 2 feet tall and bloom most of the summer. Plant 1–1½ feet apart.

VEGETABLES

them, eating the thinnings in salads. Keep picking it, to keep fresh young leaves coming, and sow more every few weeks for a fresh crop.

GOURDS. *Cucurbita pepo ovifera, Lagenaria siceraria* and others. Most gourds are simply squash that you can't eat. They are found in many shapes, sizes and colors. Some are beautiful to look at, some are funny, and some can have a lid cut in them so that you can store things inside. There is even a gourd called *Trichosanthes cucumeroides* that is shaped like a snake! It is long, like its name, and looks like it is coiled to strike; some claim it will even scare away the critters that are after your lettuce. Plant gourd seeds in the garden after danger of frost, or start a month early indoors in peat pots or milk cartons. Either way, you should plant 5 or 6 seeds right together and throw away all but the 2 tallest seedlings. They like a light, rich soil and plenty of sun. The vines also need space to run and climb. In this garden, plant them near the fence and help them climb by tying the young vines to the wire with soft twine or strips of cloth. One of the large varieties, such as the snake, could sit in the corner of the gourd patch by itself, away from the fence. Pick the gourds when they are the size and color of the ripe gourds pictured on the seed packet.

LETTUCE. *Lactuca sativa.* There are many fine lettuce varieties, but the easiest to grow are the loose-leaf types such as oakleaf or salad bowl. You might also try one with a soft, open head such as Boston or buttercrunch. They are not like the crisp iceberg lettuce you find most often in the store, and you may like the taste even better. Start sowing your lettuce seed in early spring, in a light, rich soil. When the leaves are a few inches tall you can start to thin

PEAS, EDIBLE POD (SUGAR PEAS, SNOW PEAS). *Pisum sativum macrocarpon.* This variety can be eaten pod and all. If picked when still tender (when the peas are just tiny bumps that you can feel under the skin) and cooked briefly, they have a wonderful fresh, sweet taste. They also give a higher yield than regular peas, since you eat the pods too—a big plus in a small garden. Sow them in a row along the fence in very early spring, 3 inches apart and 1–2 inches deep. The soil should be moist when you plant them, so if you are planting a little late, or it is a dry spring, give them plenty of water. They also need water while the pods are forming. You will need to remove the tough strings along one side of the pods before you eat them unless you have planted a stringless variety.

POPCORN. *Zea mays everta.* Popcorn is grown like any other corn, but it has small ears and pointed kernels that pop when heated. Plant it around the time of the last frost, 2 inches deep (3–4 inches if you plant late), and 3–4 inches apart in the rows. Rows should be 3 feet apart. When they come up, thin to a foot apart in the rows. You should always plant corn in a block or patch, not a long skinny row, or it will not pol-

linate as well. Corn likes rich soil and plenty of water. A mulch is often helpful in keeping the roots moist and in keeping down weeds, because it is easy to injure the surface roots when weeding. Let the popcorn ears dry on the stalks before picking, and save one fine ear in a cool dry place for next year's seed.

PUMPKIN. *Cucurbita pepo.* There are a number of different kinds: bush or vine, large or small fruits. Though pumpkins generally need a lot of space, you could grow a few vines in a corn patch, for corn and pumpkins grow well together, and sometimes the feel of pumpkin (or squash) leaves underfoot will keep hungry raccoons away from corn. Plant them in "hills"—groups of several seeds—4 feet apart. Your vines may take off, sneak through the fence and run all over the lawn or meadow—or all over the garden. Turn them back the way they came if they are headed somewhere you don't want them; you can also cut off the ends when the pumpkins have made a good start. The pumpkins will keep right on growing. Since pumpkins take a long time to mature it is helpful to start the seeds indoors where the growing season is short, and set them out after danger of frost. They like the same growing conditions as corn. Pick the pumpkins before the first real frost, then store in a cool place.

RADISH. *Raphanus sativus.* Choose the little red early kind. Plant first thing in the spring, about 1½ inches deep. Thinning is not necessary, but you will probably want to pull one up every now and then to see how they are doing. In 3–4 weeks you will have some big enough to eat, and you can make a small salad along with the first little lettuce leaves. Don't leave them in the ground too long or they will be tough. If you want more later on, make other sowings, with a variety suited to later crops. Radishes like a light, rich soil.

TOMATO, CHERRY. *Lycopersicum lycopersicum (Lycopersicon esculentum).* My sisters and I used to call these "burst-in-your-mouth tomatoes" because you can put a whole one in your mouth, bite down, and let it explode in your mouth. You can plant the sweet yellow oval-shaped ones as well as the familiar round red ones. Start from seed indoors or buy plants, then set out after danger of frost, when the weather is warming up. Tomatoes planted too early usually don't die, but they just don't do much of anything. Let the vines climb up wooden stakes by tying them to the stakes with strips of cloth or soft twine. Don't wait too long to do this, or the heavy vines will break when you pick them up off the ground. Plant about 2 feet apart in soil with a good phosphorus content but not too much nitrogen.

A Garden of Old Roses

When people think of their grandmothers' or their great-grandmothers' gardens, chances are they remember the old roses, the kind that grew on moundlike bushes, laden with heavy, nodding blooms. There was an abundance about them, a romantic excess, compared with the small, perky upright rosebushes you see in gardens today.

Not everyone has memories like these. In fact many people do not even know what old-fashioned roses looked like, so universal are the modern floribundas, grandifloras and hybrid teas. Those who investigate

the world of old roses are often surprised by what they find, and are so captivated that they develop a taste for these alone.

What do these flowers look like and wherein lies their charm? Actually, they vary quite a bit. An old rose you might call "typical" is one called 'Baronne Prévost.' Its blooms are about three inches wide, medium pink and flat, not high-centered like a hybrid tea. Instead of an open, sculptured arrangement of petals, the petals are very numerous and set so tightly together that the ones in the center never really open. And the center looks pulled in; this is called a "button eye." In addition, the petals are pulled in by indentations that divide the rose into

several sections; this is called "quartering." Another rose, 'Reine des Violettes,' has flowers of a similar shape, but the color is a subtle blending of lilac, gray, purple and rose. The bush, instead of making a mound, is tall, leggy and upright. 'Tuscany Superb' has petals of such a dark mahogany-purple that they are almost black. They are not tight in the center at all, but spread wide open to reveal gold stamens that stand out beautifully against the purple. 'Maiden's Blush' is a pale pink rose, almost white at the edges, with a deeper blush in the center. This delicate coloring gave to the rose its other name: 'Cuisse de Nymphe,' or Nymph's Thigh. Blooms with an especially rosy center were called 'Cuisse de Nymphe Emue,' or Passionate Nymph's Thigh.

While none of the old roses is without fragrance, some are unusually sweet-scented, or have a special scent such as the touch of raspberry in 'Mme. Isaac Pereire.'

The foliage varies too. In some the leaves are broad and glossy, in others dainty and fernlike. The rugosa roses have wrinkled leaves that are often apple-green in color; alba roses have blue-green leaves that are a perfect setting for their white or blush-pink blossoms

Old roses also have romantic names and histories. Some bear the names of queens, such as 'Empress Josephine' or 'La Reine Victoria' or 'Koenigin von Daenemark' (Queen of Denmark). Rosa Mundi is thought to be named for Rosamond, the mistress of Henry II, though the name is sometimes translated as Rose of the World. 'Fantin-Latour' was named after the French painter whose still lifes are full of pale pink roses. 'Celestial' is also called the Minden Rose, because the British troops were said to have picked it in France after winning the battle of Minden in 1759.

Quite apart from their beauty, the old roses are much hardier than modern ones, which makes them a good choice for cold climates (though there are old roses that are particularly suited to warm climates). They are also more resistant to disease than today's varieties, need very little pruning and require less care in general. Why then were they ever superseded? The answer lies mainly in one trait: their lack of continuous bloom.

With some exceptions, they give one grand show in late spring and early summer. Modern roses bloom all summer long. The color range is also more limited, lacking the yellow, orange and salmon shades that we are now used to seeing. But those who fall in love with old roses forgive these limitations gladly and become almost fanatical in their search for them, poking through abandoned gardens

© VIKI FERRENIEA

Camieux (top) shows the striping found on some old roses. Belle Amour (middle) has an elegant open form. Mme. Hardy (bottom) has a flat shape that is typical of many old roses. It also exhibits quartering and has a button eye.

THE GARDEN OF OLD ROSES

CATEGORIES OF OLD ROSES

ALBAS. *Rosa alba.* These roses are native to Europe and are thought to be a cross between *R. gallica* and some form of *R. canina.* They grow to 6–7 feet; vigorous, dense, compact. Flowers are white or pale pink. Foliage is deep bluish green, dusted white. Hips are long and scarlet.

BOURBONS. *Rosa borboniana.* This rose, discovered on the Isle de Bourbon (Réunion Island) in 1819, is a cross between the pink china and the autumn damask. It attracted immediate attention for its dependable fall bloom. The plants are compact, strong and upright, to about 5 feet. Flowers are fairly large, globular, heavy and fragrant. Foliage is sometimes purplish.

CENTIFOLIAS or CABBAGE ROSES. These were once considered ancient, but are now thought to have been bred by the Dutch during the Renaissance. They are fairly tall, with lax, open growth and slender arching canes, often needing support. Lush, heavy, button-eyed blooms form a ball as they mature and have a strong, sweet fragrance.

CHINAS. *Rosa chinensis.* These everblooming roses grow 5–6 feet tall and bear red or pink double or semidouble flowers that darken with age. They have glossy foliage and are rather tender.

CLIMBERS Roses do not actually climb the way vines do. The roses we call climbers produce very long canes (stems) with stiff thorns large enough to snag on something, enabling the rose to grow up through trees or up a fence to get to a sunnier position. Usually they need a little help, if only at first. Those called "pillar roses" grow just tall enough to be trained upright on a post. "Ramblers" are generally roses that throw out new long canes each season. "Scramblers" cover the ground on long weak stems. All these can be trained down as well as up. For example, they are often at their most beautiful when allowed to cascade down a wall or bank, like a foaming wave, laden with blossoms.

DAMASKS. *Rosa damascena.* This ancient rose, the Rose of Castile, came from Asia Minor, probably Syria. It grows up to 8 feet with arching, ·thorny canes. The nodding double or semidouble blooms in long clusters are so fragrant that they are the traditional source of attar (oil) of roses for making perfumes. The foliage is grayish, the hips large, round and red.

GALLICAS (FRENCH ROSES). *Rosa gallica.* These were grown throughout the Roman empire and are the common ancestor of most European roses. They are sturdy, almost thornless shrubs about 3 feet tall. Flowers are often deep in color, sometimes striped or spotted. The plants have rough leaves and large red hips.

HYBRID PERPETUALS. These hybrids of complex ancestry were so popular in the Victorian period that there were once as many as 3,000 varieties. They form a link between the old roses and the roses of today, some resembling the former, some the latter. They are fairly tall, with huge fragrant flowers. They are at their best in June, but some rebloom, often sparingly, in fall with a sprinkling through the summer.

MOSS ROSES. *Rosa centifolia* 'muscosa.' The moss roses came to England from Holland in the Renaissance, possibly as a sport (mutation) of *R. centifolia.* They grow to about 5 feet and are thorny. A fuzziness about the sepals, calyx, stem and even some leaflets is imparted by tiny hairlike glands which also give off a characteristic fragrance. Flowers are large and globe-shaped, usually pink.

NOISETTES. *Rosa noisettiana.* These were named for a florist in Charleston, South Carolina, in the early 19th century who propagated them from a cross between *R. chinensis* and *R. moschata.* They are quite tender, with recurrent, clustered blooms in primarily pale shades, including the yellows. The foliage is also pale in color.

RUGOSAS. *Rosa rugosa.* This Japanese species was introduced to Europe in 1789. The name means "wrinkled" and applies to the foliage, which has a hearty yellow or red fall color. They are extremely hardy, shrubby roses that can survive almost anything, but dislike chalky or clay soils. They bloom all summer with red, pink or white flowers, single or double, and their large and abundant red hips are rich in vitamin C.

TEAS. *Rosa odorata.* These ancient Chinese everblooming roses are even more tender than the chinas. They are resistant to fungus diseases and grow well in the South where other old roses often do not. Farther north they must be mounded with earth in winter to protect them from sudden changes in temperature. They were originally thought to have a fragrance like that of tea leaves. Like the modern hybrid teas, they have a broad color range including the yellow shades.

WILD OR SPECIES ROSES

This vast group encompasses natives from all over the Northern Hemisphere (and some tropical mountains). Some of the best known are the Scotch (burnet) rose, *Rosa spinosissima;* the English dog rose, *R. canina;* the sweetbrier, *R. eglanteria;* American species such as the Virginia rose, *R. virginiana,* and California rose, *R. californica;* the Asian musk rose, *R. moschata;* the Chinese *R. soulieana* and *R. moyesii;* the Japanese *R. wichuraiana,* parent of most of the modern climbers—and countless others.

HOW TO BUILD AN ARBOR

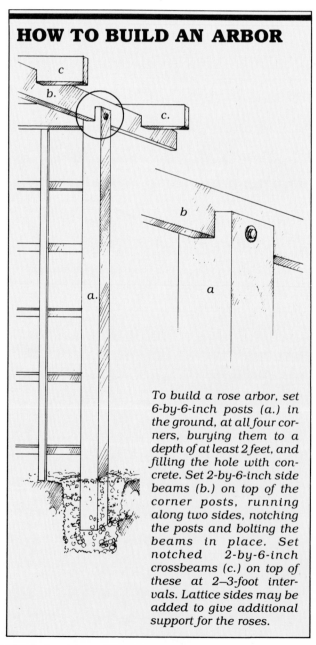

To build a rose arbor, set 6-by-6-inch posts (a.) in the ground, at all four corners, burying them to a depth of at least 2 feet, and filling the hole with concrete. Set 2-by-6-inch side beams (b.) on top of the corner posts, running along two sides, notching the posts and bolting the beams in place. Set notched 2-by-6-inch crossbeams (c.) on top of these at 2–3-foot intervals. Lattice sides may be added to give additional support for the roses.

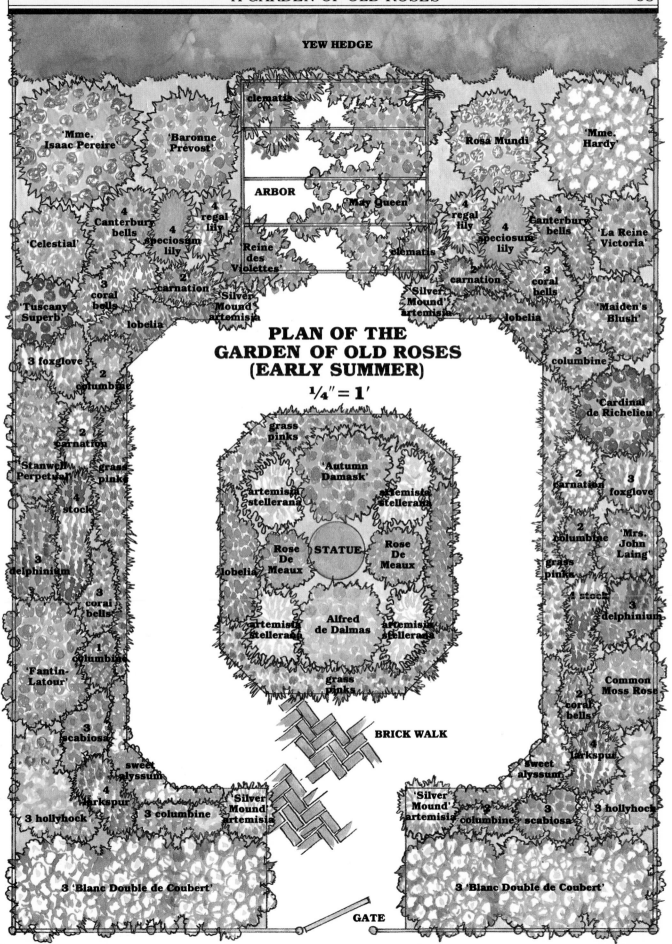

YEW HEDGE

clematis

'Mme. Isaac Pereire'

'Baronne Prevost'

Rosa Mundi

'Mme. Hardy'

ARBOR

May Queen

'Celestial'

4 Canterbury bells

4 speciosum lily

4 regal lily

Reine des Violettes'

clematis

4 regal lily

4 speciosum lily

4 Canterbury bells

'La Reine Victoria'

2 carnation

2 carnation

3 coral bells

'Tuscany Superb'

3 coral bells

lobelia

'Silver Mound' artemisia

'Silver Mound' artemisia

lobelia

'Maiden's Blush'

3 foxglove

2 columbine

3 columbine

PLAN OF THE GARDEN OF OLD ROSES (EARLY SUMMER)

¼″ = 1′

'Cardinal de Richelieu'

2 carnation

'Stanwell Perpetual'

grass pinks

grass pinks

'Autumn Damask'

artemisia stellerana

artemisia stellerana

2 carnation

3 foxglove

4 stock

2 columbine

'Mrs. John Laing'

3 delphinium

lobelia

Rose De Meaux

STATUE

Rose De Meaux

grass pinks

3 coral bells

3 coral bells

4 stock

1 columbine

artemisia stellerana

Alfred de Dalmas

artemisia stellerana

3 delphinium

'Fantin-Latour'

2 coral bells

3 scabiosa

grass pinks

Common Moss Rose

sweet alyssum

BRICK WALK

sweet alyssum

larkspur

4 larkspur

3 columbine

'Silver Mound' artemisia

'Silver Mound' artemisia

3 columbine

3 scabiosa

3 hollyhock

3 hollyhock

3 'Blanc Double de Coubert'

3 'Blanc Double de Coubert'

GATE

for sturdy old survivors and sending off to specialty nurseries for "new" old favorites.

Roses are the favorite flower of all time— and among the oldest. Some fossil remains date from 30 million years ago and are widely scattered around the world. Though their species grow almost everywhere north of the Equator, botanists say that roses began as cold-climate plants, then gradually adapted to warmer parts of the globe. They were beloved by the ancient Minoans, Egyptians, and Romans.

It is likely that the hybridization of roses—the breeding of new varieties—began in the ancient world. Several cultivated species were grown in the castles and monasteries of the Middle Ages (see the Medieval Paradise Garden, p. 169), and they were the subject of much hybridization in the Renaissance by Dutch and other European growers. The old *Rosa gallica*, or French rose, and its children—the albas, damasks, cabbage roses and others—formed the foundation of this breeding. Toward the end of the eighteenth century the introduction of the delicate but everblooming Chinese roses into European breeding changed the character of that breeding dramatically. An effort was made to combine the vigor and winter hardiness of European roses with the "remontant," or reblooming, quality of the Chinese varieties. The products were as bourbons, noisettes, portlands and hybrid perpetuals.

The period from 1810 to 1830 was a great one for roses, and its heroine was the Empress Josephine. Throughout the Napoleonic wars, Josephine combed the countries of Europe—both friend and foe—for roses to add to her magnificent collection at Malmaison. This collection was immortalized in the paintings of Redouté in a volume called *Les Roses*, commissioned by the empress and published between 1817 and 1824, with a text by the botanist C. A. Thory. Josephine's interest spurred much activity in the field of rose breeding, and in 1867 the first hybrid tea, 'La France,' was developed. By the end of the nineteenth century the hybrid teas had achieved the dominance they maintain today.

We owe much to those who developed our modern roses, but it is a shame that they are the only ones we know, particularly since

© 1979 ROBERT PERRON/KAREN BUSSOLINI

Old roses climb over arches in a turn-of-the-century garden at Elizabeth Park in Hartford, Connecticut. This view is from within a gazebo built of cedar logs and covered with Virginia creeper. Rose varieties include 'Excelsa' (1909), 'White Dorothy' (1908) and 'Crimson Rambler' (1893).

the old varieties are so easy to grow. Try a few "historical roses," as they are sometimes called. Or better yet, plant a whole garden with these roses as its theme.

PLAN OF THE GARDEN

The garden I have designed is a small rectangle planned like a traditional formal rose garden, with beds, walks and a backdrop of dark evergreen hedge at one end. In front of the hedge is an arbor on which to display climbing and pillar roses (see box, p. 92). All the roses selected are varieties introduced before 1900 and represent most of the old rose categories (see listing, p. 92) except for the less hardy varieties (gardeners in warm climates might consider adding some of these). Space has been provided for the plants to spread out, but some gardeners prefer to plant them close together "to enable the old ladies and gentlemen to hold each other up," as rose expert Gordon Edwards puts it. You need not worry if they mingle with one another. All their colors blend well, especially if you have contrasts such as pale blush roses next to mahogany-purple ones. I have tried to spread the recurrent bloomers throughout the garden so that there will always be a little bloom here and there later in the season.

Most people feel that a garden of old roses benefits from the addition of other flowers, especially for mid or late summer when the big rose show is over. It is best to use old-fashioned flowers with tidy, dignified spike-shaped blooms to complement the arching canes of the roses. Big, floppy flowers and strident colors do not blend well.

This garden includes foxgloves, delphiniums, white regal lilies, Canterbury bells, pinks, carnations, columbines and coral bells to bloom along with the roses. For later blossoms there are rose-colored speciosum lilies, annual stocks, larkspurs, hollyhocks and some edging annuals—sweet alyssum and lobelia. White artemisias are another accent. For the arbor I have suggested: one vigorous old climber, 'May Queen,' which should, in time, provide a covering sheet of flowers; 'Reine des Violettes,' grown as a pillar rose on one corner; and several clematis for summer blooms. The arbor should have a seat under it, which will offer a shady place from which to enjoy the garden and its fragrance.

This garden could be entirely enclosed by a wall or evergreen hedge, but since it is small I have left it open, because any rose appreciates good air circulation. The dark evergreens behind the arbor will set off the pink and white of the roses and lilies. These

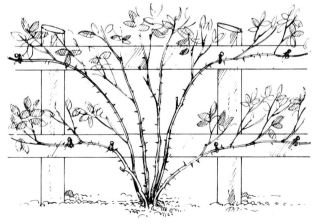

Ill. 4. Tying rose canes to a fence.

might be yew, holly, arborvitae or hemlock. At the rear corners sit two ladies of somewhat ample girth, 'Mme. Hardy' and 'Mme. Isaac Pereire.' The rest of the garden is lower, except for two clumps of tall hollyhocks in the other two corners. A hedge of the double white rugosa, 'Blanc Double de Coubert,' frames the entrance. A wooden fence is suggested for three sides of the garden, which will give some support to the roses when they need it. Canes can be tied to it horizontally to induce upright branching.

The central island contains two recurrent varieties, 'Autumn Damask' and 'Alfred de Dalmas.' This would also be a good place for a statue or other ornament. The paths could be made of flagstone, brick, gravel or even mown grass with a brick, flagstone or metal edging. English rose gardens often have edging plants, such as pinks, that spill out over paved walkways with studied informality. Controlled informality should, in fact, be the guiding style of this garden. The arbor can be of a rustic construction (rough larch poles were often used in Victorian England) but well built. The foxgloves, columbines, hollyhocks and annuals can be allowed to self-sow here and there, but only the ones that dispose themselves artistically should be retained. The garden should not look untended.

SITE

The site should be sunny, although in hot climates some shade for part of the day will be appreciated. There should also be good circulation of air, as mentioned. The site should not be in a frost pocket, especially if you are growing varieties that are tender for your region. As for soil, roses are less fussy than many people think; they like a slightly acid pH (5.5–6.5) but are not adamant about it. The soil should be fertile, but not overrich. A clay soil is better than a sandy one, unless it is so heavy that water does not drain from it. Poor drainage is the one intolerable condition. If you have it, correct it with a layer of gravel under the soil, or by raising the beds (see box, p. 45).

GROWING INSTRUCTIONS

Since your local nursery probably does not carry many old roses you will probably have to rely on mail order sources, of which there is a partial list in the back of this book. The varieties suggested are all available by mail in the U.S. and Canada (see Where to Order Plants, p. 215).

Most plants will be two-year-old shrubs and will arrive bare-root. Plant them (see box, p. 20) or heel them in as soon as possible (see illustration, p. 18); failing this, open the package to make sure there is plenty of moist packing material around the roots, then re-wrap and store in a cool place.

The question of whether to plant in fall or spring is much debated among rose growers. Both seasons are acceptable, but a lot depends on the climate in your area. The choice in some cases will be made according to which nurseries you order from. Those in warm climates may not ship plants to cool climates in fall, because their roses do not go dormant soon enough, and roses can be

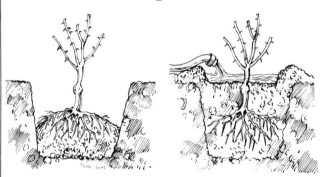

Ill. 5. To plant a rose, dig a hole about 1½ feet deep and wide enough to accommodate the roots without crowding. Make a mound of soil and compost in the bottom of the hole, and spread the roots out over the mound. Water the plant.

Fill the hole with soil, tamping firmly to get rid of air pockets. Make a saucer-shaped rim of earth around the plant and water again, filling the saucer.

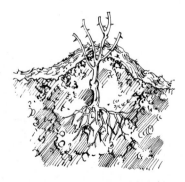

Ill. 6. To mound a rose bush, heap soil gently on top of the plant, then cover with several inches of mulch. In early spring, remove mulch, then gently remove soil mound, replacing mulch.

shipped and planted only when dormant. Whenever you plant, follow the practices illustrated in this chapter. In fall or very early spring, mound some earth around the bushes in cold climates to help the new plant adapt to freezing and thawing (see illustration below). Use some superphosphate or bone meal to start, but do not fertilize with readily available nitrogen until after danger of frost has passed, otherwise the plant will produce new growth that may be injured by the cold. Soil mounds may also be used in cold climates as winter protection for tender varieties. Some gardeners use a bark or peat mulch, mounding it around the plant, or supporting it with a collar made of newspaper or a bottomless basket. This material is then spread around the bed as mulch in spring.

A three-inch mulch in summer is a good way to conserve moisture; roses also like a good morning soaking in hot dry weather. Feed with a balanced rose food weekly or semi-monthly until the end of summer in warm climates, midsummer in cool ones. If a gypsy moth infestation is expected, spray plants with a product containing carbaryl before the roses put out their first growth. Japanese beetles may be controlled with pheromone traps, with milky spore disease or by picking the insects off and dropping them in kerosene. Aphids can be banished with a soapsuds spray. A product such as Benomyl will aid against black spot and mildew. Some gardeners think that they must spray roses with insecticides and fungicides all summer long, but many of the old varieties are so vigorous and abundant that you may not find it necessary to use any poisonous sprays whatsoever.

Pruning is at your discretion. Some gardeners don't ever prune the old shrub varieties. On the other hand there are those that cut them back by a third each spring. I find that the best practice is to remove a few old canes at the base of the plant early each spring from the second or third year onward, and also cut out any dead or twiggy growth in early spring as soon as you can tell how much winter damage—if any—has been done. If you are one of those people who is simply a pruner at heart, remember that you must prune roses either while they are still dormant or just after they have finished flowering. This means that

Ill. 7. Two methods of pegging down roses.

if a variety is the recurrent sort, you must wait to prune until it is completely finished blooming, removing only spent blossoms during the season. By and large, with old roses it is more important to concentrate on pegging down and training horizontally (see above) than to spend time pruning. Pegging forces new upright shoots along the canes, and hence more flowers.

Some old roses are grown on their own roots, i.e., not grafted to an understock. If there is a bud union indicating a graft, however, remove any suckers that start below the graft as part of your pruning routine. These shrubs should be planted with the graft two inches into the ground in cool climates, and at the level of the soil surface in warm ones.

ADDITIONS AND SUBSTITUTIONS

It may not always be possible to find the old rose varieties you want, so you must be open to substitutions, using the general principles set forth here as a guide. In warm climates you can grow some prize varieties that are tender in the North, such as the bourbon 'Souvenir de la Malmaison' (of which there is a hardy climbing variety), or the lovely climber 'Félicité et Perpétue'—in addition to a selection of chinas, noisettes and teas. You might also try other tender climbers such as climbing 'Cécile Brunner,' the climbing tea 'Gloire de Dijon,' the Banksian roses, and the pillar rose 'Zéphirine Drouhin.' If you like climbers, you could extend the arbor into a pergola—an alleyway of continuous arches or arbors—covered with climbing roses. You can hang chains between the posts of the arbors, and let roses grow up the posts and along the chains to make garlands.

You could also mix modern roses with old ones, either by adding some hybrid teas to the side borders or by filling the center island with them for a continuously blooming focal point. You could add some modern climbers if you have the space. If you have lost your heart to old roses and simply want to add more and more of them, here are some other fine varieties that are available.

Gallicas: Apothecary Rose (*R. gallica* 'Officinalis'), 'Camaieux,' 'Belle de Crécy,' 'Charles de Mills,' 'Empress Josephine.'

Moss roses: 'Deuil de Paul Fontaine,' 'Comtesse de Murinais,' 'Gloire des Mousseux,' 'Mme. Louis Lévêque,' 'Salet.'

Damasks: 'Belle Amour,' 'Marie Louise,' 'Rose du Roi,' 'Celsiana.'

Albas: 'Félicité Parmentier,' 'Koenigin von Daenemark.'

Bourbons: 'Honorine de Brabant,' 'Mme. Ernst Calvat,' 'Mme. Pierre Oger,' 'Variegata di Bologna,' 'Louise Odier.'

Cabbage roses (Centifolias): 'Tour de Malakoff,' 'Chapeau de Napoléon' (*Rosa centifolia cristata*), 'Petite de Hollande.'

Hybrid perpetuals: 'American Beauty,' 'Baron Girod de l'Ain,' 'Baroness Rothschild,' 'Frau Karl Druschki,' 'Général Jacqueminot,' 'Georg Arends,' 'Marchioness of Lorne,' 'Souvenir du Docteur Jamain,' 'Empereur du Maroc.'

Rugosas: 'Delicata,' 'Belle Poitevine,' or the ordinary *R. rugosa* 'rubra' and *R. r.* 'alba.'

For a bright color accent, somewhat out of place in this subdued garden but charming elsewhere, plant 'Austrian Copper,' *R. foetida* 'bicolor'—a single red-orange blos-

Rose 'Constance Spry' at Mottisfont Abbey in Hampshire, England.

som with yellow on the reverse side. It is easily obtainable, as is Father Hugo's rose, *R. hugonis*, with dainty foliage and very early yellow flowers.

Many other garden flowers would also go well with these roses: peonies, pansies, iris, bellflowers, forget-me-nots, hostas, rosemary, lavender, other varieties of *Dianthus*, other white-leafed plants such as lamb's ears, primroses, verbena, baby's breath, sweet william. Old-fashioned spring bulbs such as narcissus and hyacinths would be a colorful way to usher in the season. And you could add some late-blooming asters in blue and lavender, or chrysanthemums in shades of pink, lavender and pale yellow.

PLANT LIST FOR GARDEN OF OLD ROSES

ANNUALS

ALYSSUM, SWEET. *Lobularia maritima.* Purple, white or pink varieties. Grows 4–6 inches tall and blooms from late spring to frost. Tiny fragrant blossoms make a carpet. Easily grown from seed by sowing in the ground in early spring or starting indoors. Can be readily transplanted to fill any gaps in the border. Cut back for lush recurrent bloom. Often self-sows.

LARKSPUR, ANNUAL. *Consolida ambigua (Delphinium ajacis).* Most varieties grow 3–5 feet tall, in shades of blue, lavender, purple, pink and white. Long spikes of florets, similar to those of perennial delphiniums. Plant seeds outdoors in fall or early spring. Do not transplant, but thin to 1–1½ feet apart.

LOBELIA, EDGING. *Lobelia erinus.* Any blue, white or pink shades. Likes moist, rich soil. Start seeds indoors in February and set out after last frost, or buy started plants.

STOCK, COMMON. *Matthiola incana* 'Annua' hybrids. Plant trysomic strain in hot climates. Stock grows 1–3 feet tall and bears showy spikes of mostly double flowers, in shades of pink, purple, red and white. It prefers sun and a fairly rich soil, ample moisture. Sow seeds in the ground in March or April; thin out the weaker (usually single-flowered) seedlings so that the plants are 10–12 inches apart. Plant in fall in warm climates for winter and spring bloom.

PERENNIALS AND BIENNIALS

ARTEMISIA (DUSTY MILLER, BEACH WORMWOOD, OLD WOMAN). *Artemisia stellerana.* Zones 4–9. Deeply toothed aromatic white foliage. Grows ½–2 feet tall and sprawls widely. Pinch at 6 inches to encourage branching. Cut off flowers in midsummer and any straggling foliage. Prefers light, sandy soil, good drainage.

ARTEMISIA, SILVER MOUND. *Artemisia schmidtiana nana* 'Silver Mound.' Zones 4–9. Silver-gray foliage, very soft to the touch. Grows 6–8 inches high and about a foot wide. Cut back hard in midsummer when straggly.

CANTERBURY BELLS. *Campanula medium.* Zones 4–10. Biennial. Either the single, the cup-and-saucer, or the hose-in-hose variety, in which one set of cuplike petals grows inside another. Usually blue, white or pink. Grows up to 3 feet tall. Sow seed in early summer to bloom the following summer.

CARNATION, BORDER. *Dianthus caryophyllus.* Zones 6–7. In other zones grow as an annual. Grows 1–3 feet high. Grayish foliage. Flowers in many shades, clove-scented, blooms all summer.

CLEMATIS. *Clematis.* Any variety. To zone 6; 5 with protection. There are many shades—purple, lavender, pink, mauve, white and even the yellow *C. tangutica.* All blend well with old roses; most bloom throughout the summer. They twist readily around a trellis or arbor, even around rosebushes, and would look good mixed in with climbing roses. Plant with a cupful of lime mixed well into fertile soil with a mulch to shield the roots from the sun's heat and the winter's cold. Replenish the lime and mulch each year. Those varieties that bloom on new wood should be cut back to a foot or two in the spring. Those that bloom on old growth should be pruned sparingly and only after blooming.

COLUMBINE. *Aquilegia* hybrids. Zones 3–10. The old-fashioned blue *A. vulgaris* or *A. caerulea* would be appropriate here, as would the showy, brightly colored McKana hybrids. Most grow 2–3 feet tall and bloom in May and June. Prefer moist but well-drained soil. Set about a foot apart. They will self-sow, and should be allowed to, within reason, in this garden.

CORAL BELLS. *Heuchera sanguinea,* any shade. Zones 4–9. Tiny, bright red or pink bell-like flowers dangling from wiry stems all summer. About

18 inches tall. Very vigorous. Plant a foot apart and divide every few years.

DELPHINIUM. *Delphinium*, Pacific Coast hybrids. Zones 3–7. Or you might plant the garland delphinium, *D. belladonna*, or the lower-growing Chinese delphinium, *D. grandiflorum*. In general, the taller and more magnificent a delphinium variety is, the harder it is to grow. Find the one that suits you best. The blues will look best, but mauves, pinks and whites will also be effective here. Plant 1½–2 feet apart, depending on how tall the variety is, and cut back in early summer after blooming for more blossoms later in the summer.

FOXGLOVE. *Digitalis purpurea, D. mertonensis, D. grandiflora* and others. Zones 4–9. The Excelsior or Shirley hybrids are the showiest, with tall spikes of beautifully marked florets in pinks, white and other shades, carried on

several sides of the stem and at right angles to it. They grow up to 4 feet tall and bloom in June and July. They are biennials in most zones, but will self-sow. Let them come up among the roses; their spikes are the perfect foil. There are also annual foxgloves called 'Foxy' that bloom the first season they are sown. All prefer soil that is moist in hot weather, but not too wet in cold weather. For perennial varieties a winter mulch is helpful, but do not mulch if you want them to self-sow.

HOLLYHOCK. *Alcea rosea* (*Althea rosea*). To zone 3. Plant the old-fashioned single varieties if you can find them. They are more appropriate for this garden than the modern doubles, and the powder puff hollyhocks are so heavy that they tend to fall off in the rain, strewing the ground like soggy Kleenex. Plant 2 feet apart, and stake against summer storms. Even if they do not survive the winter, they are dependable self-sowers.

LILY. *Lilium regale*, improved strain. Grows 3–6 feet tall and blooms in June and July. Red speciosum lily, *Lilium speciosum* 'Rubrum,' grows about 6 feet tall and has red-streaked recurved blooms in August–September. Both to zone 5. Plant lilies in spring or fall, 6 inches deep in very well-drained soil. Stake just before blooming if needed. May not attain full height the first year.

PINK, GRASS (SCOTCH PINK, COTTAGE PINK, BORDER PINK). *Dianthus plumarius* 'Semperflorens.' Zones 4–7 as a perennial, 8–10 as a biennial. Grows about a foot tall and blooms all summer. Foliage forms a blue-gray mat. Likes full sun, somewhat dry soil.

SCABIOSA (PINCUSHION FLOWER). *Scabiosa caucasica*. Zones 3–9. Grows 2–2½ feet tall. Flowers are light blue or lavender and come in summer and into fall. Likes sun, manure. Water in drought. Propagate by division every few years or so. You may sow seeds in summer to bloom the following season.

ROSES

(Dates are the presumed dates of introduction or earliest record.)

'ALFRED DE DALMAS' (MOUSSELINE). *Rosa centifolia* 'muscosa'), HYBRID MOSS. To zone 4. 1855. Compact, bushy plant, 2–3 feet tall. High-centered, cupped double blooms, pale pink and moderately fragrant. Free-flowering and long-blooming.

AUTUMN DAMASK (FOUR SEASONS ROSE). DAMASK. *Rosa damascena* or *R. d. bifera* 'semperflorens'. Zone 4. Probably known to the ancient Romans. Vigorous, growing 3–4 feet tall. Flowers deep pink, crumpled, not ex-

ceptionally beautiful, but continuous, especially in mild climates. Olive-green leaves, long red hips.

'BARONNE PRÉVOST.' HYBRID PERPETUAL. Zone 5. 1842. Compact and erect, to 5 feet. Flat, large double flowers in a clear pink with silver on the reverse side. Button-eyed, quartered, fragrant. Repeats until frost.

'BLANC DOUBLE DE COUBERT.' Zone 4. *Rosa rugosa* hybrid. 1892. Grows to 7 feet; average about 5. Large semidouble flowers with good fragrance bloom all summer.

'CARDINAL DE RICHELIEU.' GALLICA. 1840. Zone 4. Lax mound about 5 feet tall. Ball-shaped flowers with rolled petals of a deep velvety purple, almost black, that darken with age and are moderately fragrant. Smooth dark green foliage. Appreciates some thinning.

'CELESTIAL' (CELESTE). ALBA. Zone 4. Late 18th century. Well-shaped plant, growing 5–6 feet tall, sturdy and

erect. Semidouble pale pink flowers, beautifully shaped, with gold stamens. Moderate fragrance. Grayish blue leaves.

COMMON MOSS (OLD PINK MOSS, 'COMMUNIS'). MOSS ROSE. Zone 4. Circa 1696. Vigorous shrub, usually 4 feet tall. Well-formed double blossoms are clear pink, open in a globe shape, then flatten out, with button center. Very fragrant. Medium green foliage, long mossy sepals. Needs to be pegged down.

'FANTIN-LATOUR.' Variously classed as a BOURBON or a CENTIFOLIA. Zone 4. Circa 1850. Lax, rounded bushes 4–6 feet tall. Light pink flowers flat, double, button-eyed and fragrant.

'LA REINE VICTORIA.' BOURBON. Zone 5. 1872. Slender, erect bush to 6 feet. Clusters of double dusty-pink flowers that are full and rounded,

with a cupped shape. Intensely fragrant. If pegged down, it will send up fresh flowering shoots all summer.

'MAIDEN'S BLUSH' (CUISSE DE NYMPHE). ALBA. Zone 4. 1797. There are "great" and "small" varieties; most nurseries have the smaller, which nonetheless grows to 6 feet, outward arching and freely branching, with many sweetly fragrant flowers. These are pink, flat, with pale edges and deeper pink centers (the "blush"). Foliage gray-green. Responds well to pegging.

'MAY QUEEN.' *Rosa wichuraiana* hybrid. Zone 5. 1898. This vigorous rambler is part bourbon, and therefore repeats. It can grow 25 feet and more if not cut back, with interlocking twigs that keep building on each other. Dusty-pink flowers, very double, with an applelike fragrance; flat and quartered, often with a button eye. Good on a wall, on a fence, or even as a large moundlike shrub. Leaves are fresh green and glossy.

'MME. HARDY.' DAMASK (sometimes considered an ALBA). Zone 4. 1832. Tall, abundant bush, 5–6 feet tall. Flowers pure white, flat (almost concave) and very double with a button eye and often a green spot in the center. Excellent fragrance, once used in

perfumes. Luxuriant dark green foliage.

'MME. ISAAC PEREIRE.' BOURBON. Zone 5. 1881. Grows 6–8 feet tall; can almost be considered a pillar rose. Huge pink quartered flowers with the color and fragrance of ripe raspberries. Lax growth, needing support.

'MRS. JOHN LAING.' HYBRID PERPETUAL. Zone 5. 1887. Fairly tall, up to 6 feet, and thornless. Profuse large double flowers medium pink, look more like those of a modern rose. Popular because of its strong fragrance and long bloom.

'REINE DES VIOLETTES' (QUEEN OF THE VIOLETS). HYBRID PERPETUAL (sometimes classed as a BOURBON). Zone 5. 1860. Thornless shrub that will grow as tall as 8 feet. Can be pegged down, trained as a climber on a wall or fence or kept to a 5-foot shrub by pruning.

ROSA MUNDI. *Rosa gallica* 'Versicolor.' Zone 4. 16th cen-

tury, possibly ancient. Grows 3½–5 feet tall. Semidouble flowers of moderate fragrance, crimson splashed with white or pink. These markings are more pronounced if the soil is not too rich.

'ROSE DE MEAUX.' CABBAGE ROSE. *Rosa centifolia* 'Pomponia.' Zone 4. 17th or 18th century. Miniature cabbage rose, named for a 17th-century bishop. Bushes only 1½–3 feet tall. Flowers tiny pink pompons, moderately fragrant. Pale green leaves.

'STANWELL PERPETUAL.' *Rosa spinosissima* hybrid. Zone 4. 1838. Grows to 3 feet or more, but spreads widely in a prickly tangle. Flowers blush-pink, flat, double, moderately fragrant. Dainty grayish foliage. One parent was a damask perpetual, which causes this rose to be a good repeater. Several bushes planted close together make a good, dense shrub.

'TUSCANY SUPERB.' GALLICA. Zone 4. Before 1848. Small, sturdy, upright shrub, to about 4 feet. Flowers are large, semidouble, dark crimson-purple, and spread wide open to reveal beautifully contrasting gold stamens.

A Zen Garden

There may come a time when you decide to put aside a number of worldly cares and create a simple little garden, tucked away in a sheltered spot—outside your kitchen door or study window, perhaps, or even on the balcony of your city apartment. It might contain nothing more than two or three of your favorite plants and a special rock that you picked up on a walk in the woods.

Because this garden is so understated, you had to think a long time before arranging each piece of it, and it has become your favorite vista and a focus of contemplation. You may be no philosopher—chances are your gardening goals have always run along such lines as: "death to the slugs," or "more bloom for August"—but what you have created, perhaps without knowing it, is something like a Zen garden. (You could not construct an authentic Zen garden unless you were a longtime student of that discipline.)

The philosophy and practice of Zen is a subject quite beyond the scope of this book, but there are a few things about it that might give inspiration to a gardener. The

word "Zen" means "meditation," and it is a discipline by which the mind is emptied of the chaos of daily life and brought to a state of peace and harmony. In this state, you attempt to experience a wholeness of self, and you are able to experience yourself as part of the whole of creation. A small, quiet, beautiful garden from which anything chaotic or disharmonious is excluded is a fit setting for such meditations. Indeed, this spirit encompasses even the maintenance of the garden; since Zen makes no distinction between a goal and the process by which it is achieved ("getting there" is the same thing as "there" for instance), the act of gardening itself is an important part of the discipline. Tasks such as pruning, weeding and raking should be performed with care and humility. Skill and efficiency of motion are in the proper spirit. A weed is not yanked out of the ground thoughtlessly, but with the respect due to any living thing. Even inanimate objects such as water and stone are handled as if they had a spirit, for in Zen thinking, they do.

Zen masters developed gardens as special settings for a ceremony which celebrated the drinking of tea. Tea is said to have entered Zen as something to keep one awake while meditating, but it became much more. The tea ceremony, the teahouse and the tea garden were stylized expressions of the unity with nature that these masters had found in mountain retreats, and an entire aesthetic was developed around them. In the fourteenth and fifteenth centuries the tea garden was brought to perfection by masters of the art, such as Soami and the great painter Sesshu, and it was still alive in the seventeenth in the hands of Kobori Enshu.

The tea garden, briefly described, is a series of small landscapes through which a visitor walks before entering a teahouse, as if he were walking down a woodland path into a rustic hut, and accepting tea from an old hermit. These landscapes, which are part of the ceremony itself, contain natural stones, woodland plants and certain artifacts such as a lantern to light the guests' way and a stone basin for rinsing the mouth. These objects should have the mellowness that comes with old age and long use—old lanterns are often lichen-covered; old gates are often

weathered by the elements. The same aesthetic extends to stones, which are lichen-covered, and even to plants. It is considered beautiful, for example, for old trees to need props to support them, and no attempt is made to hide these aids.

Shibusa is a word the Japanese often use to describe gardens. Translators have found the word rich in connotations—restraint, truth, nobility, good taste, simplicity, elegance. It is a word that speaks on the plane of religion, morality, art and etiquette, all at the same time.

There is another quality peculiar to the Zen garden that comes from the heart of Zen thought and is the thing that sets a Zen garden apart. It is the quality of incompleteness—a minimal or shorthand approach to design that forces the viewer to complete the picture himself. It originates in the Zen concept of clearing the mind and relaxing the effort of the will, in order to gain a clearer vision.

Japanese gardening is very metaphorical—a pond with a tiny island in it, for example, might represent the eternal sea and the isle of the immortals. Zen gardens abbreviate things even further. Small stones represent whole mountain ranges; small plants symbolize vast forests. An area of gravel raked into patterns might represent water. This style of gardening moves closer to the pure abstraction of mind that meditation aims for in all mystical religions, but at the same time it forces the eye to see with almost supernatural clarity the essence of a single beautiful thing in nature. And it never de-

This stone garden is at the teahouse of the Japanese embassy in Washington, D.C. Moss, stones, gravel and a few plants, enclosed by a simple wall, invite relaxation and tranquillity.

parts from the basic foundations of all Japanese gardening: water, plants and stones. In recent years, Zen gardens have become familiar to the West chiefly through the purest and most famous of all Zen gardens, the flat garden of Ryoan-ji in Kyoto. Ryoan-ji is nothing more than a rectangle of sand, fifteen carefully placed stones and a little dark moss. Some gardens even eliminate the moss.

The manner in which this abbreviation is carried out has a subtle quality, and it cannot be achieved by direct imitation, only learned and absorbed. This quality underlies the "Japanese simplicity" that has contributed so much to our modern sense of good design. Try to learn just a little of it and apply it in setting up your own garden; this would be a far better approach than simply acquiring lanterns, bridges or pagodas in a misguided attempt to an Oriental look.

The importance of stones can hardly be underestimated. A western gardener might search to find an attractive stone for a rock garden, one that was handsome and appeared natural in the setting. But a Japanese gardener would search relentlessly for one that was nothing short of perfect, perhaps even hiring a stone broker to find one. He might place the stone in such a way that it represented something else, a mountain perhaps, and possessed a personality of its own. There might be a whole language of stones being spoken in his garden, each stone making its own eloquent statement. Some kinds of stones are of course more expressive than others, especially dark colored ones on which lichens stand out well; rough-textured stones with crevices where moss and other small plants can grow; stones with elegant or fanciful shapes.

The most obvious difference between Japanese and western gardens is the attitude toward plants. While we are very concerned with flowers, the Japanese emphasize foliage and overall design. Plantings are considered permanent, and must be attractive in all seasons. Trees and shrubs are of primary importance, especially evergreens, and great care goes into pruning and training them. Some are even shaped to catch the snow in beautiful ways. This does not mean that the Japanese dislike flowers; on the contrary,

In the Japanese garden at Fanhams Hall in Hertfordshire, England, tranquil water reflects the dazzling red foliage of maples in fall.

they prize them. But they might be content with one cherry tree blooming in its season, and not worry about what kind of other blossoms follow. They might plant just one clump of iris in the garden and then keep a cutting garden in an inconspicuous spot, so as to always have a perfect flower for the tea room. Plants in the landscape bloom only incidentally, and buds are often snipped off in the course of pruning, since it is the basic form that matters most, not the decoration.

Such a strict aesthetic is not to everyone's taste, but it is worth learning about, if only to see your own standards in a different perspective. The art of Oriental gardening is very old, whereas ours has only recently separated itself from agriculture and medicine. Renaissance or Colonial gardens, with their businesslike herb beds or burst of bright flowers next to a fence, seem like peasant gardens, or childish enthusiasms, when compared to practices that have been a self-conscious art for many centuries.

The maintenance of a Japanese garden is also in keeping with the spirit of meditation—unhurried, but efficient and without wasted motion. It is a meticulous, thorough craft, requiring patience and expertise. Pruning is the most important task, for not only does careful pruning produce beauti-

THE ZEN
GARDEN

fully shaped plants, it is the reason why the plants are always in just the proper scale for the size of the garden.

Since raking and weeding are done with ceremonial care, these gardens always look clean, tidy and ordered. Nonetheless there is a fine line between order and unnaturalness. In an oft-told tale, the tea master finished raking up the red leaves that had fallen from his maple, then shook the tree so that just a few leaves would fall to the ground, as appropriate to the season.

PLAN OF THE GARDEN

The garden in this chapter is what the Japanese would call a sand garden. There are only five kinds of growing things here, and two stand outside the borders of the garden proper. It is a tiny rectangular area surrounded by a wooden fence. A third of this area is composed of a stone terrace. The only entrance is from this terrace, and the plant picture is viewed from there; you do not walk in the garden except to tend it. A Japanese maple and Japanese black pine can be seen over the fence, lending their height and some shade. Some of their branches should sweep gracefully over the scene below.

Within the fence is a simple composition of plants and stones. It need not be copied precisely; use your own imagination and sense of composition. Some stones are carefully placed, with dark, mound-shaped Japanese hollies behind them. Among the rocks are clumps of epimedium, a hardy but slow-spreading ground cover with small heart-shaped leaves and dainty, pale flowers. In crevices in and among the stones are ferns—maidenhair spleenworts (*Asplenium trichomanes*)—that grow only four to six inches tall. This grouping should please the eye simply as a combination of natural materials—the gray stones, the light green epimedium, the dark hollies, the bright medium green of the ferns, the dark green of the overhanging pine. Shapes and textures also vary—the slender pine needles, the delicate, deeply indented maple leaves, the small glossy leaves of the holly, the wood of the fence, the lobed leaves of the ferns. The rest of the area is simply raked gravel—yet another texture.

One way to look at this garden is as a river flowing down from mountains into the sea. The rounded hollies are tree-covered hills; the rocks are smaller hills closer to the sea, where salt winds prevent most trees from growing. The epimedium with its forest of little long-stemmed leaves represents the wooded valleys between the hills. The ferns are clumps of rugged trees that grow even on a rocky hillside. And the gravel is the river winding down through the valleys and emptying into the sea below. A single rock with its own epimedium "forest" and fern clump is an island in this sea. The concept behind the picture is a typical one, and not hard to improvise yourself. On the other hand, you might want to make a design that is wholly

THREE WAYS TO MAKE "FLOWING BRANCHES"

To make a branch overhang the garden in a graceful, flowing arc, tie a thin rope to the branch and then to the trunk, making just enough of a bend so that the branch is pulled downward but doesn't drag on the ground. To protect the tree, thread the rope through sections of an old garden hose or plastic tubing wherever it is wrapped around the tree.

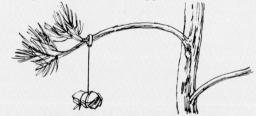

A stone or other weight can be suspended from the end of a branch to make it arch slightly.

Another method is to tie the end of the branch to a small wooden stake sunk in the ground. This and the above devices may be removed once the arching habit has been established.

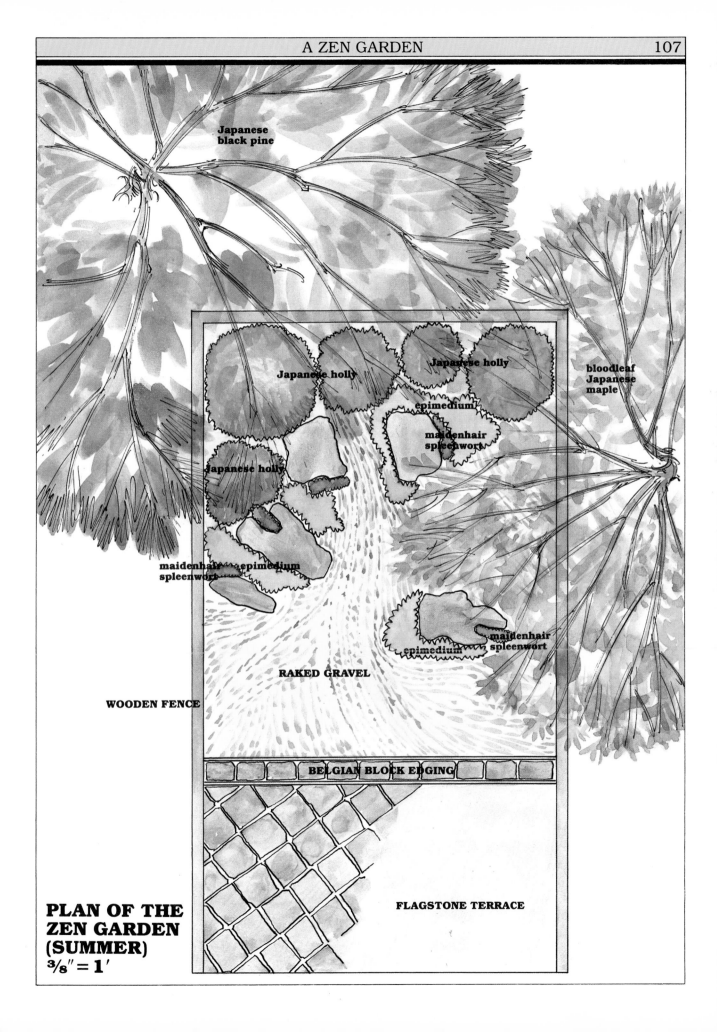

Japanese black pine

Japanese holly

Japanese holly

bloodleaf Japanese maple

epimedium

maidenhair spleenwort

Japanese holly

maidenhair spleenwort

epimedium

epimedium

maidenhair spleenwort

RAKED GRAVEL

WOODEN FENCE

BELGIAN BLOCK EDGING

FLAGSTONE TERRACE

PLAN OF THE ZEN GARDEN (SUMMER)
$^3/_8'' = 1'$

abstract, not a "representational" picture at all. You might even decide you prefer no plants whatsoever, just gravel and stones.

The kinds of rocks available to you depend, of course, on where you live. You may live in a region that is positively strewn with interesting-looking rocks—or you may have to do some hunting. Because it has more crevices and ridges where moss, lichens and other plants can thrive, in general metamorphic rock such as granite is preferable to the sedimentary kind. Natural rocks are always better than cut stones; they should all be of a single type.

The "sand" in sand gardens is usually fine gravel; it blows around less, stays cleaner and keeps its raked contours better than sand would. Quarter-inch stone is ideal, and the kind with angular rather than smooth surfaces is better for raking. But a number of other materials have been used in sand gardens, from black Mexican beach pebbles to turkey grit.

Since you will not want to walk on this carefully raked pattern, you will need a place from which to view the garden. A terrace is recommended here. It is made of flagstones set in diagonal rows and edged in front with a row of Belgian block, a rather choice paving stone that looks like a large rectangular cobblestone. You could also make a terrace in the old Japanese style, with clay tiles set in a diagonal pattern, or substitute a simple wooden platform instead. To build a terrace, lay a wooden edging, put in a bed of sand and lay both the flagstones and the block as you would for the brick terrace on page 165. The fence should be of a simple, tasteful design, made of wood and painted a dark neutral color such as gray; better yet, treat it with a wood preservative and let it weather to a natural color.

SITE

This garden should have a fairly shady location. The plants within the garden enclosure are shade-loving and will be partly shielded by the pine and the maple. Shade from other surrounding trees is fine, as long as the pine and maple do not have to compete with them too much for light. The maple likes part shade but is attractive when some sun

shines through its leaves from behind, giving it a red glow. Shade will contribute to the restful quality of the garden, although it is nice to have some sun there in cold weather; this is best achieved by using the deciduous maple, and possibly other deciduous trees near the garden.

Ideally the terrace will project from a door that leads only to the garden. If it is a door used for coming and going, however, make a gate in the fence in such a way that you exit by way of the terrace, to one side. It would be an attractive garden for an entry, though it will serve as a true meditation garden only if it is private. You could achieve this by placing the garden at some distance from the house, reached by a path. Another good spot for the garden would be a courtyard within a house or other building, where it is visible from several rooms.

GROWING INSTRUCTIONS

This garden requires very little upkeep, but it is very important to perform the tasks that are necessary. Imagine the "mountains" growing shoots of greenery in odd directions, islands of crabgrass coming up all over the "sea," and a sand pattern showing evidence of a place where two cats have had a fight. You should prune the hollies several times during the growing season, beginning with early spring, and whenever they start to lose their smooth, round form (see below). If, upon

Ill. 8. To prune Japanese holly, trim each branch individually, making your cut just above a branchlet. Remove any twigs that are dead or winter burned. Give the shrub a smooth, moundlike form.

© BARBARA DAMROSCH

The stark simplicity of a single stone is an aid to meditation in the garden designed by Eido Roshi at the New York Zendo, New York City.

planting, you have added humus and a fertilizer for acid-loving plants, you should not have to feed them any more unless they are under stress. This plant does not like wind and hot sun in winter; like many broad-leafed evergreens it is easily burned by the sun reflecting off the snow. But this sheltered, shady location is in its favor.

The epimedium, like the holly, will appreciate a woodsy soil with plenty of humus. It will need no other care. Plant the maidenhair spleenwort in pockets or crevices in the rocks where it will be visible from the terrace

Ill. 9. When "candles" appear at the ends of branches of Japanese black pine in spring, break the central candle about halfway down its length. This will produce bushier needle clusters. Remove branches to maintain a pleasing, symmetrical form.

and not get lost in the epimedium. It adapts readily to a spot where there is very little soil, as long as there is shade and some moisture in very hot weather. Plant the trees according to the instructions in the Garden Primer (see pp. 20 and 21) and stake as needed. Prune when necessary.

You will have to remove autumn leaves and other debris from the plants and gravel from time to time, raking the gravel anew whenever it has been walked on. A steel one will do the job, or a homemade wooden one with sawtooth-shaped notches. Drag the rake smoothly through the gravel, using only the pressure of its own weight. You may enjoy experimenting with different patterns.

ADDITIONS AND SUBSTITUTIONS

There are so many plants that are suitable in Japanese gardens that it would be impossible to list them here; they include a large number of our commonest plants. I shall just suggest a few alternatives to the five plants I have recommended for this garden. Instead of epimedium you could use a moss. The Japanese consider moss almost essential in their gardens, particularly those with rocks and sand. It is not commonly cultivated in the West; however, if you live in a region where there are native mosses that grow well, you could transplant some to a moist shady site. The Japanese would use a moss such as *Polytrichum commune*. You might try Irish moss *(Arenaria verna)* or flowering moss *(Pyxidanthera barbulata)*, though neither is a true moss. Other substitutes for moss include baby's tears *(Soleirolia soleirolii)* or various ground covers such as ajuga *(Ajuga reptans)*, wintergreen *(Gaultheria procumbens)*, or dichondra *(Dichondra repens)* (dichondra and baby's tears in warm climates only). Wild ginger *(Asarum canadenses)* would be a fine substitute for the epimedium. You could also use the native club moss, also called ground pine *(Lycopodium clavatum)*, though you must not take this plant from the woods in states where it is protected.

Many small ferns could be used, such as the Pacific maid maidenhair *(Adiantum raddianum* 'Pacific Maid'), the ribbon brake fern *(Pteris cretica* 'Albo-lineata') and some of the *Woodsia* species. There are slightly larger ferns that would look beautiful in the setting, such as the increasingly popular Japanese painted fern *(Athyrium goeringianum* 'Pictum').

Instead of Japanese holly you could use evergreen azaleas, especially the dwarf ones. Boxwood is another good choice. Both of these can be trimmed in the appropriate shape. There are also a multitude of trees that could be substituted for the ones chosen; for example, cherry, plum, apricot, crab apple, quince, a weeping cherry or birch, ginkgo, mimosa (silk tree) or laburnum (golden rain tree). A choice form of the Japanese maple called the cutleaf *(Acer palmatum* 'Dissectum') is very popular in gardens and might be substituted for the taller Japanese maple I have suggested. But since the cutleaf has a low, spreading umbrellalike shape it is less in scale with the garden and could not be placed outside the fence—though if you love it you could surely find a way to include it if you give the matter some quiet reflection.

PLANT LIST FOR ZEN GARDEN

PERENNIALS

EPIMEDIUM. *Epimedium grandiflorum.* Zones 3–8. If possible, find the dwarf species, *E. diphyllum,* which grows 6–8 inches tall and blooms white in early spring. The more usual species is 9–12 inches tall. The color of the flowers varies from white to yellow to rose or violet; they appear in late spring or early summer. The leaves are pinkish in spring, green with red veins in summer and bronze in fall and even into winter in a protected spot or warm climate. Epimedium spreads slowly; it likes part shade and rich, moist soil with humus. Plant in spring or fall and divide in summer if you want clumps in different places.

MAIDENHAIR SPLEENWORT. *Asplenium trichomanes.* Zones 3–8. This fern needs shade, but will tolerate more dryness than most ferns. Grows in clumps, in small amounts of soil. Likes lime. Increase by division.

SHRUBS AND TREES

HOLLY, JAPANESE. *Ilex crenata* 'Convexa,' 'Helleri' or 'Microphylla.' Zones 6–10. These are small-leafed, compact varieties. They like winter shade and protection from wind, appreciate moist soil in summer. Fertilize in spring around the roots as needed with an acid fertilizer, and mulch around the roots in winter. Prune in early spring with hedge shears, and thereafter when needed to retain proper shape. Grows well in the city.

MAPLE, BLOODLEAF JAPANESE. *Acer palmatum* 'Atropurpureum.' Zones 5–9. Another good variety is scarlet Japanese maple, *A. p.* 'Sanguineum.' The bloodleaf variety is a hardy tree that grows to be up to 20 feet tall, and keeps its reddish purple leaves all season. It likes rich, moist, well-drained soil enriched with organic matter. Plant it in spring in sun or very light shade, pruning only as needed to maintain view of the garden.

PINE, JAPANESE BLACK. *Pinus thunbergiana.* Zones 5–9. Grows to 90 feet tall, with a dense, spreading, irregular growth habit. The name refers to the color of the bark, though the needles are also very dark. Grows quickly while young; responds well to pruning. Needs sun, well-drained soil, but not too rich. It will thrive in harsh situations, such as the seashore. Prune for this garden and do not feed much, if at all.

A Shakespeare Garden

Shakespeare's fairy kingdom in *A Midsummer Night's Dream* is a kingdom of flowers. Its queen, Titania, chooses a flowery woodland bank for her bed, and to such a "flowery bed" she brings Nick Bottom, her lover.

No matter that fairy magic has transformed him into an ass—fairy magic has also made her blind to this defect (like many lovers before and since). A spell worked with a flower has caused her passion, and with flowers she decks Bottom's grizzled head.

Shakespeare's plays and poems abound with flowers and gardens. His city dwellers flee to the blossoming countryside in spring, looking for a pastoral simplicity. And important scenes take place in walled gardens: lovers meet, games are played, wars begin. There are English cottage gardens, royal palace gardens, town gardens in Italy—always planted, though, with English flowers. Shakespeare's language is rich in plant and garden metaphors, so much so that some scholars suggest that he was something of a gardener himself. As Caroline Spurgeon puts it, in *Shakespeare's Imagery,* "One occupation, one point of view, above all others, is naturally his, that of a gardener; watching, preserving, tending and caring for growing

things, especially flowers and fruit. All through his plays, he thinks most easily and readily of human life and action in the terms of a gardener." Historians note that Shakespeare grew up loving the countryside and wildlife surrounding his native Stratford-on-Avon, and the rustic gardens of the little town. They note that he had a garden of his own when he returned to live in Stratford his later years.

Actually, there is no proof that Shakespeare himself ever so much as touched a spade. We are sure of very little about his life, in fact; all we know is that the mentions gardening often in his works in a way that shows some knowledge of the subject. More importantly, that he uses that knowledge as a way of understanding the rest of life. He also assumes that his audience knows something about gardening, and one has the impression that it was a popular enthusiasm among the people of his time. They would also have known the silent language of plants and flowers—the symbolic meanings acquired over the centuries (see Uses and Meanings of Plants and Flowers, p. 120 for some examples).

People who like Shakespeare and also enjoy gardening are often intrigued with the idea of building a garden around the plants mentioned by the Bard. Many such gardens have been planted over the years, from simple herb or cottage gardens to the rather elaborate grounds that are maintained at Shakespeare's Stratford home. For the garden here, I have focused on several flora-filled scenes or passages from the plays, and designed a garden with these in mind. I have tried to do justice to the variety of Shakespeare's plant lore: the plants of the countryside, the traditional garden herbs and the emblematic use of flowers in the history plays.

Titania's bower, in *A Midsummer Night's Dream*, with wild thyme and violets underfoot, flowering vines above, is a romantic woodland setting:

> *I know a bank where the wild thyme blows,*
> *Where oxlips and the nodding violet grows,*
> *Quite over-canopied with luscious woodbine,*
> *With sweet musk-roses with eglantine*
> *There sleeps Titania sometime of the night*
> *Lull'd in these flowers with dances and delight.*

The "bank" is a fragrant bed to lie on, and the canopy of vines provides shade and con-

Anne Hathaway's cottage in Stratford-on-Avon, England, is a colorful jumble of flowers. It is typical of the country gardens that Shakespeare knew, and that one can see in England today.

cealment. "Sleep thou," she tells Bottom, "and I will wind thee in my arms . . . so doth the woodbine the sweet honeysuckle gently entwist." Even the twining of the vines is an image of entangled lovers. Such hideaways appear in other plays, too, such as the "pleached bower" in *Much Ado About Nothing*, "Where honeysuckles ripen'd by the sun Forbid the sun to enter" (III, i).

Such woodland settings might seem hard to incorporate into an Elizabethan garden. Not so. The gardens of medieval and Renaissance England often contained pieces of wild nature, though tamed and enclosed—thyme-covered banks, turf seats, flower-dotted lawns or "meads" (see Medieval Paradise Garden, p. 169)—and arbors with flowering vines carefully woven in imitation of lush forest growth. These conventions provided town and castle dwellers with the means to enjoy the natural world in a safe, civilized setting.

The pruning and weaving of trees and vines to make such arbors or walkways was a highly developed art. Trees such as linden or hawthorn were planted close together, then "pleached" (their side branches trimmed close, to form a hedge) and "plashed" (their small top and side branches woven together). Hedges such as these could take various forms; sometimes briers and flowering vines were woven into them, either for decoration or to make the hedges more effective barriers against livestock. In the light of such practices, it seems likely that most of Shakespeare's "woodland bowers" are such as might be found in a well-kept garden.

Meadows dotted with wild flowers also provided plenty of inspiration for Shakespeare; like Chaucer and so many other English poets, he sang their praises as images of joy and rebirth. Witness this song from *Love's Labour's Lost* (V, ii):

> *When daisies pied and violets blue*
> *And lady-smocks all silver-white*
> *And cuckoo-buds of yellow hue*
> *Do paint the meadows with delight.*

Or this, from *The Winter's Tale* (IV, iii):

> *When daffodils begin to peer,*
> *   With heigh! the doxy over the dale*
> *Why, then comes in the sweet o' the year;*
> *   For the red blood reigns in the winter's pale.*

And this one, from *Cymbeline* (II, iii):

> *Hark! Hark! the lark at heaven's gate sings,*
> *   And Phoebus 'gins arise,*
> *His steeds to water at those springs*
> *   On chalic'd flowers that lies;*
> *And winking Mary-buds begin*
> *   To ope their golden eyes."*

The last is an *aubade*—a song to wake up a lady in the morning. Mary-buds, also then called marigolds, are what we would call calendulas, and are known for their habit of opening in the morning and closing at night. Like most flowers with "Mary" in the name, they are associated with the Blessed Virgin. So are flowers with "lady" in the name, such as the lady-smocks mentioned above, a pinkish-white wild flower. Here again, there are conventions that enable you to use these flowers in a civilized Elizabethan garden; a small version of the flowery mead in the Medieval Paradise Garden (see page 169) would be the way to do it.

Far less cheerful is the collection of wild flowers that Ophelia picks in *Hamlet* (IV, vii). Wandering out to "where a willow grows aslant a brook," she drowns while trying to hang "fantastic garlands" on the tree. These garlands, we are told, contain "crow-flowers, nettles, daisies and long purples." Such a list might have had a symbolic significance, or even spelled out an allegorical message. Esther Singleton interprets these four to read, "Fair maiden—stung to the quick—her virgin bloom—under the cold hand of death." We already know that Ophelia speaks the language of flowers. In an earlier scene she has gathered herbs and flowers, probably from the castle garden, presenting the king and queen with rosemary "for remembrance," pansies "for thoughts," then rue, fennel and columbines (IV, v). Her choice of flowers for her death scene is thus all the more poignant after this discourse. You could re-create this scene by planting a willow aslant a brook, but a willow is a large tree for a small garden. There will surely be a place for at least three or four of Ophelia's flowers in your garden.

The wild flower that Shakespeare mentions more than any other is the primrose. (as well as cowslips and oxlips, its cousins). Its associations vary in the plays. In *A Midsummer Night's Dream* (I, i), Hermia reminds her former lover, Lysander, of the place "where often you and I Upon faint primrose beds were wont to lie." In *Cymbeline*, (IV, ii), Arviragus names the flowers he would strew on his sister Imogen's grave, among them "the flower that's like thy face, pale primrose." Primroses often had sad connotations because though gay in their bloom, they bloom early and then fade—like beauties who die young. But they also had their roguish side, as in the "primrose path of easy dalliance" referred to in *Hamlet* (I, iii) and also in *Macbeth* (II, iii).

A Shakespeare garden should also include some cultivated flowers, the sort that grew in cottage gardens. Such a garden is humbly displayed by Perdita, the lost princess raised as a shepherdess in *The Winter's Tale*. Greeting her visitors, one of which is the king in disguise, the father of her lover Florizel, she offers them herbs (IV, iii):

> *Rosemary and rue; these keep*
> *Seeming and savour all winter long;*
> *Grace and remembrance to you both.*

Perdita's herbs, like Ophelia's, bear symbolic messages that are inseparable from their beauty and usefulness. She offers her guests what her plants signify—grace and remembrance. Teasing her, they take her offer of "flowers of winter" (i.e., herbs) as a reference to their advanced years.

Perdita's "rustic garden," as she describes it, is primarily an herb garden, with lavender, mints, savory, marjoram and the marigold already mentioned, which was eaten in Shakespeare's time as a salad green. She does not, she says, grow "streak'd gillyvors" (gilliflowers), the carnations so frequently hybridized in the Renaissance, calling them "nature's bastards." Her visitors defend the gilliflower and the wedding of "wild and cultivated stock": though hybridizing is an art practiced by man in imitation of nature's own art, it too is part of nature—a natural act for man to perform. The passage is full of the irony of Perdita's own station in life. As a young princess, she was accused of being illegitimate, hence her banishment; now, as a humble shepherdess, she is destined to marry the prince, wedding wild and cultivated stocks, and gilliflowers themselves are emblems of marriage. As for the parentage of gilliflowers, knowledgeable gardeners will catch the drift of Perdita's coy protest. The *Dianthus* genus is notorious for the production of natural hybrids—plant two different colors and you may get a third, a chance occurrence much sought after by gilliflower breeders. Like these "nature's bastards," Perdita herself is an unexpected prize found in a rustic garden. In any case, you should not exclude them as she does, for they are one of the great Elizabethan flowers.

Perdita goes on to talk about the spring flowers: daffodils, "violets dim," "pale primroses that die unmarried," "bold oxlips," crown imperial, "lilies of all kinds/The flower-de-luce being one"—all of which might well have been blooming earlier in her garden, and could be included in yours.

The flower-de-luce, mentioned often in Shakespeare, is one of great historical import. We would not call it a lily as Perdita does, but an iris, the fleur-de-lis that is the emblem of France. Louis VII adopted it as his battle insignia during the First Crusade, in the twelfth century, when he was looking for a place to ford a river. The wild iris he saw in the distance, the water-loving *Iris pseudacorus*, gave him a sign that there was a shallow, wet place where his army could cross.

Other flowers make political statements in Shakespeare's plays, too. Best known of all was the rose, which has figured in British heraldry since the time of Edward I. One of the most famous garden scenes in Shake-

speare comes in Act II of *Henry VI*, Part I. It is set in the Temple Garden in London (the garden of the Order of Knights Templars, who fought in the Crusades). Here Richard Plantagenet, Duke of York, plucks a white rose, and the Earl of Somerset a red one, urging those who would follow their respective factions to pluck the appropriate rose as a symbol of loyalty. The argument that follows adds more symbolic association—the white face of fear, the red color of courage, red blood from thorns, the canker worm that hides in a rose blossom and destroys it (one of Shakespeare's favorite images of corruption). The scene ends with a declaration of war "between the red rose and the white." Though this incident is only legend, the conflicts that followed—the Wars of the Roses—were real, the House of Lancaster adopting the red rose as its badge, the House of York the white.

These roses are usually said to be the red Apothecary Rose (*Rosa gallica* 'Officinalis') and the Great Double White (*Rosa alba* 'Maximum') or possibly *R. a.* 'Semiplena'). There is also a rose known as the 'York and Lancaster' rose, which bears both pink and white flowers on one bush, with some individual flowers a mixture of both. It was so named as early as 1551, and Shakespeare describes this rose in Sonnet XCIX:

> One blushing shame, another white despair;
> A third, nor red nor white, had stolen of both.

But whichever roses actually grew in the Temple Garden on that day in 1455, a bed planted with all three will be a handsome picture, as well as a nice historical allegory.

Shakespeare's history plays as a whole have much to say about gardening. Shakespeare loved to compare good horticulture with good government. In *Richard II* (III, iv), a gardener and his helper discuss the downfall of their beloved king while they are doing their work. Why, the servant asks, should they bother to keep order in the castle garden when "our sea-walled garden," England:

> Is full of weeds, her fairest flowers chok'd up,
> Her fruit trees all unprun'd, her hedges ruin'd,
> Her knots disorder'd, and her wholesome herbs
> Swarming with caterpillars? (III, iv, 43–47)

Richard's flaw, the elder gardener claims, was that "he hath not so trimm'd and dress'd his land As we this garden," by pruning out those who weakened it. In a similar passage in *Henry V*, the Duke of Burgundy laments the effects of war on "this best garden in the world, our fertile France."

The queen overhears the conversation, her first news of the king's overthrow. Calling the gardener "old Adam's likeness," she curses his plants because he bears such news. Compassionately, the gardener answers:

> Poor queen! so that thy state might be no
>   worse,
> I would my skill were subject to thy curse.
> Here did she fall a tear; here, in this place,
> I'll set a bank of rue, sour herb of grace;
> Rue, even for ruth, here shortly shall be seen,
> In the remembrance of a weeping queen.

In planting rue "he" signifies his repentance for having caused the queen grief, and extends its meaning to include ruth, or pity, for her plight, thus using the gentler language of plants (and his own trade) to counteract the harm that his spoken words have done.

PLAN OF THE GARDEN

This garden is designed as an enclosure, a pleasure garden. If it is within your means, a brick or stone wall would be appropriate and would look good. But you can still enclose the garden in the Renaissance style by building a wooden fence, at a height that suits you. This will also give you a structure on which to grow climbing plants such as roses. This garden can be entered from two sides, with a simple wooden gate at each entrance. The paths can be brick, but gravel is also a material that might have been used in Shakespeare's time, and it is easy to lay and to maintain. A combination of fine gravel and sand is comfortable to walk on and can be laid to a depth of three to four inches within a brick or metal edging. Using such an edging for all the beds will give the garden a tidy appearance.

As you walk through the garden, you encounter what are almost a series of little stage settings, connected by a meandering path. Elizabethan paths did not often meander in small gardens like this; they were geometrical, like the ones in the Colonial Garden and the Medieval Paradise. But I arranged the garden in this way in order to let groups of plants evoke the mood of several of Shakespeare's garden passages, rather than just providing a catalog of the plants he mentions.

The garden falls roughly into two parts, the wild and the cultivated. A crab apple tree in the center separates them. Why a crab apple? Although many trees appear in the plays, I chose this one because it is small—just the right scale for this area. It is also hardy and easy to grow, and looks beautiful covered with blossoms in spring or small fruits in fall. It is these fruits that most often drew it to Shakespeare's attention. There are many references to their use in an old Celtic drink called "lambs wool," in which hot, roasted crab apples are tossed sizzling into a bowl of spiced ale. In *The Taming of the Shrew* (II, i), Kate calls Petruchio a wrinkled "crab" when he chides her for her sour looks. As luck would have it, one of the best available crab apple varieties is called 'Katherine.' By all means plant it.

The "wild" or pastoral end of the garden contains Titania's bower and a little patch of flowering meadow. Most of the plants in this section are natives of the English countryside, or their equivalents.

The plants that canopy Titania's bower are musk roses, honeysuckle and eglantine, a much-loved rose that grew wild in Shakespeare's England. His musk rose was probably *Rosa moschata*. It is not clear from the text whether honeysuckle and woodbine are two different plants or one and the same. (What we call woodbine is Virginia creeper, *Parthenocissus quinquefolia*.) Most likely, Shakespeare's was an old European honeysuckle, *Lonicera periclymenum*. The best combination might be some modern climbing roses that bloom all summer and a Hall's honeysuckle (*Lonicera japonica* 'Halliana'). But eglantine (*Rosa eglanteria*) is worth taking the trouble to obtain from a supplier of old roses (see Where to Order Plants. p. 215), with its old-fashioned single pink flowers and apple-scented leaves. If you want to embark on the project of pleaching and plashing, you could prune and weave a bower out of plants alone, planting some small saplings to support the vines and climbing roses. But a

THE SHAKESPEARE GARDEN

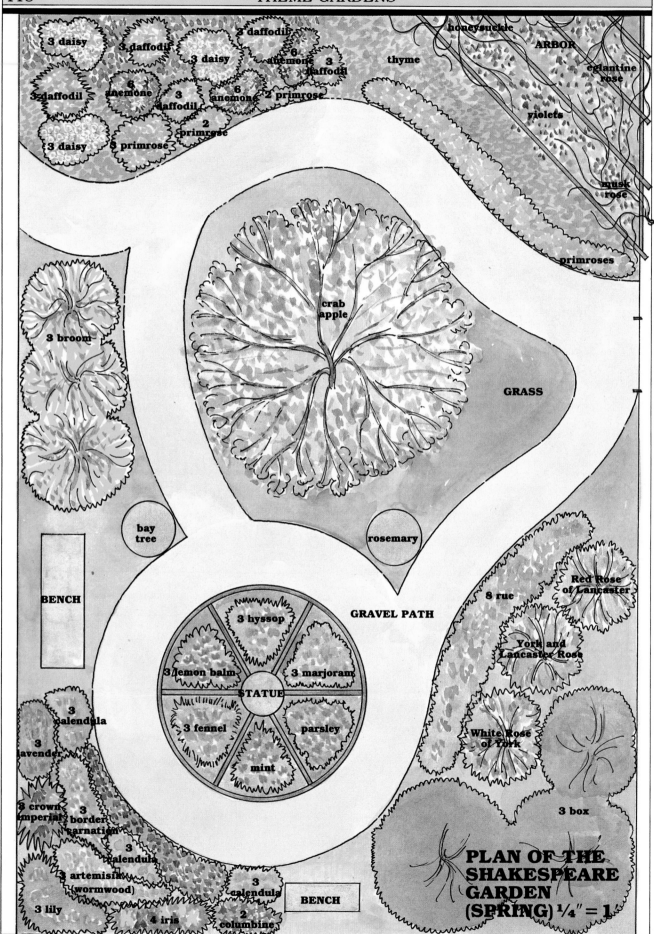

3 daisy
3 daffodil
3 daisy
3 daffodil
6 anemone
3 daffodil

3 daffodil
6 anemone
3 daffodil
6 anemone
2 primrose

3 daisy
2 primrose
8 primrose

honeysuckle
ARBOR
thyme
eglantine rose
violets
musk rose
primroses

crab apple
GRASS

3 broom

bay tree
rosemary

BENCH

GRAVEL PATH
8 rue
Red Rose of Lancaster

York and Lancaster Rose

3 hyssop
3 marjoram
3 lemon balm
STATUE
3 fennel
parsley
mint

White Rose of York

3 calendula
3 lavender

8 crown imperial
3 border carnation
3 calendula
3 calendula
3 box

3 artemisia (wormwood)
3 lily
4 iris
columbine
BENCH

PLAN OF THE SHAKESPEARE GARDEN (SPRING) 1/4" = 1'

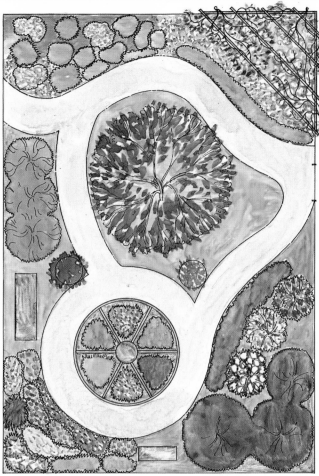

THE GARDEN IN SUMMER

too, and the anemones that spring from the blood of Adonis in *Venus and Adonis*. The "purple flower . . . chequer'd with white" suggests several species, but the most satisfactory one would be *Anemone blanda*, which grows from little tubers, or possibly *A. pulsatilla*, a hardy perennial that blooms very early in the spring. These could all grow among grass, or you could just continue the bower-carpet of thyme and violets like a ground cover, with these other flowering plants among them.

Passing the meadow, you come to several broom plants. These are the "broom groves" that Iris talks about in *The Tempest*, in whose shadow the "dismissed bachelor" can hide when he is "lass-lorn" (IV, i). Broom is a handsome shrub, popular in England and can be grown in most of the United States. It bears yellow or pink flowers in early spring, and a little grove of it is appropriate to a small garden.

After the broom, you enter a cottage garden modeled on Perdita's, but with a little poetic license. Following Gervase Markham's advice in *The Countrie Farm*, written in 1616, flowers for "nosegays" go on one side of the path, and useful herbs on the other. In the flower garden on the right are Perdita's spring flowers—flower-de-luce, crown imperial, lilies, marigolds (calendulas) and lavender, as well as the gilliflowers she scorns. Hamlet's *Artemisia absinthium* (wormwood) is included for a gray-leafed accent. Here also are Ophelia's "pansies" (johnny-jump-up) and columbines.

The round herb bed is divided into six sections, like the slices of a pie. This is a good way to grow herbs, because it enables you to keep them separate. Some herbs are notorious spreaders, and among the worst are Perdita's "mints." Here also is her marjoram—the "sweet marjoram of the salad" to which a lady is compared in *All's Well That Ends Well* (also mentioned in Sonnet XCIX: "And buds of marjoram had stolen thy hair"). The rest of the bed includes Ophelia's fennel (also eaten with eels in *Henry IV, Part II*), and parsley from *The Taming of the Shrew*: "I knew a wench married in the afternoon / as she went to the garden for Parsley / to stuff a rabbit." There is the soothing balm mentioned so often Shakespeare, and finally hys-

wooden arbor like the one in the Garden of Old Roses (see box, p. 92) would be simpler; build it on the diagonal in a corner, as an extension of the fence.

The bank beneath the arbor, where the queen reclines, can be built up in several ways. You could make thyme seats out of wood or masonry, or just by mounding up the earth, using a few large stones here and there to help retain the soil, until you have sculpted a natural seat. Plant it immediately with thyme to make a fragrant bower. (If one part of your bower is shadier than the rest, plant the violets there.) The paths in this part of the garden could be lined with primroses to make a "primrose path," for this is where scenes of "dalliance" are played—along with some of the "cowslips tall" that are Titania's "pensioners" (guards).

The meadow next to the bower is carpeted with the daffodils and daisies of Shakespeare's spring songs. Mary-buds can live here

THE MEANINGS AND USES OF PLANTS AND FLOWERS

The plants in this list once had a wealth of associations, many of which are all but lost today. Many of them were symbolic meanings that date back to pagan Greece and Rome. These were overlaid with Christian meanings in the Middle Ages, or altered to conform with Christian doctrine. A plant that signified physical love to the pagans, for example, might have come to mean spiritual love by medieval times. During the late Middle Ages and Renaissance, the courtly "religion of love" turned some of these meanings back the other way. Though shades of meaning overlap at various times, in this listing I have tried to give an idea of the associations these plants might have gathered by Shakespeare's time. Most of them would apply to the medieval and Colonial periods as well.

Many of their old medicinal functions are now considered useless, even dangerous, for a good many of these plants are now known to be poisonous. Those that still have value should be used medicinally only by those trained to do so. For decoration, of course, they have as much charm as ever.

Plant	Use	Significance
ANEMONE (Pasqueflower). *Anemone pulsatilla.*	Green dye for Easter eggs; also as a sedative and analgesic.	For the pagans, death and mourning, since the flower sprang from the blood of the dead Adonis, or the tears shed for him by Venus. For Christians, similar associations: it sprang from Christ's blood or Mary's tears.
APPLE. *Malus* species.	Eaten raw or in cooked dishes, but most popular in cider.	Symbolized the Fall of Man and all that went with it: sin, lust, temptation, sourness, rottenness.
BALM, LEMON (COMMON). *Melissa officinalis.*	Used in potpourris and scented baths; in cordials, teas, tonics and liqueurs such as Benedictine and Chartreuse; as a mild sedative and for colds and gout; to attract bees.	Sympathy and social pleasantries.
BOX. *Buxus sempervirens.*	Made, as name suggests, into boxes and other wooden articles; bark used in some perfumes; oil used to treat epilepsy and other ills.	Constancy, stoicism.
COLUMBINE. *Aquilegia vulgaris.*	Extracts were drunk with ale, and used against measles, "pox," impotence and nervous ailments.	Since the petals are thought to resemble a ring of doves bending toward the center of the flower, it was a symbol of the Holy Ghost.
CROCUS, SAFFRON. *Crocus sativus.*	Prized for yellow color of stamens, for cosmetic dyes, food coloring and inks. Also used as an aphrodisiac, and to treat stomach complaints.	Mirth.
CROWN IMPERIAL. *Fritillaria imperialis.*	Decorative garden flower, imported from the Middle East.	Pride of birth, power, majesty.
DAISY. *Bellis perennis.*	Innocent of medicinal virtues, except perhaps herbal baths. Used for garlands and for playing "He loves me—loves me not."	Known as "the measure of love" and also the "eye of day," more because of its diurnal blooming habit than its sunlike appearance. In Christian phraseology, the "eye of God" or "eye of Christ."
FENNEL. *Foeniculum vulgare.*	Licorice-flavored herb used in salads and other dishes (seeds especially); also a digestive and antidepressant.	Strength and praiseworthiness.
GILLIFLOWER (pink and carnation). *Dianthus* species.	"Clove gilliflower" used as spice, in sweet syrups and in wine (one of its names was "sops-in-wine"). Often woven into garlands.	Pinks in general stood for betrothal, marriage and fidelity. Carnations stood for "pure motherly love," especially the Virgin Mary's.

Plant	Use	Significance
HAWTHORN ("thorn" in Shakespeare). *Crataegus monogyna.*	The key ingredient in May garlands—another name for the tree is "may." Its wood was used to make boxes; the berries for an alcoholic beverage.	Spring, fertility, hope. Christ's crown of thorns. Somewhat bewitched, it was bad luck to cut it down.
HYSSOP. *Hyssopus officinalis.*	Hyssop had many medicinal uses—for stomach trouble, colds, bruises and as a purgative for worms. It flavored soups and other dishes, and scented perfumes, drawers and chambers.	A holy "bitter" herb for Lent, its purgative powers gave it connotations of cleansing, penitence and humility.
IRIS. *Iris germanica, I. florentina, I. pseudacorus.*	Irises were used to weave chair seats and for strewing. They cured colds, insomnia and stomachache. The root of the Florentine iris (orris) yielded perfumes, dyes, inks and a fixative used in potpourris.	Most likely the flower represented in the fleur-de-lis, the emblem of French kings and royalty in general, also England (for a time), the city of Florence and the Virgin Mary. Sometimes called the "sword lily."
IVY, COMMON (English). *Hedera helix.*	Used as a cough suppressant, as a purgative and against evil spirits—as well as for other medicinal uses.	Sacred to the god Bacchus and still associated with wine in Christian times. Symbol of fidelity and married love because of its clinging habit.
LAUREL (BAY). *Laurus nobilis.*	Mostly a cooking herb, used to flavor many dishes from meats to sweets. Used to scent clothes, and in water for hand-washing at meals. Sometimes employed to treat deafness and other maladies.	The ancient Greeks and Romans crowned victors with bay at athletic and other contests. Vestal virgins wore it as an emblem of chastity. It remained a victor's crown in the Renaissance, especially for poets, and kept its association with chastity. It also stood for constancy and immortality because of its evergreen leaves.
LAVENDER. *Lavandula angustifolia angustifolia.*	Important strewing herb for clothes, rooms and chests; it not only scented them but was said to keep them free of moths. Used for perfumes and bath oil; an ingredient in sweet syrups and condiments. Taken internally, a sedative; externally, a stimulant. Important bee plant.	Sacred to the Virgin Mary because of its associations with cleanliness and chastity. Later came to signify distrust.
LILY, MADONNA. *Lilium candidum.*	Treasured as a church decoration and as a source of perfume. Also a balm for wounds and stings; as a decongestant, and other medicinal uses.	A fertility symbol in classical times, the lily became a Christian symbol of chastity and purity, one of the chief emblems of the Virgin, innocent beauty and immortality.
MARIGOLD. *Calendula officinalis.*	Good all-purpose plant: cooked as a vegetable and used for color and flavor in soups. Made into garlands, used as a yellow hair dye. It was considered good for the eyesight and to heal ulcers inside and out.	Called "St. Mary's gold" and sacred to the Virgin. Meant "sacred affection," later "grief."
MYRTLE, COMMON. *Myrtus communis.*	Used chiefly for its aromatic properties, for perfume and for seasoning in cooking; sometimes as a salve.	Myrtle was sacred to Venus and stood for peace and love. Even in Christian times used for wedding garlands.
MYRTLE (PERIWINKLE, VINCA). *Vinca.*	Used as a ground cover and for garlands. Once used to crown condemned criminals and for children's graves. Said to ward off the devil, discord and snakes.	Though known as "joy of the ground" in the Middle Ages for its cheerful blue flowers, it had associations with death.

Plant	Use	Significance
PANSY. *Viola tricolor.* (The plant we call johnny-jump-up.)	Diuretic, and other medicinal uses.	As its French name, *pensée*, suggests, it stood for "thoughts"—in a Christian sense, remembrance of the Blessed Virgin and meditation; in a romantic sense, thoughts of the beloved. Its colors—blue, white and yellow—were emblematic of the Trinity.
PARSLEY. *Petroselinūm hortense.*	Popular seasoning in cooking; also drunk in a tea.	An aphrodisiac in Greece and Rome, parsley kept its sexual associations;
PRIMROSE. *Primula veris.* Also cowslip, *Primula vulgaris.*	Leaves were eaten as a vegetable, the buds in salads, the flowers in puddings, the root as a headache remedy. Cowslips, closely allied, were made into wine and used as a sedative, for respiratory problems and against paralysis.	Known by the unromantic names of "horse-blobs" and "cow-sloppes," these cheerful flowers were much loved in the Middle Ages and the Renaissance. Primroses, suggested freshness and innocence, youth and pride. They were also called "keys of heaven" or "St. Peter's keys." Cowslips suggested pensiveness or winning grace.
ROSE. *Rosa* species.	Though rose syrup was thought to fortify the feeble, the major use of roses was cosmetic and culinary; they provided color and fragrance for jellies, confections, lotions, balms, garlands and potpourris.	In pagan times, the flower of Venus and sexual love—also secrecy, triumph, pride victory, death and rebirth. Christianized as the flower of Mary and martyrdom, then as a symbol of the beloved lady of love poetry. Individual species had their own significations, white for purity, yellow for papal benediction, red for martyrs' blood, and the pink-and-white York and Lancaster for war.
ROSEMARY. *Rosmarinus officinalis.*	Important closet herb (against moths), for strewing and for sweetening bath water. Steeped in wine and with meats. Powerful against heart ills and other complaints. Laid on graves for "remembrance."	Remembrance, friendship.
RUE. *Ruta graveolens.*	A powerful magic herb, against witches and a host of physical troubles such as "ill humours and phlegms." Hung in houses to ward off plague. Used as a purgative, as a strewing herb, and as a bitter seasoning in beverages.	"Herb of grace o' Sundays," suggestive of penitence, regret. Later disdain.
VIOLET, SWEET. *Viola odorata.*	Used for strewing, for soothing baths, perfumes, and both an emetic and purgative. Leaves used in salads, the flowers as a candied confection (as they still are today).	Humility and modesty, especially that of the Virgin Mary.
WOODBINE (honeysuckle). *Lonicera periclymenum.*	Antiseptic for the skin.	Married love and fidelity.
WORMWOOD. *Artemisia absinthum.*	Banished fleas and various worms, both internal and external. Used as disinfectant. Said to cure constipation, stomachache. Strong hallucinogen, used in some alcoholic drinks such as absinthe and vermouth.	Bitterness, later absence. Said to have grown in the path of the serpent in the Garden of Eden.

sop, from one of the best gardening passages in the plays (*Othello*, I, iii):

> 'tis in ourselves that we are thus or
> thus, Our bodies are our gardens;
> to which our wills are gardeners; so
> that if we will plant nettles or sow
> lettuce; set hyssop and weed up thyme;
> supply it with one gender of herbs, or
> distract it with many; either to have
> it sterile with idleness, or manured
> with industry; why, the power and
> corrigible authority of this lies in our wills.

You could set these words of Iago's in wood or stone on a pedestal in the center of the herb bed—they are an apt motto for the garden. That center would also be a good spot for a statue of the Bard, or just a large pot of a nonhardy but significant herb such as rosemary "for remembrance" or bay (laurel) with which to crown a poet.

Next to the herbs is a tiny rose garden. Here are planted the red, white and varicolored roses, for York and Lancaster. And I have added a "bank of rue" for Richard's weeping queen, even though this incident takes place in 1399, years earlier than the Temple Garden scene, and the fate of a different Richard is at stake. The blue-green foliage of rue looks good with roses. Three box shrubs stand in the corner. Box is also a good foil for roses and is traditionally grown in rose gardens, trimmed into tidy and often imaginative forms. It will winter-burn badly in cold climates unless you wrap it up in burlap, but it is worth the trouble: not only is box a good English shrub, but its thick foliage on top and open growth habit at the bottom make it a good hiding place, as it was for Sir Toby Belch, Sir Andrew Aguecheek and Fabian in *Twelfth Night*, when they hid in Olivia's garden to spy on Malvolio ("Get ye all three into the box-tree").

SITE

Any sunny, well-drained site would suit this garden. If there is a spot in the garden where drainage is poor, plant Ophelia's "long purples" and the wild flower-de-luce (*Iris pseudacorus*). A level site will make the paths easier to lay. Eglantine is especially fine in a site where a warm, moist wind can blow the apple scent to where people gather. Another thing to bear in mind is that the herb garden needs more sun than the bower. So if the apple tree will cast a shadow on the garden, let it fall on the bower, not on the herbs.

GROWING INSTRUCTIONS

Most of the plants in this garden are easy to grow. In general, herbs like slightly dry, sandy soil of only moderate fertility, but mint likes plenty of water. Contain the mint with a strip of metal flashing sunk in the ground so that it won't creep all over the herb bed. Cut all the herbs back if they become unruly. Prune the crab apple when it becomes too dense, removing branches that grow vertically or crisscross each other. All the beds can be planted in spring, except for the daffodils and crown imperials, which are planted in fall. Treat the flower bed like any perennial border, with annuals filling in with summer color.

The rose bed should be dug at least a foot deep and humus added to it. If you use the hardy old historical varieties you should not need to mound them in winter, but if you substitute modern hybrids, you should mound them with soil in winter in cold climates (see illustration, p. 96).

All the beds will look tidier with a shallow mulch—pine needles or leaf mold, for example. Try to avoid a mulch that is very light in color, such as wood chips, or very modern in appearance, like stones or bark nuggets.

The plants in the woodland area can be allowed to spread naturally into a thick carpet. Primroses and their relatives like a moist, rich, humus-filled soil, as do violets, and the others there will not protest. Honeysuckles

In the Renaissance, a bed divided into small sections with wooden dividers was—and still is—a good way to keep herbs tidy.

are easy to please, as are most climbing roses. At first you will want to supervise their "entwisting," tying them where you want them to go. But soon they will make a forestlike tangle that will give shade and a sense of mystery to your bower.

ADDITIONS AND SUBSTITUTIONS

There are many more plants in the works of Shakespeare that you could add to a garden. Here are some of them: *Rosa centifolia* (from *Hamlet*); scarlet martagon lily (*Lilium chalcedonicum*); saffron crocus; hawthorn; ivy; a cherry tree, for the "cherry nose" that Thisbe thinks Pyramus has; "aconite" or monkshood (*Aconitum* species), which is a good late-blooming plant for the border; the myrtle tree under which Venus and Adonis meet (*Myrtus latifolia*); the "wild hyacinth" or harebell; peony; the leek that Fluellen wears in his hat on St. Davy's Day in *Henry V*; and one of my favorite images, the "furr'd moss" that Arviragus wants to plant on Imogen's grave in winter "when flowers are none."

PLANT LIST FOR SHAKE-SPEARE GARDEN

ANNUALS, BIENNIALS AND TENDER PERENNIALS

BAY (SWEET BAY). *Laurus nobilis.* Perennial in zones 8–10. Bay is grown outdoors in warm climates, where it becomes a tall tree if left unpruned. North of zone 8, and for this garden, grow in a large pot or tub and bring indoors before the first hard frost. The plant produces the classic "bay leaf" used in cooking. Buy a small nursery-grown specimen and move up to successively larger pots as it grows, shearing it to keep it attractive and a movable size. Fertilize in spring and summer. Can be kept fairly dormant through the winter. Dislikes dry heat, either indoors or out, and can be stored over the winter in a cool basement or garage where there is some light. In Shakespeare's time bay was often trimmed into ornamental shapes.

CALENDULA (MARIGOLD, MARY-BUD). *Calendula officinalis.* The single yellow or orange varieties would be most appropriate for this garden. The plant grows 1–1½ feet tall. Sow seeds as soon as the ground thaws in spring; set plants 1 foot apart. Easy to grow, it can be sown in succession through the season, especially in warm climates where winter flowering is possible.

FENNEL. *Foeniculum vulgare.* Tender perennial or biennial, usually grown as an annual. Grows up to 4 feet tall, with threadlike foliage similar to that of dill. Large yellow umbel-shaped flowers, borne in early summer, produce aromatic brown seeds. All parts of the plant are licorice-flavored. Sow seeds in the garden in early spring, and thin to 8 inches apart. Likes rich, well-drained soil.

MARJORAM, SWEET (KNOTTED MARJORAM). *Majorana hortensis* (sometimes called *Origanum majorana*). Perennial in zones 9–10, usually grown as an annual. Grows 1 foot tall. Seeds are usually sown indoors, then transplanted to the garden about 10 inches apart. Likes lime and well-drained, dry soil.

PARSLEY. *Petroselinum hortense.* Plant either the curly type, *P. h. crispum* or the broad-leafed Italian type, *P. h. filicinum.* Sow seeds in the garden as soon as the ground can be worked; they germi-nate slowly. The plants like moist, rich soil. Often self-sow, acting as a biennial.

PANSY (HEARTSEASE). *Viola tricolor.* Perennial in zones 6–8. This species is also known as johnny-jump-up, because of its self-sowing habit. Best grown as a biennial, sowing in late summer. Prefers light shade and moist soil, rich in humus.

ROSEMARY. *Rosmarinus officinalis.* Hardy in zones 8–10, and up to zone 6 with winter protection. Otherwise winter indoors. Grow in pots in this garden, with well-drained soil and a sprinkling of lime.

BULBS

ANEMONE. *Anemone blanda.* Zones 6–9; zone 5 with protection. These anemones come in many colors— red, blue, pink, purple and white. They bloom in May and grow 4–6 inches tall. Soak the small bulbs in water for a day or two before planting in early spring, in clumps, 2–3 inches deep. In cold zones you can either mulch them in winter or treat them as annuals and replace them (they are inexpensive).

CROWN IMPERIAL. *Fritillaria imperialis.* Zones 6–10. A member of the lily family, this

bulb produces a spectacular head of bright flowers on a 3-foot stalk in April and May. Flowers can be yellow, orange or red. Prefers gravelly, well-drained soil. Plant 6–8 inches deep and divide every few years.

DAFFODIL, HOOP-PETTI-COAT. *Narcissus bulbocodium.* Zones 6–10. Any *Narcissus* would look good, but this and other old-fashioned species such as *N. triandrus* would be the most appropriate. This 8-inch daffodil has a large cup and tiny petals. Plant in late summer or early fall, in clumps, 3–4 inches deep. Fertilize with bone meal or superphosphate.

LILY, MADONNA. *Lilium candidum.* Zones 3–10. Grows 3–4 feet tall and bears large snow-white flowers in June and July. Plant by covering the bulb with only 1 inch of soil in late summer. Set the bulbs 1–1½ feet apart. Keep the soil damp but not wet. These lilies like lime and gravelly soil. The bulbs develop some leaves in the fall.

PERENNIALS

ARTEMISIA (WORMWOOD). *Artemisia absinthium.* To zone 3. Grows up to 4 feet tall with feathery white foliage. Prefers well-drained soil.

BALM (LEMON BALM). *Melissa officinalis.* Zones 4–10. Mintlike herb about 2 feet tall. The lemon-scented foliage is good in meat dishes and teas. Sow seeds in the garden in fall or very early spring. Do not overfertilize. Easily divided and shared with friends.

CARNATION, BORDER (GILLIFLOWER). *Dianthus caryophyllus.* Zones 6–7; farther north with winter protection. Can also be grown in colder zones as an annual, or plant other *Dianthus* sorts such as *D. deltoides* or *D. allwoodii.* Grows 1–3 feet tall, with clove-scented flowers in many shades and grayish foliage. Blooms all summer. Prefers well-drained light soil; too much moisture around the crown can lead to diseases.

COLUMBINE. *Aquilegia vulgaris.* Zones 3–10. Plant the old-fashioned blue variety that grows 2–3 feet tall and blooms

in May and June. Prefers moist but well-drained soil. Set about a foot apart.

DAISY, ENGLISH. *Bellis perennis.* Zones 6–10 as a perennial or biennial. Grows 6 inches tall and blooms in spring. Try to find the old-fashioned single white variety with the yellow "eye." Likes sun and moist, peaty soil.

HYSSOP. *Hyssopus officinalis.* Zones 3–8. Shrublike plant about 2 feet tall with dark green narrow leaves. Flowers are usually blue, sometimes pink or white, and appear from June throughout the summer. Seeds are best sown in the garden in very early spring, though nursery-grown plants can also be used. Plant in well-drained soil. Cut mature plants back to the ground in early spring to prevent them from becoming too woody.

IRIS, TALL BEARDED. *Iris* hybrids. Zones 3–9. (Or plant one of the original species known to Shakespeare, such

as *Iris germanica florentina,* also known as orris root.) Grows 2–4 feet tall and blooms in May and June. Will thrive in most soils, but good drainage is essential. Plant groups of 3 in a triangle, mounding the soil slightly and setting the rhizome just below the soil surface, with the feeder roots deep in the soil. Feed with a low-nitrogen fertilizer. Divide every few years, discarding and burning any roots with signs of iris borer (small holes) and/or soft rot (mushy roots). Borers encourage the fungi that cause soft rot. If they are a problem, spray plants with an insecticide containing dimethoate in spring. As a precaution against fungi, shake roots in a bag with fungicide dust before planting.

LAVENDER. *Lavandula angustifolia angustifolia (L. officinalis).* Zones 6–9. Most varieties grow between 2 and 3 feet tall, with flowers that give the color its name, and bloom from June or July onward. Winter in a cool, light place indoors in cold climates. Grow in well-drained soil (wet will kill it faster than cold) and prune back in early spring to just above the previous year's growth.

MINT (PEPPERMINT). *Mentha piperita.* (Other varieties such as spearmint—*M. spicata*—may be used.) Zones 3–9. Stands up 2–3 feet tall, with spikes of lavender flowers in midsummer. Thrives in sun or shade, but prefers some shade, and moist, fertile soil, although manure should not be used, since it may lead to a rust disease. Vigorous spreader that needs to be contained.

PRIMROSE. *Primula vulgaris.* Zones 4–8. Low clump of broad, bright green leaves, with midspring flowers on stalks 6–10 inches tall, usually yellow. Prefers moisture, part shade and woodsy soil.

RUE (HERB OF GRACE). *Ruta graveolens.* Zones 4–9. Rue is grown for its dainty blue-green foliage that keeps its color well into the winter. Usually grows 2 feet tall. Rue is a "strewing herb" and should not be eaten. Easily grown from seeds sown in early spring or late summer. Thin to 1 foot apart. Cut back to encourage bushiness.

THYME, CREEPING. *Thymus serpyllum.* Zones 3–9. Any of the creeping thymes would be suitable, as they form a carpet, sweet to walk or lie on, and different varieties can be mixed attractively. Flowers are rosy, lavender or white in late spring or early summer. Thyme prefers light, well-drained soil and sun. Best planted from started clumps and propagated by division.

VIOLET, SWEET. *Viola odorata.* Zones 6–10. Fra-

grant, usually purple flowers in late spring. Obtain plants from a nursery or a friend. Prefers light shade and moist soil, rich in humus.

SHRUBS AND VINES

BOX. *Buxus sempervirens.* Zones 6–10, farther north with protection. Grows to 20 feet if unpruned. Needs protection from extreme winter cold and drying winter winds. Burlap screens are usually effective. The roots like a cool, moist situation. Winter-damaged growth can be pruned out in spring, and the plant sheared in ornamental forms.

BROOM. (SCOTCH BROOM). *Cytisus scoparius.* (Hybrids such as Warminster broom, *C. praecox,* could also be grown.) Zones 5–10. Arching green stems bear yellow flowers in May. Plants grow to 6 feet, sometimes taller. They like sun and well-drained soil. Prune just after flowering.

CRAB APPLE. *Malus* 'Katherine.' Zones 4–10. This tree

grows to 20 feet tall and is covered with double, pale pink flowers in May, followed by tiny red apples. Spreading in habit. Likes sun, well-drained acid soil, manure.

HONEYSUCKLE, HALL'S. *Lonicera japonica* 'Halliana.' Zones 4–10. A vigorous vine that bears white fragrant flowers in June and has a bronze fall color. Grows in most soils, in sun or shade.

ROSE, EGLANTINE (SWEETBRIER). *Rosa eglanteria.* To zone 4. Native rose of England, growing to 6 feet and more. Bears single, pale pink flowers in June, red or orange hips in fall. The foliage has an applelike scent after rain. Can be grown as a pillar rose (see Climbers, p. 92) or clipped as a hedge. No special requirements except adequate drainage.

ROSE, MUSK. *Rosa moschata.* To zone 5. Climbing rose, 20–30 feet high. Vigorous and hardy. Bears profuse single white blooms with a musky fragrance in June.

Train on trellis or arbor; prune back if too rampant.

ROSE, RED OF LANCASTER (APOTHECARY ROSE). *Rosa gallica* 'Officinalis.' To zone 4. Ancient shrub rose, suckering freely when grown on its own roots. It has lush dark green foliage and semidouble light crimson blossoms in early summer. Grows to about 4 feet. You may need to prune out the suckering shoots; do this below soil level and give them to friends.

ROSE, WHITE OF YORK. (GREAT DOUBLE WHITE). *Rosa alba* 'Maxima.' To zone 4. Very old rose that grows to 6–8 feet and bears white blossoms in June. Has dark blue-green foliage. You can prune back the long canes after flowering to keep it the same height as the other roses in this bed.

ROSE, 'YORK AND LANCASTER.' *Rosa damascena* 'Versicolor.' Zones 4–10. Usually grows about 5 feet tall, bearing clusters of semidouble blossoms that are white, pink or a combination of both. It has one long flowering in late spring, a moderate fragrance, light gray-green foliage. It appreciates fertilizer.

A Gray Garden

O ne of the most exciting things about planning a garden is the many and varied ways there are to play with color—from blending great masses of color to highlighting the gemlike glow of a single blossom.

Even more subtle is the palette provided by the tones of the foliage. Plants have leaves not only in every imaginable

shade of green, but in shades of red, purple, blue, gray—even white.

When you see its full design possibilities, foliage becomes much more than just something that sprouts out of the stalk below the flower, and the color scheme of your garden is not limited to a sea of green with bright spots of color in it. You can even have a garden with almost no green at all—or with no flowers.

Why are plants gray? Actually, the leaves themselves are not gray in color, but are covered with tiny hairs that catch the light and give them a gray cast. Often the plant looks hairy or woolly. The function of these hairs is to prevent loss of moisture, and in coastal regions to trap salt in the air before it can burn and scour the leaves' surface. Other "glaucous" plants have a gray-blue waxy covering that keeps moisture in and salt out. These are adaptations that the plants have made to life near the coast or in dry, harsh climates.

Gray plants are a popular choice for seaside gardens. Look at the plants that grow wild by the ocean and you will see a gray garden in nature. Plants such as sea holly, sea buckthorn, lyme grass and Russian olive have leaves that range from gray-green to gray-blue to silver. Not surprisingly, many garden plants with foliage in these shades are cultivars of these wild plants, and a collection of them makes a fine seaside garden. As well as looking "right" for the shore because of their origins, they go well with weathered gray beach cottages, gray wooden fences and driftwood. Their soft, subtle colorings change with the variable seaside light, one day shimmering silver in the sun, the next day a subdued blue or green in swirling fog and mist.

But not many of us live right on the sea, and you may want to have a gray garden for the sheer beauty of it—because you like the subtle shadings you can create. You can grow one in a benign climate that lacks the harsh conditions I have described, and the plants will thrive, as long as you provide proper drainage and plenty of sun.

Gray gardens are something of a tradition, especially in England. Lamb's ears and lavender are great favorites in English perennial borders, as accent plants or as foils for brightly colored flowers such as roses. Vita Sackville-West's great gardens at Sissinghurst, planted in the 1930s, included a garden of gray foliage plants and white flowers.

There are many ways of using gray-leafed plants. By including all the whites, blue-grays, silvers, gray-greens and so forth, you can plan a whole garden around them. Often people mix in flowers of pastel lavender, rose and yellow—the flower shades most commonly produced by the gray plants themselves. The result is a lovely misty effect.

Since plants with gray, white or silvery foliage are similar to one another in the demands they make of a gardener, they are easy to care for as a group. These species owe their existence to conditions that not many plants will tolerate. If you live near the shore, or in a hot, dry, windy place, you will not have to coddle them the way you would many common garden plants. Most of them need plenty of sun and excellent drainage, and they prefer a sandy soil that is alkaline and low in nutrients. They dislike winter moisture, and they hate air pollutants, which can become trapped in their fine hairs.

PLAN OF THE GARDEN

The first step in planning a gray garden is to decide how gray you want it to be. The one I have planned here is a small, easily tended border, with many bright spots of color. While you could plant it in many situations, I imag-

Here the grays of rocks and gravel blend with that of herbs, creating a garden of subtle contrasts.

ine it as a welcoming garden for the entrance to a cottage, perhaps. As such, I think that all grays would be too much of a good thing, especially in cloudy weather. This scheme also gives you the chance to try the effect of bright flower colors without the masses of green that would normally go with them; the soft, misty-gray foliage of this garden is a pleasant setting for that brightness. Not only are these leaves muted in hue, but their growth is never lush or overwhelming. Most of them are needlelike, grasslike or willowy—the better to withstand harsh winds.

This is a summer-blooming garden, and might well suit a house that serves as a summer retreat. If you live by the sea, you know that spring comes late there, though the blooming season may extend longer into fall than it would in inland areas of the same latitude. Despite the fact that many gray plants are native to warm places such as the Mediterranean, a good many are easy to grow in this country as far north as Cape Cod, because frosts on the coast are later and less severe than inland, and because the good drainage and dryness of a sandy soil in winter keeps them from perishing. If you live inland, you can still grow nearly all the plants in this garden even in regions where winter temperatures fall to −30° F.

Tall bearded iris, with their stiff grayish leaves, start the season, joined by bright oriental poppies and accented by the sprouting tufts of new gray foliage around them. When the iris are cut back and the poppies die down, their leaves will be hidden by the other plants coming along. Through July and August the colors will be at their height: tall blues and purples toward the back, and pinks, yellows and oranges in the foreground, with all the grays, whites and silvers among them. Most of these plants are perennials, but the annual California poppies and bachelor's buttons provide a solid mainstay of color, together with the annuals in the window boxes—pink sand verbenas (a trailing plant resistant to wind) and *Cineraria maritima,* a woolly white annual or tender perennial that is one of the many plants confusingly called "dusty miller."

Two shrubs are included, both with grayish foliage and lavender flowers: fountain buddleia 'Argentea' blooms in May and

In this English foliage garden, lamb's ears, Gypsophila *and grasses border the path; the trees are blue atlas cedars.*

© SMITH COLLECTION

June, and chaste tree (*Vitex agnus-castus*) in August. These serve as a visual frame for the garden and also help to shelter it from the wind. A gray wooden fence—picket or split rail, perhaps—enclosing the garden and a patch of lawn on either side of the walk would add to this garden's cozy, enclosed feeling. Gray flagstones lead up to the door, with white pussytoes growing between them.

SITE

If you live by the shore, the most important site consideration is shelter from wind. Even the most seaworthy plants need a little protection. Where the garden is situated will, of course, depend on a number of factors. As long as there is sun, the best spot is in the lee of the house, usually on the opposite side from the water, where the wind is less severe. You can also extend the barrier formed by the house by planting trees or tall shrubs at the corners. But you can have a seaside garden between the house and the water; this will almost always require a wall or hedge for shelter. If the house casts too great a shadow on the garden, choose a spot across the lawn and against the fence, planting shrubs at either side for extra protection. But bear in mind that sunlight near the ocean is very intense, so even half a day's sun may be suf-

THE GRAY
GARDEN

PLAN OF THE GRAY GARDEN (SUMMER)
³⁄₈″ = 1′

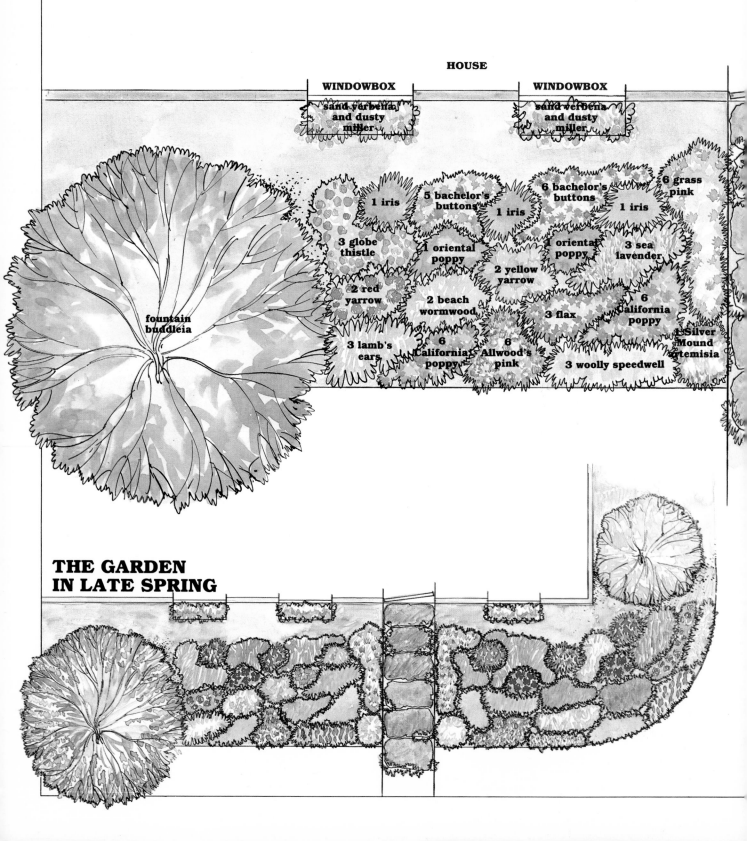

HOUSE

WINDOWBOX

sand verbena and dusty miller

WINDOWBOX

sand verbena and dusty miller

1 iris

5 bachelor's buttons

1 iris

6 bachelor's buttons

1 iris

6 grass pink

3 globe thistle

1 oriental poppy

1 oriental poppy

3 sea lavender

2 red yarrow

2 yellow yarrow

2 beach wormwood

3 flax

6 California poppy

3 lamb's ears

6 California poppy

6 Allwood's pink

3 woolly speedwell

1 Silver Mound artemisia

fountain buddleia

THE GARDEN IN LATE SPRING

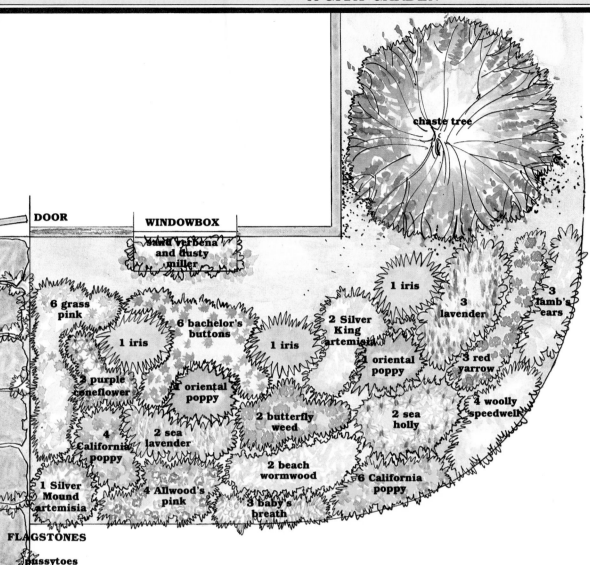

chaste tree

DOOR

WINDOWBOX

sand verbena
and dusty
miller

6 grass
pink

1 iris

6 bachelor's
buttons

2 Silver
King
artemisia

1 iris

1 iris

3
lavender

3
lamb's
ears

2 purple
coneflower

1 oriental
poppy

1 oriental
poppy

3 red
yarrow

4
California
poppy

2 sea
lavender

2 butterfly
weed

2 sea
holly

4 woolly
speedwell

1 Silver
Mound
artemisia

4 Allwood's
pink

2 beach
wormwood

6 California
poppy

3 baby's
breath

FLAGSTONES

pussytoes

ficient. On the other hand, if the garden is too shaded the plants will look green, because the leaf hairs will not reflect enough light to seem gray. The bed has been set out from the house a little, to allow more sun to reach it, and to provide access to the window boxes.

A site with good drainage is very important, especially in winter. Not all seaside areas are dry, or even sandy. Some are marshland or woodsy loam. If there is mud or standing water in your yard in winter and spring, or if there is hardpan close to the soil surface, you would do best to grow the plants in raised beds (see box, p. 45). Edge them with a retaining wall, railroad ties or boards and fill them with a good sandy loam.

GROWING INSTRUCTIONS

The perennials here, as in most gardens, will look impressive most quickly if you buy them from a nursery as started plants in spring. For some, you can also take divisions or cuttings in the spring from a neighbor's garden, or grow them from seed if you don't mind the wait. Be careful, however, about which plants you divide. Many of these plants have deep taproots in order to reach down to moisture below the dry soil surface, and cannot be moved without risking fatal damage. Some may be propagated by division: yarrow, thyme, artemisia, lamb's ears, iris, coneflower, globe thistle, creeping baby's breath, speedwell and pinks. These cannot without difficulty: flax, sea holly, butterfly weed, lavender and oriental poppies. Increase these by seeds (except for most lavender hybrids, which won't breed true) or cuttings.

Plant the annuals as indicated in the plant list, setting some aside in pots to fill in gaps. Plant the shrubs by digging a generous hole and working in a few shovelfuls of peat or other humus. Even with sand-loving shrubs it is good to provide some moisture-holding humus to get root development off to a good start. Water all the plants well when you plant them. Fertilize them with a food high in phosphorus such as bone meal to encourage rooting, but go easy on the nitrogen; it will lead to lush, weak growth. Remember that these plants like barren places. But they do need some nutrients, and these leach out of sand more quickly than other soils. The best way to feed them is lightly but regularly—every spring. Though most of the plants like lime, don't add it indiscriminately. Test your soil and aim for a pH of about 6. A mulch is not necessary except in the space at the back of the bed.

Pruning is important in any garden that emphasizes foliage. Many gray plants, like artemisia, will produce bushier foliage if you do not let the flowers develop at all. But you will probably want to let them bloom at least once, then decide whether you want that effect or not. If you do let them bloom, remove spent flowers right away, as with all of the flowering plants here. All will benefit from spring pruning to encourage bushy growth, but do not cut back living stems after August, or new growth will appear, only to be injured by frost. You should, however, remove dead leaves and stems in fall to discourage rot from winter moisture. Some of these plants will keep their gray color in winter: lamb's ears, yarrow, some of the artemisias, the gray-green points of iris. You may want to leave these unpruned. Instead of losing its mass of lush greenery in fall, your garden will change slowly and subtly, aging gracefully as it were, adding its own muted tones to those of frost and snow, matching the grays of winter.

ADDITIONS AND SUBSTITUTIONS

Most of the plants I have selected for this garden will grow on any U.S. coast and most inland sites, but there are many special things you can plant if you live in the South or in warm parts of the West Coast. In the West, try California bayberry (*Myrica californica*), *Ceanothus* species, California tree poppy (*Romneya coulteri*) and *Phacelia* species such as California bluebells. In the South you can grow *Helichrysum* species, *Convolvulus cneorum* and horned poppies (*Papaver glaucum*).

There are many trees and shrubs that will go well with a gray garden. Russian olive (*Elaeagnus angustifolia*), with its long silvery-green leaves, silver flowers, and silvery fruit, is a good choice. It is very hardy by the sea. There are other *Elaeagnus* species that would do well (some with red berries), and a

DRYING FLOWERS FOR WINTER BOUQUETS

There are many different techniques for drying flowers; here are a few simple methods. Many of the plants in this garden will dry well, retaining their form and color. Especially attractive in bouquets are sea holly, globe thistle, the yarrows, lavender, sea lavender, the artemisias, butterfly weed, bachelor's buttons, baby's breath and pussytoes.

To dry flowers, cut them with long stems at or just before their peak of bloom. Remove foliage and hang upside down in small bunches in a dry, dark place for several weeks or until dry.

Another method is to dry them in sand, one flower at a time. Use sand that is clean and dry. (Special smooth sand for drying flowers can be obtained; silica gel may also be used.) Place a few inches of sand in a flowerpot or coffee can, put the flower in, then trickle sand slowly until it fills in around the petals and buries the flower. Flowers may be dried upside down this way, with stems sticking up, but some will work better right side up with stem protruding through a hole in the bottom of the container. Leave the flower in the pot or can in a dry place for about 2 weeks or until dry. Remove sand with great care, brushing it from petals with a soft brush.

Dried flowers are an attractive display even while they are hanging upside down for drying. These pictured are at Caprilands Herb Farm in Coventry, Connecticut.

© ROBERT PERRON

number of gray-leafed willows (*Salix* species); also the willow-leafed pear (*Pyrus salicifolia*). To form a stout windbreak for your garden, plant red cedar (*Juniperus virginiana*), tallhedge (*Rhamnus* 'Columnaris'), beach plum (*Prunus maritima*), or Japanese black pine (*Pinus thunbergiana*) planted along with the shrublike bayberry (*Myrica pensylvanica*) to fill in beneath its spreading branches. Other suitable shrubs are tamarisk (*Tamarix* species), rugosa roses (called "sea tomato" because of their red hips), sea buckthorn (*Hippophae rhamnoides*), heather (*Calluna*), *Caryopteris* and groundsel bush (*Baccharis halimifolia*). If you are never at the house until summer, plant the butterfly bush that blooms in August, *Buddleia davidii*, instead of *B. alternifolia*.

There are many good choices among the evergreens, for example blue spruce (*Picea pungens* 'Glauca'), Canada hemlock (*Tsuga canadensis*), Japanese black pine, mugo pine (*Pinus mugo mugo*) and some of the low-growing junipers such as *Juniperus horizontalis* 'Bar Harbor' or shore juniper (*J. conferta*).

For the lawn, the seed you use will depend on what part of the country you live in, and it is wise to investigate what does well in your area. You may also use a lawn substitute like woolly thyme or woolly yarrow (to extend the gray effect), turfing daisy (*Tripleurospermum tchihatchewii*, also called *Matricaria tchihatchewii*) or Irish moss (*Arenaria verna caespitosa*). Between the flag-

stones you can add woolly thyme (*Thymus serpyllum tomentosum*), snow-in-summer (*Cerastium tomentosum*) or wall cress (*Arabis caucasica*). If there is a shady place where you can keep the soil a bit moist, plant some *Hosta sieboldiana*; its big blue-green leaves will be a lovely contrast to the fine, wispy foliage of the other plants in the garden. For the window boxes there are many possibilities; try a new one each year. *Gazania* 'Silver Beauty' has silvery foliage and bright yellow flowers, though these tend to close on gray days. Other good annuals are African daisy (*Arctotis grandis*) and sea marigold or ice plant (*Mesembryanthemum crystallinum*).

Good perennials to add or substitute include lavender cotton (*Santolina chamaecyparissus*), catnip (*Nepeta* species), rue (*Ruta graveolens*), the *Salvia* species, sea thrift (*Armeria maritima*), other *Achillea* and *Artemisia* species, mullein (*Verbascum* hybrids), beach goldenrod (*Solidago sempervirens*), blue fescue (*Festuca ovina glauca*), sea lyme grass (*Elymus arenarius*) and the white pearly everlasting (*Anaphalis margaritacea*)—the last an excellent choice if you are making dried bouquets. Other good drying flowers for this garden are the taller baby's breaths, *Gypsophila paniculata* and *G. repens* 'Bodgeri'.

If you live north of zone 5 you can grow all the plants in the garden plan except lavender, chaste tree and, in most cases, fountain buddleia. Two good perennials, hardy in zones 4 to 10, that you can substitute for lavender are catmint (*Nepeta faassenii*), which bears mauve flowers in early summer, and blue salvia (*Salvia azurea*) which has tall blue spikes in late summer. One of the tall, blue late-blooming veronica varieties such as 'Blue Peter' would also do well. For a hardy, late-blooming flowering shrub, try five-stamened tamarisk (*Tamarix pentandra*), hardy in zones 2 to 10, with feathery pink flowers in mid and late summer; its gray-green foliage would look fine in the garden. It does need about twelve feet to spread, however, so if space is limited you might plant hills of snow hydrangea instead (*Hydrangea arborescens grandiflora*). This is hardy to zone 4 and needs only three to four feet to spread.

PLANT LIST FOR GRAY GARDEN

ANNUALS

BACHELOR'S BUTTON (CORNFLOWER). *Centaurea cyanus.* Tall variety such as 'Blue Boy,' 2½–3 feet. Sow in garden in fall, or start indoors in early spring. Set out started plants 1 foot apart.

DUSTY MILLER. *Cineraria maritima (Senecio cineraria).* Perennial in zones 9–10. Usually about a foot tall, with stark white woolly foliage. Start seeds indoors very early, or buy nursery plants. Set in window boxes after danger of frost is past.

POPPY, CALIFORNIA. *Eschscholzia californica,* mixed shades. Perennial in zones 8–10. Grows about a foot high and sprawls widely. The native variety is yellow, but hybrid mixes also contain pink, red, orange, white, bronze and bicolors. Fernlike, silvery-green foliage. Easy to grow, and easily self-seeds. Sow seeds in fall or early spring

in beds; thin to 6 inches apart. Sow the seeds where you want the plant to grow, because it is difficult to transplant.

VERBENA, SAND. *Abronia umbellata.* Perennial in zones 9–10. Not a true verbena, though it looks and smells like one. Bears dainty pink trailing flowers. Sow indoors and transplant when very small to peat pots. Set out in window boxes after danger of frost is past, or buy started plants. Water windowboxes in hot, dry weather.

PERENNIALS

ARTEMISIA. *Artemisia schmidtiana nana* 'Silver Mound.' Zones 4–9. Silver-gray foliage, very soft to touch. Grows 6–10 inches high and about a foot wide. Cut back hard in midsummer when straggly. All artemisias prefer well-drained soil, but keep them moist in very dry weather.

ARTEMISIA. *Artemisia ludoviciana (A. albula)* 'Silver King.' 3 feet tall. Feathery, silver-white foliage. Zones 4–9. Prefers well-drained soil, but keep moist in drought.

BABY'S BREATH. *Gypsophila repens* or *G. r.* 'Rosea.' Zones 4–8. Low-growing variety, 4–6 inches high. Pale blue-green foliage, narrow leaves, tiny white or pink flowers in June and sporadically

throughout summer. Likes sun, lime and poor soil.

BEACH WORMWOOD. *Artemisia stellerana.* Zones 4–9. Grows 1–2 feet and sprawls widely. It has toothed, woolly white foliage. Pinch the terminal shoot when the plant is 6 inches tall to encourage branching, and cut it back when straggly.

BUTTERFLY WEED. *Asclepias tuberosa.* Zones 3–9. Grows about 2 feet tall and blooms in flat red-orange umbels from mid to late summer. Prefers slightly dry, sandy soil that is low in nitrogen. It is taprooted and, except when young, is extremely difficult to transplant. It can be grown from seed, but it will take 4–5 years to produce plants mature enough to flower. Even nursery-grown plants are slow to produce bushy clumps. But if provided good drainage the clumps will grow large, persist a long time, and often self-sow. New growth is late to appear in the spring, so watch for it and don't dig up the plants by mistake.

CONEFLOWER, PURPLE. *Echinacea purpurea.* Zones 3–10. Grows up to 3 feet tall, bears flowers similar to black-eyed Susan *(Rudbeckia)* but

purple, from July to September. Plant 1½ feet apart and divide when crowded.

FLAX. *Linum perenne* 'Heavenly Blue.' Zones 4–9. Grows 1–1½ feet tall and bears bright blue flowers all summer. Likes full sun and well-drained soil. Propagate by seed, not division. Plant 12–14 inches apart.

GLOBE THISTLE. *Echinops* 'Taplow Blue.' Zones 3–10. The flowers are prickly blue balls that bloom in July–August and grow 2–4 feet tall. Plant 2 feet apart. Divide clumps when crowded.

IRIS, TALL BEARDED. *Iris* hybrids. Zones 3–9. Choose clear, bright-toned varieties like 'Grand Alliance' (purple), 'Glazed Orange' (bright apricot), 'Big League' (blue) and 'Rainbow Gold' (yellow). Grows 2–4 feet tall. Flowers in May–June. Will thrive in most soils, but good drainage is essential. Plant groups of 3 in a triangle, mounding the soil slightly and setting the rhizome just below the soil surface, with feeder roots deep in the soil. Feed with low-nitrogen fertilizer. Divide every few years, discarding and burning any roots with signs of iris borer (small holes) and/or soft rot (mushy roots). Borers encourage the fungi which cause soft rot. If they are a problem, spray plants with an insecticide containing dimethoate in spring. As a precaution against fungi, shake roots in a bag with fungicide dust before planting.

LAMB'S EARS (WOOLLY BETONY, SAVIOUR'S FLANNEL). *Stachys byzantina (S. lanata).* Zones 3–9. Grows a foot tall with white, woolly leaves. Bears small mauve flowers all summer if cut. Remove all dead leaves and new ones will appear.

LAVENDER. *Lavandula angustifolia angustifolia* 'Twickel Purple.' Zones 6–9. This is a 3-foot purple variety, but you may substitute any variety, allowing for heights. Blooms from June or July onward. Winter the plants in a cool, light place indoors in cold climates. Grow in well-drained soil (wet will kill it faster than cold) and prune back to just above the previous year's growth in early spring.

PINK, ALLWOOD'S. *Dianthus allwoodii.* Zones 4–7. Biennial in warmer zones. Usually a foot tall. Small, fragrant flowers in shades of pink, red, bicolors or white. Gray-green tufts of foliage which should be cut back to keep a

tidy appearance and encourage summer-long bloom. Plant 1 foot apart.

PINK, GRASS (SCOTCH PINK, COTTAGE PINK, BORDER PINK). *Dianthus plumarius* 'Semperflorens.' Zones 4–7 as perennial, 8–10 as biennial. This variety, which grows about 1 foot tall, blooms all summer. Foliage forms a blue-gray mat. Likes full sun, dry soil.

POPPY, ORIENTAL. *Papaver orientale.* Zones 3–8. Any bright varieties such as 'Helen Elizabeth' (pink), 'Beauty of Livermore' (crimson) or 'Bonfire' (dark red-orange). Grows 2½–3 feet high. Blooms in June. This garden is the perfect situation for oriental poppies, which like sun and sandy, well-drained soil. Plant in late summer or early fall with crowns 3 inches below soil surface. Remove spent blooms. They are very difficult to transplant; propagate by root cuttings taken in midsummer or buy new plants.

PUSSYTOES. *Antennaria rhodantha* or *A. dioica.* To

zones 2–3. Weedy perennial gound cover for dry, sandy places. 6–12 inches tall, with white, woolly leaves, small white flowers that can be dried. (*A. d.* 'Rosea' has pink flowers.)

SEA HOLLY. *Eryngium amethystinum.* Zones 4–10. Grows 1½–2 feet tall. Bears spiny blue flowers in July–August. Grows wild on dunes in Europe. Prefers dry, sandy soil. Plant 1–1½ feet apart.

SEA LAVENDER (STATICE). *Limonium latifolium.* Zones 3–10. Tiny lavender or mauve flowers in July–August. Likes sunny, sandy, well-drained location. Plant 18 inches apart and do not transplant or divide.

SPEEDWELL, WOOLLY (VERONICA). *Veronica incana.* Zones 3–10. Silvery foliage, blue flower spikes a foot tall. Blooms in July–August. Well-drained soil is important; place gravel under leaves if soil stays damp. Plant 1 foot apart.

YARROW. *Achillea millefolium* Zones 3–10. 'Fire King.' 2 feet tall, blooms rosy-red in summer and fall; light gray-green foliage in low mats. Choose a yellow variety also, such as *A. taygetea,* which has even grayer foliage. Plant 1–1½ feet apart.

SHRUBS

BUDDLEIA, FOUNTAIN. *Buddleia alternifolia* 'Argentea.' Zones 3–10. Grows to 12 feet tall with an even greater spread. It is covered with long lavender spikes of flowers in late spring. Prune after blooming. Likes fairly rich soil.

CHASTE TREE. *Vitex agnus-castus.* Zones 6–8. Grows up to 9 feet. Bears fragrant lavender-blue flowers from July to September and has gray aromatic foliage. Dies back in winter in northern areas.

A Garden of Love

"Come into the garden, Maud," urged the poet Alfred, Lord Tennyson, like so many ardent suitors before—and after—him. "I am here at the gate alone." Though truly determined lovers will meet almost anywhere, the garden is their natural trysting place, just as it was for Romeo and Juliet, Pyramus and Thisbe, Adam and Eve.

Some gardens are more suited to lovers' trysts than others. If you were to imagine

the ideal lovers' garden you might think of something like the Garden of Shalimar, which was built by the great Mogul emperor Jahan in 1637. Covering eighty opulent acres in Kashmir, it was filled with huge shade trees, elegant pavilions, the heady scent of roses and the sparkle of several hundred fountains. Or you might conjure up a more intimate version—a pavilion for shelter from the hot sun, strewn with silk cushions, carpeted with an Oriental rug as richly patterned as the flowered lawns surrounding it, and hung with the sweetness of jasmine and golden

roses. Nightingales would be singing in the trees; the wine, brought by bronzed serving men or smoky-eyed maidens, would be sweet; the Persian melons would always be ripe.

Such gardens did exist, long ago. Those master gardeners, the ancient Persians, perfected the art of pleasure gardens, and their efforts were widely imitated throughout the Middle East. Even in the West the gardens of Persia have been the chief models for gardens built solely for love and delight. Part of their fame can be ascribed to the Crusades, from which European warriors returned with tales of perfumed gardens, and the seeds and bulbs with which to plant them.

Equally important were the Persian poets of the mystical Sufi sect, whose works found a ready audience in Europe in the Middle Ages. (It is from these poets that the idea of "wine, women and song" originally came—despite the fact that these poems are actually more religious than hedonistic.) Many centuries before Tennyson's lovesick hero beckoned to his Maud, poets such as Runi, Hafiz, Sa'di and Firdausi (whose adopted name means "of the garden") were singing to maidens couched in rose bowers, or enticing them there. Runi's line, "When I enter the rose-showering garden of union with you," is typical of the poetic praise the Sufis lavished on ladies and flowers in such a way that both blend together into one sensuous image—something love poets have been doing ever since. It is no wonder that Persia was known as "the land of poets and gardens."

Gardens were sacred to the inhabitants of the parched lands of the Middle East. The Koran promises the followers of Islam an afterlife spent in a "garden of pleasure" under which cooling rivers flow; it is much like the pleasure gardens the poets talk about, filled with wine and good things to eat, and even "large-eyed maids like hidden pearls" to attend the pious. With water so precious, it is not surprising that desert folk should think of heaven as an oasis. The paradise in the Koran is based on real manmade gardens that were built many centuries before the birth of Islam. Even, as we have seen, the word for paradise came long before the concept of the luxurious afterlife, and simply meant "garden." The Koran's version is simply more

beautiful, and eternal. In later times it became customary to compliment a real garden by calling it a "paradise."

To the western mind, the Islamic paradise seems to be a very earthly one, because we tend to think of heaven as a place where one leaves behind the joys of the flesh, particularly such delights as "large-eyed maids like hidden pearls." But ancient Islam held all earthly joys sacred. In the early fifteenth century there lived an Arabian sheik named Nefzawi about whom little is known except that he wrote a famous manual of erotic love called *The Perfumed Garden*. It is a good example of the Islamic reverence for sex; the sheik aimed, in his book, to gladden men's and women's souls as well as their bodies, and invoked the Lord's aid in writing it. The book was not seen by western eyes until the mid-nineteenth century, when the volume both shocked and fascinated the Victorian world; nevertheless, the "perfumed gardens" of the Orient have been a western erotic fantasy for centuries, and remain so today.

What were these earthly paradises like? From the ancient Middle Eastern gardens that have been preserved we know that they were a mixture of voluptuous beauty, wealthy extravagance and hard practicality. They were essentially natural water sources controlled by man so that plants could be grown and the water's coolness could be enjoyed. Of

The wooden gazebo in this garden at Hershey, Pennsylvania, looks out over tall purple foxgloves, blue delphiniums and yellow yarrow in early summer. White foliage of lamb's ears is to the right.

THE GARDEN OF LOVE

course, the idea was not simply to provide water but to display it in elaborate ways: water spouting into the air, water reflecting the sky or surrounding plants, water brimming over in huge raised pools that seemed to hover above the ground, water gushing down a carved slope—called a *chadar*—that broke it into patterns of foam. It was profligate water; it was water showing off, doing things that you would least expect it to do in a land where there was little of it. Often, water entered the garden from a higher and more distant source, then separated into four separate channels that represented the four rivers that flowed out of paradise (an image found in the Christian Eden). These four formed a cross, or grid—originally just a logical way to provide irrigation. Sometimes there was a long, narrow pool—up to half a mile long, or longer—an exquisite and practical way both to display and transport water.

Pools, fountains, doorways, arches, walls, floors were often lavishly carved or tiled. It is because of these structures that some of these gardens are still extant today. However, we know that these masters of water and stone did breathtaking things with flowers, too. Jonas Lehrman describes an ancient garden where a pool was divided into many sections, with flowers floating on the surface of each one. And no doubt there were "bowers" (originally just a place that housed women) filled with the scent of jasmine and roses, such as the poets described.

The Persians were skilled horticulturists who collected species from many other lands. While those in other cultures grew plants with their utilitarian medicinal uses foremost in mind, the Persians took delight in the fragrance and color of flowers alone. Sacred among them was the rose; in fact "rose" and "flower" even had the same name—*gul*. Jasmine and lilies were also favorites. Flowers were grown in many different ways: in pots, in formal beds, climbing on walls or sprinkled informally in grassy plots within a walled enclosure. Among this efflorescent splendor a sultan might hold court, a poet might meditate on wisdom (as Sa'di did in his great poem, the *Gulistan*—the word means "rose garden")—or two lovers might meet secretly in the cool of the evening.

THE GARDEN IN SPRING

BUILDING A WATER LILY POOL

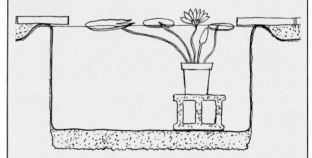

This cross section of the pool and terrace shows several inches of sand at the pool's bottom. A layer of polyvinyl chloride sheeting covers the bottom and sides, then extends underneath the sand that forms the bed of the flagstone terrace. For information about laying flagstones, see pp.165 and 197. The ones in this garden overhang the pool by several inches in order to hide the plastic sheeting. A concrete block keeps the potted water lily at the proper depth in the water.

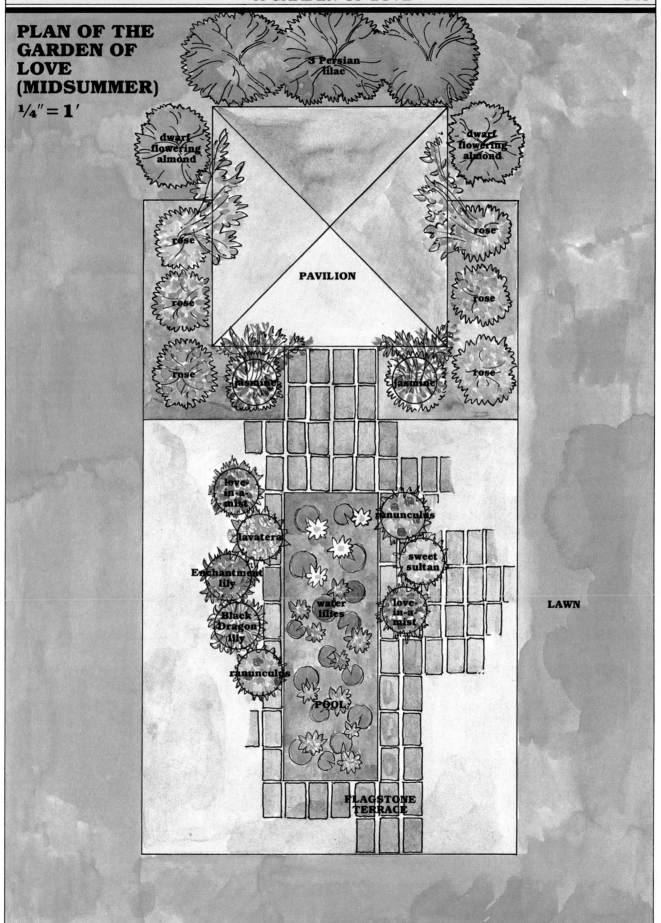

PLAN OF THE GARDEN OF LOVE (MIDSUMMER)

¼″ = 1′

3 Persian lilac

dwarf flowering almond

dwarf flowering almond

rose

rose

PAVILION

rose

rose

rose

rose

jasmine

jasmine

love-in-a-mist

ranunculus

lavatera

sweet sultan

Enchantment lily

water lilies

love-in-a-mist

Black Dragon lily

ranunculus

POOL

LAWN

FLAGSTONE TERRACE

You do not have to be Cyrus of Persia or live in the Taj Mahal to have a garden of love. Begin with a simple pavilion that shelters you from the rain or hot sun but is open at the sides so that you can look out at your garden. Add a reflecting pool filled with tropical water lilies that can be seen from the enclosure. Then plant an array of flowers for fragrance and color, choosing ones that come from the Middle East or the Mediterranean region. The combination of these ingredients can give you a bit of Arabian Nights splendor in your backyard, or even on a tiny terrace in the city. Of course, you may have to make a few compromises. Perhaps dark-eyed houris are unavailable in your particular corner of zone 7. Or, instead of nightingales, you will have to settle for a chorus of "Katy-did, Katy-didn't," or the sound of your neighbor's television. But the course of true love never did run smooth.

You may also want to adjust the concept according to the architecture of the house where you live. If it is Colonial, Victorian or Tudor, for example, your pavilion should probably be built in a corresponding style, or else in a "neutral" style—one with simple lines—such as I show in this chapter. The flowers could just be your favorites—the ones you consider to be the most romantic, or some of those in the Fragrance Garden (see p. 25). (Grow aphrodisiacs, too, if you have faith in them; Sheik Nefzawi swore by asparagus, chickpeas and onions.) If you live in a part of the country such as the West Coast or the Southwest, a Middle Eastern oasis may be quite appropriate, with glazed blue tiles in the Moorish style, or Indian arches. How you build your garden, and how elaborate you make it, will depend on how much time and money you can spend on features such as paving, pools and fountains. Fortunately this need not be a great amount. With very little means you can build a simple terrace, pavilion and ornamental pool for your perfumed garden.

PLAN OF THE GARDEN

The main feature of this garden is a small pavilion. There are many different ways to build one, depending on time and budget. A relatively simple one might be a wooden,

Nymphaea 'Bob Trickett,' a tropical water lily.

roofed platform with open sides. You could add railings and seats, or just spread a rug and cushions on the floor. You can, of course, add whatever furnishings suit your own needs. Plans for garden pavilions and gazebos can be found in many books on garden construction, or you might consult with an architect. You could also construct an arbor like the one in the Garden of Old Roses (see p. 92), and spread a piece of decorative canvas over the top for shade and protection from rain.

Flowering vines and shrubs are planted around the little structure, so when you are inside you are enveloped in color and scent. In front of you is a long, narrow pool with water lilies, and alongside the pool are planters filled with spring and summer flowers. The area around the pool is a terrace paved with flagstones. To be a true *pairidaeza*, the garden should be enclosed in some way, either with a masonry wall or fence, or by a line of tall shrubs or trees. (You could pave all of it, extending the terrace to fill a large space, or you could make grass lawns dotted with spring bulbs and other flowers.) Dwarf flowering almonds bloom in early spring at the rear cor-

Nymphaea marliacea albida. *One of hardy water lilies.*

paving material you use should project over the side of the pool for several inches to hide the plastic liner. If your terrace is made of small tiles, brick or gravel, you can set larger pavers such as flagstones along the side of the pool in order to achieve this overhang. Preformed plastic or fiberglass pools are also available. These can simply be set in the ground. They are more expensive than polyvinyl chloride lining, but less than poured concrete. Whatever kind of pool you build, a dark color is best, preferably black. A dark pool will look deeper and give better reflections. The pool that I've suggested is a rectangle, four feet by twelve feet and two feet deep.

The pool is planted with tropical water lilies. These are easy to grow, need little care and grow in shallow water. Even a tiny pool made from a washtub or a barrel can be a home for water lilies. You could grow as many as four in a pool the size I've specified here, but you may want to plant fewer in order to leave enough open water; you will want to make sure the pool does not become clogged with plants; otherwise they will neither look good nor grow well. If you will be using your garden by night as well as by day, plant both day-blooming and night-blooming varieties.

In arranging planters around the pool you can use your creativity. Vary their sizes and the materials of which they are made: terra cotta, metal, stone, wood and so on. They can be pots, tubs, boxes, urns and other kinds of containers. The smaller they are, the more easily you can move them around, to vary the look of the garden, and replace spring bloomers with summer ones and then with fall ones. For spring there are fragrant hyacinths and tulips in bright shades. These are followed by ranunculus (a summer bulb, also known as Persian buttercup) and 'Enchantment' lilies. Also for summer are three annuals that might be unfamiliar to you, but are available from many seed companies: sweet sultan, a lovely fuzzy-headed flower; love-in-a-mist, which blooms in early summer, then later on if you make another sowing in a second pot; and lavatera (tree mallow), which looks like a large pink hollyhock, but grows only three or four feet tall. Finally, there are 'Black Dragon' lilies for a spectacular show

ners of the pavilion, followed by a row of Persian lilacs, whose foliage will form a backdrop even after their flowers have finished blooming. Persian lilacs are very fragrant, shorter than our common lilac and not hard to obtain. Roses, the traditional flower of love, are planted at the front and sides, to provide color all summer long. Some should be climbers; they can ramble over the pavilion. Sweet white jasmine vines, grown in pots or tubs, frame the structure's entrance, and will give off a delicious scent throughout the summer.

The kind of pool you make is entirely dependent on your taste and your pocketbook. It could be made of concrete; it could be tiled; it might contain fountains; it might have lily pads and goldfish; perhaps you want a pool that simply reflects the sky in its many moods. You might even want to put in a swimming pool. The one suggested here is very simple, however. It is inexpensive to build, and you can probably do the work yourself (see box, p. 142). The terrace is composed of rectangular flagstone slabs laid in sand, but you might also want to use tiles or gravel; or else set the terrace material in concrete instead of just sand, if you desire. Whatever in late summer (add some potted chrysanthemums if you want a show of color through the fall). All these plants are easy to grow in containers. If you prefer, you can grow any of these in beds, perhaps adding a few other plants such as iris and Oriental poppies. But the pot scheme makes your garden more variable. This plan also lets you create the garden in a very small space, or a place where little soil is available. It also makes it an easy garden to take care of. You do not have to worry about plants competing with or hiding one another; you don't have to think about their colors clashing, or their foliage being in the way before or after blooming. Simply rearranging the pots will solve all these problems, leaving you more time for dalliance.

SITE

The most important requirement for these plants is full sun—that is, at least six hours of sun each day. If you have a choice of exposures, choose the sunniest and the one with the least wind. As well as being pleasant to sit in, a garden with still air is more apt to have the fragrance of flowers hovering in it than a breezy garden. To ensure privacy, the site could be a courtyard, a back or side yard (not a front yard), a rooftop or even a spot quite far from the house.

You can choose a site with relatively poor soil, because the growing areas are small and can be easily enriched and lightened with humus. Roses like a site with good drainage, however. And ideally the site should be level; it is easier to lay a pool and set potted plants on flat ground. If your site is uneven or on a slope, however, use it to advantage by terracing it in different levels, perhaps placing the pool and pavilion at the lowest point, and allowing water to cascade down to it, either naturally or by means of a recirculating pump. A flight of wide stone steps with potted plants placed on the sides could be very charming, especially if the steps curve around to a glade that is concealed from view from the top.

GROWING INSTRUCTIONS

The lilacs and flowering almonds can be planted in either spring or fall. Plant them as you would any shrub (see box, p. 20), with humus and fertilizer, watering well and making a saucerlike depression around them to

Nestled among ferns and azaleas, this garden seat at Winterthur in Delaware is a romantic spot in springtime.

hold water. A mulch will reduce the need for weeding and watering. For the roses, dig the soil deeply and add plenty of humus; mound them with soil or mulch in winter if you live in a cold area.

The annuals can all be sown directly in the planters, either indoors before the last expected frost, or outdoors after frost danger has passed. The spring bulbs can be planted in the containers in fall, then stored in a cool cellar or outdoors in a cold frame and set out on the terrace in early spring. Lilies can be treated in this way or planted directly in the planters in early spring. Be sure you bring all your planters indoors in winter in cold climates if they are made of terra cotta, china or any other material that will crack if frozen. The jasmine must also be wintered indoors north of zone 7.

The water lilies can be grown in several ways. To plant them in a natural pond, make sure there is some rather heavy, rich soil at the bottom, and plant the roots in it, wrapping them first in clumps of sod or tying them up in a soil-filled burlap bag. For this artificial pool, however, it is best to grow them in plastic pots (the one- or two-gallon size should be sufficient) or wooden boxes filled with rich soil. After planting the lilies, place about an inch of gravel on the surface to keep the soil from muddying the pool. Then set the container on bricks or blocks in the pool to keep the plants at the proper depth: when young, a lily should be covered by four to six inches of water; after it has matured it can be covered by six to twelve inches. Plant tropical lilies only when the water temperature has reached 70°F; otherwise they will not flower. Feed them with slow-release tablets, obtainable from the same sources that supply you with lilies. Tropical lilies must be removed from the pool before frost. They can be wintered-over in a greenhouse pool or tank, or they may be wrapped in a moist burlap sack surrounded by plastic and stored in a cool basement. But many gardeners treat them as annuals in cold climates and simply replace them each season. There are hardy lilies that are lovely, though smaller and less showy than the tropical varieties. These can be wintered in the pool, but only if it is deep enough or protected enough to keep the water from freezing solid. Water lilies may become the pride and joy of your garden; there are so many varieties available that you may want to try several new ones each year.

ADDITIONS AND SUBSTITUTIONS

I have tried to keep this garden simple and uncluttered. You might prefer an even sparser look, with only one or two potted plants, or only roses and water lilies. On the other hand, you may feel that a sense of sensuality and luxury comes only through abundance. If so, you could add more pots around the pool and in other parts of the garden, or lay out beds of flowers. You could plant vines at the corners of the pavilion and string unobtrusive wires for them to climb: clematis, grapes, sweet peas and other species of jasmine. Winter jasmine (*Jasminum nudiflorum*), which blooms in early spring, will grow as far north as zone 6. There are also many fragrant tropical jasmines such as Goldcoast jasmine (*J. dichotomum*), which blooms at night, Arabian jasmine (*J. sambac*) and primrose jasmine (*J. mesnyi*).

If there are grassy areas in your garden, dot them with small spring bulbs such as grape hyacinths or anemones, and use some flowering ground covers such as creeping veronica (*Veronica prostrata*) and some of the others described in the Medieval Paradise Garden (see p.169). Other garden flowers that would be appropriate include carnations, geraniums, calendulas, iris, cyclamens, violets, chrysanthemums, hollyhocks, larkspur, crown imperial (*Fritillaria*), lily of the valley, tulip poppy (*Papaver glaucum*), other varieties of *Lilium* such as the Turk's cap (martagon hybrids), and the peonies that are so

prevalent in Persian miniatures.

You could grow herbs such as sage or marjoram, and other flowering shrubs such as quince (*Chaenomeles japonica*). If you are a grower of houseplants, you could place some of them around the pool in summer—a night-blooming cereus on the rare night that it blooms, for instance, would be wonderful. Instead of water lilies, you might plant one sacred lotus (*Nelumbo nucifera*) to glow in the center of the pool. If you have goldfish or other decorative fish in the pool, you will need some floating aquatic plants that fish need. Fish, by the way, will not only add beauty, but will also help to keep mosquitoes from breeding in your paradise.

PLANT LIST FOR GARDEN OF LOVE

ANNUALS

LAVATERA, TREE MALLOW. *Lavatera trimestris.* Grows about 4 feet tall. Flowers are light, medium or dark pink and resemble those of hibiscus or hollyhock. The plant likes sun and well-drained soil. For summer bloom, sow seeds as soon as the soil can be worked. Thin to 2 feet apart in the garden, or plant 2 or 3 in a 24-inch planter. In mild climates you can sow in September. Do not transplant.

LOVE-IN-A-MIST. *Nigella damascena.* Another name for this plant is "devil-in-a-bush." It comes in shades of pink, purple, blue and white, and there are mixtures available such as the one called 'Persian

Jewels.' It grows about 1½ feet tall and has threadlike foliage similar to fennel. The flowers look like those of bachelor's buttons. Plant in average soil. Make an early sowing in spring for early summer bloom, and a later sowing for bloom in late summer. In warm climates, sow in fall. Thin to 8 inches apart and do not transplant.

SWEET SULTAN. *Centaurea moschata.* Purple, yellow, pink or white flowers, 2 feet tall. A taller variety usually called *C. imperialis* or *C. suaveolens* grows up to 4 feet tall. All have fuzzy flowers like soft thistles. Sow in the garden or pots as early as soil can be worked, thinning to about 8–10 inches apart.

BULBS AND TUBERS

HYACINTH. *Hyacinthus orientalis.* Zones 4–10. The familiar, large-flowered kind, 8–12 inches tall, in any color that pleases you. Plant in fall, 6 inches apart and 5 inches deep. Division is not necessary.

LILY. *Lilium* 'Black Dragon' and *Lilium* 'Enchantment.' Zones 5–9. 'Black Dragon' lilies are large and trumpet-shaped, with white inside the petals and dark red outside. They grow 5–6 feet tall and do not need staking, even when container-grown. They bloom in July and August and have a strong fragrance. 'Enchant-

ment' lilies are an old classic hybrid, very hardy, with orange-red, upward-facing trumpets. They grow only 3 feet tall and bloom in June and July. Both are true lilies, not day lilies. Plant in spring or fall, 6 inches deep, in very well-drained soil. They may not reach their full height until the second year.

RANUNCULUS (PERSIAN BUTTERCUP). *Ranunculus asiaticus.* This plant grows

from tubers to a height of 1½ feet. It flowers in winter or early spring in warm climates, and early summer in cool ones. The flowers are shades of yellow, orange, red, pink and white. Prefers full sun. Soak the tubers overnight before planting. From zone 7 north plant in early spring for summer bloom, and dig up the tubers for winter storage in fall, or replace each year. In warmer climates plant in November and leave them in the ground permanently.

TULIP. *Tulipa.* To zone 4. Any of the large-flowered tulips would look good, including the exotic parrot tulips, if these are to your liking. Shades of rose, gold and apricot would mix beautifully. Most tulips grow about 2 feet tall and bloom in May. In this garden they are best planted in pots in fall and stored in a cool place for the winter. After blooming, move the pots to an inconspicuous spot and let the foliage continue to grow until it dies naturally. After foliage is brown, dig up the bulbs and store them in a cool dry cellar or a similar place until planting time in fall. Or you may replace them each year as you would annuals. Plant the bulbs 6 inches apart, fertilizing them with bone meal or superphosphate.

SHRUBS AND VINES

ALMOND, DWARF FLOWERING. *Prunus glandulosa.*

Zones 4–9. This is not the nut-bearing almond, but an ornamental shrub related to it. It rarely exceeds 5 feet in height. The branches are covered with small round pink flowers in early spring before the leaves appear. Its only requirements are full sun and well-drained soil. Prune after flowering to stimulate bushy growth.

JASMINE, COMMON WHITE. *Jasminum officinale.* Zones 7–10. This plant can be grown as a shrub, clipped like a hedge or allowed to ramble like a vine over trellises and other structures. Native to Iran and other parts of the Orient, it has fragrant white flowers in summer and semievergreen leaves. North of zone 7, grow in tubs, then cut back before frost, wintering it in a greenhouse or in a cool spot where it can stay dormant until spring. Bring it outdoors again after danger of frost has passed.

LILAC, PERSIAN. *Syringa persica.* Zones 5–9. This lilac grows up to 5–6 feet tall and bears light purple flowers in late May. The clusters are smaller than those of the common lilac. Like the common one, it is easy to grow. It is valued for its profuse bloom and low-growing habit.

ROSE. *Rosa* hybrids. Choose varieties of the hybrid teas, hardy to zone 6, farther north with winter protection. Any shades that suit you would look good in this garden, but the Persians were especially fond of yellow roses. You could blend these with pinks and salmons with good effect. You could also grow the old tea roses *R. odorata*, a yellow climber such as 'Golden Showers,' or even the original Persian Yellow rose, *R. foetida* 'Persiana.' Grow all these according to the instructions in the Garden of Old Roses (see p. 88), but mound tender varieties with earth in winter if you live north of zone 6.

WATER PLANTS

WATER LILY. *Nymphaea,* tropical variety. Not winter hardy except in frost-free climates. Water lilies come in many sizes, from the pygmy lilies, suitable for very small tubs, to the giant ones, one of which will fill a pool of 50 square feet. Most medium-size varieties require at least 12 square feet of pool surface. They can be found in just about every color that it is possible to find in a flower. Many are fragrant. Some bloom only at night. They stand on rigid stems above the water. The leaves are the familiar flat, round "lily pads." For planting and care, see the "Growing Instructions" section of this chapter.

A Hummingbird Garden

In my family a hummingbird in the garden was considered a great compliment. Conversation on the lawn would cease at the sound of its whirring wings, and someone would say, "Oh, look—there's the hummingbird."

We would all watch as the tiny creature buried itself in one of my mother's lilies. We took its coming as a tribute to the brightness, sweetness and abundance of our flowers.

Actually it is not hard to make hummingbirds visit, and there is nothing mysterious about what attracts them: they have a sweet tooth. Although a large part of their food consists of tiny spiders and aphids, they also crave the sweet nectar of flowers the way children crave candy, and they will feed on almost any flower that has an ample supply.

Given a choice, hummingbirds will gorge

on a flower that is tubular or trumpet-shaped, be it wide open and showy like the hibiscus or tiny and closed like the coral bell. This is a classic case of coevolution between plant and animal: many trumpet-shaped flowers are designed to be pollinated by creatures with long, sucking mouthparts, like the proboscis of a butterfly or a hummingbird's long, hollow, pointed bill. There are even a few flowers, like the trumpet vine, whose flower tubes are so deep that only the hummingbird's long bill can penetrate and pollinate them. Nature has made the flowers, in turn, irresistible to hummingbirds, to ensure that pollination takes place.

Hummingbirds also prefer flowers in shades of bright red and orange. They will sample flowers in other shades, but red and orange catch their eye first. According to hummingbird expert Norma Lee Browning, they will even investigate the lipstick on a woman's mouth, to see if she is a flower. As for fragrance, it makes little difference, though some of their favorites, like honeysuckle, do smell sweet.

If you fill your garden with a good supply of the flowers that hummingbirds love dearly, they will not pass it by. Trumpet vine is a prime choice, and so is bee balm, whose flower heads are nests of tiny tubes. Another favorite is wild native columbine. Among the flowering shrubs, an excellent choice is Japanese flowering quince. You can make sure that there will always be ample temptation for the birds all spring and summer long, from their earliest appearance (in New England) in April—when they migrate north from Central America—to their departure in mid-September. If the hummingbirds like your garden, they will visit often. They may even nest in the limbs of nearby trees; the nests are so tiny that you have to be extremely sharp-sighted to find them.

PLAN OF THE GARDEN
This garden has been designed as a haven for the ruby-throated hummingbird, which is the one found east of the Mississippi. It may, however, be adapted to other parts of the country—see Additions and Substitutions.

A garden that is all red and orange might please a hummingbird but probably not you; it would be too intense. Some cooler shades of the flowers hummingbirds favor will tone things down a bit. So while the garden I have designed here is still a blaze of bright red and orange, it is tempered with blue, blue-violet and white. Small and easily managed, it includes annuals, perennials, shrubs and vines. In the main bed, clematis and tall perennials form a backdrop for the shorter perennials and annuals. In front of this bed is a small island of flowering annuals and perennials. A fuchsia hangs at the far right, and at the left a stone wall is covered with trumpet vine. Beyond the wall is a small shrub border.

The annuals in this garden serve several important functions. They help ensure a long season of continuous bloom, something that is hard to achieve in a garden restricted to a single theme. (Some of the best season spanners, like the sunflower group, have little attraction for hummingbirds.) Annuals can also fill a gap left by a perennial that has died, is diseased or for some other reason hasn't worked out—and this is liable to happen despite your best efforts. Annuals can also balance out the color scheme to suit your own preferences. If you must have some yellow, plant a few marigolds. Although they won't attract hummingbirds, they won't repel them.

Some people put out small tubular feeders filled with red sugar water for hummingbirds to drink, but if your garden includes even a third of the plants listed here they won't need this artificial food supply. In fact, there is evidence that natural, unrefined plant nectar is more nutritious for the birds.

The first spring migrants will find your azaleas and quinces, then stay to sample your columbines and other early bloomers, followed by the range of midsummer flowers like coral bells, day lilies, bee balm and phlox. The birds will still be on hand to feed from the latest bloomers—rose mallow and false dragonhead. The annuals will bloom until the first frost, when the hummingbirds are departing.

SITE
In selecting a site for the garden, choose a sunny open place, preferably facing south. You will need something for the clematis to

climb on, ideally a trellis. One could be built against a house, garage or barn; or it could be freestanding. Twining vines like clematis will not grow directly on a flat surface the way clinging vines will, and you can lay both the trellis and the vines on the ground when it is time to paint the house (usually a sunny week in August when vines are blooming). You could also string vertical wires between the eaves and a bracket projecting from the building at ground level; or you might want to set wooden posts in the ground and grow a vine on each. But a trellis would also give you a support to tie delphiniums and rose mallows to; they will need no other staking.

The varieties of azaleas and quinces used here have been selected for their small size. The weigela will need eight or nine feet to spread if left unpruned, but you can confine it to a six- or seven-foot space if you prune it back after flowering.

Prepare the soil well, adding lime and humus as needed (see Garden Primer, p. 11). Bone meal or superphosphate will aid in root development, but be sparing in the use of manure or other fertilizers that are high in nitrogen. A soil too rich in nitrogen will produce a garden whose main color scheme is green, with only tiny spots of color.

GROWING INSTRUCTIONS

No matter how carefully you fertilize and cultivate your plants, you will have to keep an eye on how tall they grow. Although the garden is planned to rise from the low-growing pinks in front to the giant rose mallows in the background, most plants will grow to different heights under different conditions. A fast-growing annual may engulf a perennial next to it that has not taken hold as vigorously as it should have or has not attained its full height the first year. If you are not careful you might forget the perennial is there, and later find that it has died from crowding. Thin the aggressor before it is too late, and prune it so that it will grow low and bushy.

This is a garden to be tended weekly; to be kept tidy and well supervised. Think of it as a gathering of strong personalities in a small room. You may apply mulch for easy weed control, but don't bury the plants with it; they could rot.

ADDITIONS AND SUBSTITUTIONS

Most of the plants in this garden are hardy to zone 5 (see Zone Map, p. 215) and can be adapted to any area within the bird's range. Choose the plants that will survive in your zone, as indicated in the plant list for this chapter. In far northern areas a few of the perennials will do well if treated as annuals or as perennials that need replacing after a few seasons, as the plant list indicates.

Several other varieties of hummingbird migrate to the United States, among them the rufous, Anna's, Costa's, Allen's, black-chinned and broad-tailed. These can be attracted by planting a garden similar to the one we suggest for the Northeast, using as many plants as will grow in your zone. In addition, there are hummingbird delicacies peculiar to specific regions. Californians should grow hummingbird's trumpet, also called California fuchsia *(Zauschneria)*, as well as true fuchsias, since these are hardy and thrive in California's subtropical regions. Gardeners in Texas and Louisiana should grow hibiscus and salvia in plenty; the rufous hummingbird sometimes winters there and loves these flowers. Another superb hummingbird plant for zones 8 through 10 is red-hot poker *Kniphofia (Tritoma)*; it

The weigela, coral bells and columbine in this spring garden are sure to lure hummingbirds.

THE HUMMINGBIRD GARDEN

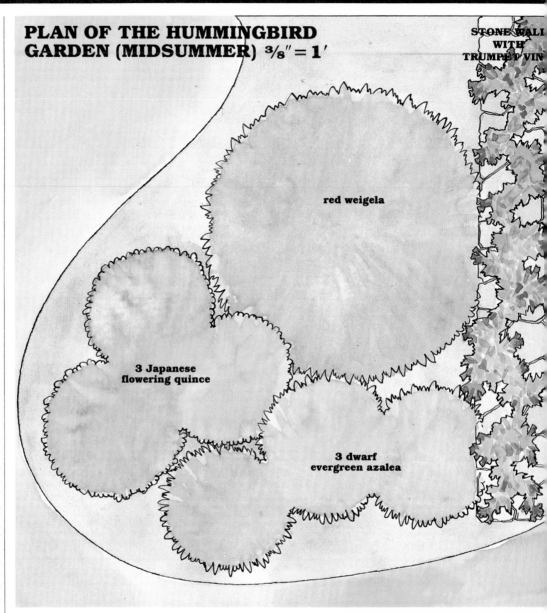

PLAN OF THE HUMMINGBIRD GARDEN (MIDSUMMER) ⅜″ = 1′

STONE WALL WITH TRUMPET VINE

red weigela

3 Japanese flowering quince

3 dwarf evergreen azalea

HOW TO BUILD A TRELLIS

The entire trellis should be built flat on the ground, then erected in desired location in one piece. Build a sturdy frame out of 2-by-4-inch posts, using lapjoints and screws to join posts together. There should be an upright post for every 8 or 10 feet of trellis. Leave 2 feet of post at the bottom, to sink into ground. Use either a rot-resistant type of wood or lumber that has been treated.

Use 1⅛-inch lattice for crosspieces. Place them every foot or so, and nail to frame at top, bottom and sides with short, thin nails. Lattice can be woven for extra stability.

Paint trellis the same color as the building behind it. If freestanding, paint it any desired color or paint with wood preservative and let it weather. The trellis can be re-painted whenever the plants are cut back. If vines are grown that will remain on trellis, however, do not use paint, since it will peel and not be repaintable.

Set trellis a foot or so from building, and sink posts. For extra sturdiness, secure to building with wood or metal brackets at the top.

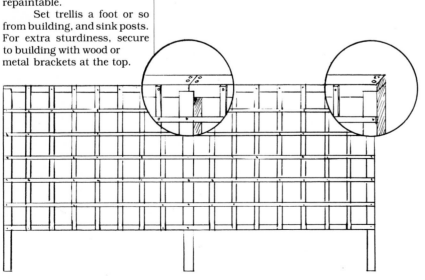

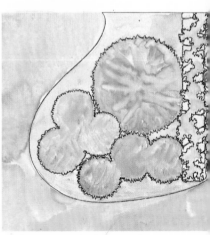

THE GARDEN IN SPRING

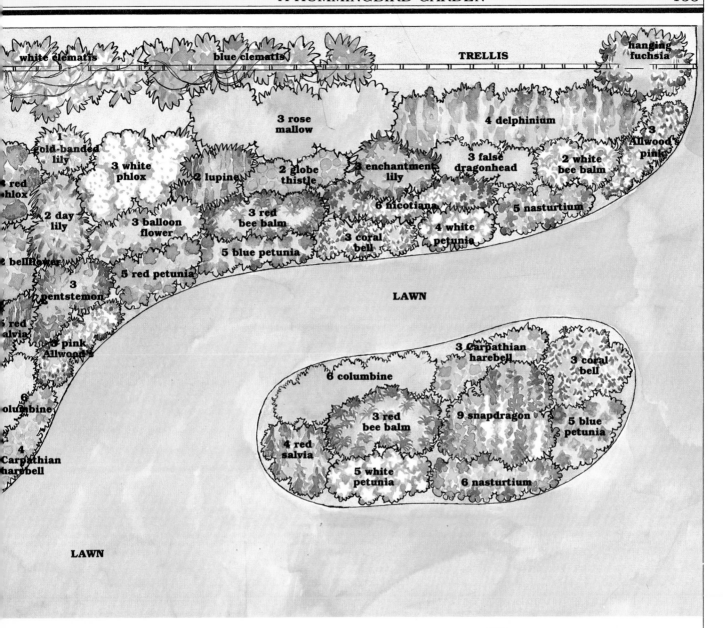

white clematis

blue clematis

TRELLIS

hanging fuchsia

1 gold-banded lily

3 red phlox

3 white phlox

2 day lily

3 balloon flower

2 bellflower

3 pentstemon

red salvia

5 pink Allwood's

columbine

4 Carpathian harebell

2 lupine

3 rose mallow

2 globe thistle

3 red bee balm

5 blue petunia

5 red petunia

3 enchantment lily

3 coral bell

6 nicotiana

4 white petunia

4 delphinium

3 false dragonhead

2 white bee balm

5 nasturtium

3 Allwood's pink

LAWN

6 columbine

4 red salvia

3 red bee balm

5 white petunia

3 Carpathian harebell

9 snapdragon

6 nasturtium

3 coral bell

5 blue petunia

LAWN

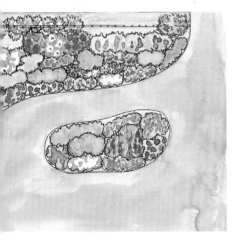

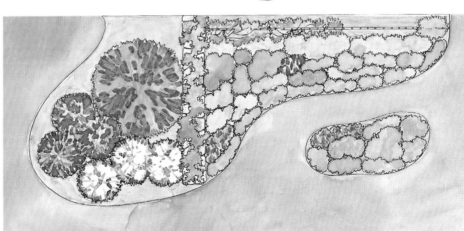

THE GARDEN IN FALL

can be grown in zones 6 and 7 with a protective mulch and the leaves tied together in winter. Substitute it for the snapdragons in the small island bed.

In the South a number of trees can be grown to lure hummingbirds: mimosa, buckeye, horse chestnut, the citruses. In the Deep South several of the suggested plants, such as delphiniums and lupines, will not tolerate the heat, and you will have to alter the basic garden, building it around plants that do well where you live. Just make sure you have a gradation in heights, a pleasing balance of color, a selection that will span the growing season and have arranged your plants so that something is always blooming in each section of the garden.

You may have to make other adaptations to suit your particular terrain and the availability of plants in your area. If you don't have a stone wall, for example, or don't want one, you can grow trumpet vine on a low slope or a tree. Although trumpet vine is the classic hummingbird plant, you might want to substitute trumpet honeysuckle (*Lonicera sempervirens*) if you don't have much room. Its flowers are a smaller version of the trumpet vine's and have a longer blooming period (June to September). It is less rampant, and is twining as opposed to clinging. It could be grown on the trellis. You could also plant it in place of clematis if your garden site gets extremely hot sun. It is hardy to zone 4, and while it is susceptible to aphids, the aphid-eating hummingbirds may help you to control these pests. All the honeysuckles, both in shrub and in vine forms, are favored by hummingbirds and can be used if you have sufficient space. Shrub varieties worth noting are Morrow honeysuckle (*Lonicera morrowii*) and Tatarian honeysuckle (*L. tatarica*). Yellow honeysuckle (*L. flava*) is another excellent vine and can be grown on a trellis.

Hummingbirds also visit lilac (the common *Syringa vulgaris* or the fragrant hybrids), beauty bush (*Kolkwitzia amabilis*), fountain buddleia (*Buddleia alternifolia)* and butterfly bush *(B. davidii).* One way to use these large shrubs would be to plant them in a sunny area next to a lawn, where you will be able to see the birds up close. Don't plant them right next to the house where they will grow up and block the windows.

If you have a lot of space and want to enlarge this garden, it would be better to make it longer, rather than wider. Use more of everything—or more of the things you like best—but again, allow for heights, colors and periods of bloom. You might want to enlarge the shrub area either by planting more of what has been suggested or by adding more varieties, such as the showy Exbury azaleas.

If you need to make this garden smaller, you might plant just the island section with only snapdragons in it. Or plant one half of the large border, with a quince or two off to the side. Just be sure you've included some plants that the birds love best, like columbine, bee balm and quince. Hummingbirds also like geraniums. Plant some red ones on your windowsill. Geraniums, as well as other annuals like petunias and nasturtiums, can be grown well in containers. Place them on a patio, next to the door or in a gap in the border—the spot where the columbines have finished blooming, for example. They will give the garden a bright finishing touch.

PLANT LIST FOR HUMMINGBIRD GARDEN

ANNUALS

FUCHSIA. *Fuchsia hybrida.* Double red and white variety. Perennial only in zone 10. Buy a showy specimen and grow it in a hanging planter near a door or window. Bring it indoors before danger of frost, cut it back hard, and store it in a cool place for the winter, watering only occasionally. Propagate by stem cuttings.

NASTURTIUM. *Tropaeolum majus.* Mixed dwarfs, 1 foot tall. Sow seeds indoors in early spring or outdoors after danger of frost is past, thinning plants to 6–8 inches apart. Nasturtiums grow best in soil that is dryish, sandy and rather poor in nitrogen.

NICOTIANA. *Nicotiana alata grandiflora.* Nicki hybrids. Mixed shades of red, pink and white. Fragrant dwarf, 15 inches tall. Sow seeds in early spring indoors or buy nursery-grown plants and set out after danger of frost is past. Set 10 inches apart.

PETUNIA. *Petunia hybrida multiflora.* Choose single varieties in clear shades of red, blue and white. Grows 12–18 inches tall. Sow seeds indoors in early spring or buy nursery-grown plants and set outdoors after danger of frost, 8–10 inches apart. Pinch when 6 inches high to encourage branching, and snip faded blooms to encourage flowering and prevent straggly growth.

SALVIA, RED. *Salvia splendens.* Dwarf red variety such as 'St. John's Fire.' Grows about 1 foot tall. Sow seeds indoors in early spring or buy started plants and set out after danger of frost, 10–12 inches apart. Do not overfertilize.

SNAPDRAGON. *Antirrhinum majus.* Choose medium-height plants (1½–2 feet tall) in red, bronze and white shades. Buy nursery-grown plants and set out after danger of frost, 8–10 inches apart.

PERENNIALS

BALLOON FLOWER. *Platycodon grandiflorum.* Zones 3–

9. Bears bell-like flowers similar to campanula but more open. Grows 1½–3 feet tall and blooms from June to August. Plant 15 inches apart, then leave undisturbed. Slow to establish, so be patient.

BEE BALM. *Monarda didyma.* A red shade such as 'Cambridge Scarlet' and a white such as 'Snow Queen.' Zones 4–9. These July- and August-blooming plants are vigorous and spreading. Both grow to 2–3 feet tall. Plant 18 inches apart and divide often.

BELLFLOWER, PEACH-LEAFED (PEACH BELLS). *Campanula persicifolia* 'Telham Beauty.' Zones 4–10. 2–4 feet tall. Bright blue bell-shaped flowers in June and July. Plant 12–16 inches apart. May need staking.

COLUMBINE, AMERICAN. *Aquilegia canadensis.* Zones 3–9. This is the native variety that grows wild throughout most of the eastern United States. Grows 12–18 inches tall, as a rule, and blooms in May and June. Its delicate, spurred flowers will be overshadowed in the border unless planted in a fairly large mass. Sow seeds in the ground in June or July for second-year

bloom, or buy nursery-grown plants for first-year bloom. Plant 1 foot apart. Prefers rather dry soil, low in nutrients. Self-sows freely.

CORAL BELLS. *Heuchera sanguinea.* Zones 4–9. Tiny bright red bell-like flowers dangling from wiry stems all summer. 18 inches tall. Very vigorous. Plant 1 foot apart and divide every few years.

DAY LILY. *Hemerocallis* 'Bright Banner.' Zones 3–9. Red and bronze variety, blooming in August and growing 3 feet tall. Day lilies are among the easiest perennials to grow, but the clumps will become dense and should be divided about every 4 years.

DELPHINIUM. *Delphinium* Pacific Coast Hybrids 'King Arthur' and 'Blue Bird.' Zones 3–7. 5–8 feet tall. 'King Arthur' has deep purple flowers with a white "bee" or center. 'Blue Bird' is medium blue with a white bee. Both bear magnificent flower spikes in June and July and again in fall if cut after blooming. Plant 2 feet apart and stake with a sturdy dowel or green bamboo pole to keep plants from being blown over by wind. Not dependably perennial. The hybrids 'Belladonna' and 'Bellamosa' are

more permanent substitutes, though shorter and less showy.

FALSE DRAGONHEAD. *Physostegia virginiana* 'Bouquet Rose.' Zones 3–10. Spikes of pink flowers 3–3½ feet tall that bloom from August to October, even after frost. Plant 15 inches apart and divide every 2–3 years.

GLOBE THISTLE. *Echinops* 'Taplow Blue.' Zones 3–10. The flowers are prickly blue balls that bloom in July and August and grow 2–4 feet tall. Plant 2 feet apart. Divide clumps when crowded.

HAREBELL, CARPATHIAN. *Campanula carpatica.* Zones 4–10. A low-growing bellflower, 4–8 inches tall, that bears blue-violet or white flowers in July and continues into fall. Choose any blue variety and plant 1 foot apart.

LILY. *Lilium* 'Enchantment' and gold-banded lily (*L. auratum*) or one of its hybrids. Zones 3–10. This is the true lily, which grows from a bulb, as distinguished from a day lily, which grows from a rhizome. 'Enchantment' is an old classic hybrid with orange-red, upward-facing, trumpet-shaped flowers. It grows 3 feet tall and blooms in June and July. Gold-banded lily has huge white outward-facing trumpets with gold stripes and dark red spots. It grows 5–6 feet tall and blooms in August. Plant lilies in spring or fall, 6 inches deep, in very well-drained soil. Stake just before blooming. They will not reach their full height until the second year.

LUPINE. *Lupinus*, Russell hybrids, red or bronze shade. Zones 4–7. Lupines grow 2–5 feet tall and bloom in May and June. They prefer moist but well-drained acid soil. Plant 18 inches apart.

PENTSTEMON (BEARD-TONGUE). *P. barbatus* 'Prai-

rie Fire.' Zones 6–9. (In zones 4 and 5 plant 'Rose Elf.') 2–3 feet tall. Small tubular red flowers in June and July, longer if faded blooms are cut. Must have good drainage. Plant 12–15 inches apart.

PHLOX, GARDEN. *P. paniculata*. A good bright red ('Starfire' is excellent) and a white variety such as 'World Peace.' Zones 3–9. 'Starfire' is about 3 feet tall, bright red and blooms in early July and August. 'World Peace' is the same height, pure white, and blooms from midsummer into September. Both have large flower heads and make a massed display in the late summer garden. (Any good red and white varieties might be substituted.) Plant 18–24 inches apart. Thin clumps each spring, then thin shoots within each clump. This will allow better air circulation and discourage mildew. ('Starfire' is mildew-resistant.) Removal of spent blooms will prolong flowering.

PINK, ALLWOOD'S. *Dianthus allwoodii*. Zones 4–7. Biennial in warmer zones. Usually 1 foot tall. Small fragrant flowers in shades of pink, red, white and bicolors. Gray-green tufts of foliage which should be cut back to keep a tidy appearance and encourage summer-long bloom. Plant 1 foot apart.

ROSE MALLOW. *Hibiscus moscheutos*. Zones 4–9. These have huge red, pink and white flowers in August and September, similar to but larger than hollyhocks. They grow slightly shorter than holly-

hocks (5–6 feet) and are more dependably perennial. Choose a red variety such as 'Satan' and a white such as 'Ruby Dot.' Plant 3 feet apart, with the crowns 3–4 inches below the surface.

SHRUBS AND VINES

AZALEA, DWARF EVERGREEN. *Rhododendron* 'Delaware Valley White.' Hardy to zone 6, but can be grown successfully to zone 4 if well mulched to protect the shallow root system. Azaleas belong to the rhododendron genus. This variety is a small white-flowered shrub that grows eventually to 4 feet. ('Polar Bear' is an excellent substitute.) Prefers acid soil.

CLEMATIS. *Clematis lanuginosa candida* and *C. l.* 'Ramona.' To zone 6, and zone 5 with protection. These delicate-looking vines need no encouragement to twine around a trellis or other support. *C. l. candida* has huge single white flowers. 'Ramona' has single pale blue ones. Plant with a cupful of lime in fertile soil with a mulch to shield the roots from summer heat and winter cold. Do not disturb roots. Replenish the lime and mulch each year. Both varieties bloom for most of the summer on the current year's growth and

should be cut back to a foot or two in the spring.

QUINCE, JAPANESE FLOWERING. *Chaenomeles japonica* 'Texas Scarlet.' To zone 5. Blooms scarlet-red in mid-May and sometimes again in the fall. It has glossy dark foliage and gracefully arching branches. Be sure to buy *japonica*, the dwarf form, rather than *C. lagenaria* or *C. speciosa* unless you have room for a shrub that grows 6 or more feet tall.

TRUMPET VINE (TRUMPET CREEPER). *Campsis radicans*. Zones 5–10. A heavy clinging vine that can be grown on a stone wall, chimney, tree, bank or sturdy fence, but not on a wooden building or trellis. It is a very strong vine that could damage the wood and make painting difficult or impossible. It bears red-orange tubular flowers in mid-July. A rapid grower.

WEIGELA (DIERVILLA). *W. florida* 'Vanicek' ('Newport Red'). To zone 6. This shrub is covered with small tubular red flowers in late May. In cold climates it may be killed back somewhat in winter. If this happens, prune out the dead wood in spring and it will still bloom profusely. This variety may grow to 9 feet if left unpruned. If it becomes so crowded with branches that you wish to prune out live wood, you should do so just after it flowers.

A Secret Garden

Why keep a garden a secret? The one in Frances Hodgson Burnett's *The Secret Garden* was a secret from a grim adult world for the three children who played there.

They brought straggly ancient roses back to life and created a special world for themselves within its old walls. In the twelfth century, Henry II of England built a secret garden in which to woo Rosamond, his mistress. It was a bower hidden within an elaborate maze built of shrubbery.

A secret garden could serve innumerable purposes—it could be an island of quiet to escape to for peace of mind, a place to eat something not on your diet or even a place where adults could hide from children. But aside from those purposes, it is enchanting to come upon a beautiful garden quite by chance; there's something very special about a garden that is concealed.

My ideal secret garden—albeit an imaginary one—would be a small, very private enclave. To reach it you would have to thread your way down a narrow mossy path among tall shrubbery to a huge mound of two-hundred-year-old boxwood. Tucked inside the mound would be a tiny wooden door; you'd have to look to find it. There would be an old wooden latch, and iron hinges that squeaked a bit. Inside, there would be a hidden flower world in filtered sunlight, a small terrace of faded, rose-colored bricks with moss growing between them, an old iron table and chairs. In my fantasy the flowers are all soft shades of pink, salmon, peach and white. It is an image of absolute quiet and solitude except for the movement of butterflies and the sounds of birds.

Like most fantasies it is not altogether realizable. A two-hundred-year-old box hedge is hardly a stock item at the local garden center. But if I were going to build my secret garden it would be like the one in this chapter. If I could afford it, I would build a surrounding wall of rose-colored brick, or buy large heavily sheared hemlocks for an instant dense hedge. If I had patience I would buy small yews of upright growth habit, like the Hicks yew in the Winter Garden (see p. 203), and start a hedge that would be a tall enclosure in years to come. If I had neither money nor patience I would build a high wooden fence or trellis and plant climbing roses in shades of pink and white all over it. Or I would select an out-of-the-way place in a semi-wooded part of my property and plant the broad-leaf evergreens native to my own region such as mountain laurel (*Kalmia latifolia*), pinxterbloom azalea (*Rhododendron periclymenoides*, also called *P. nudiflorum*) and rosebay rhododendron (*Rhododendron maximum*). These would slowly grow and enclose the spot in a natural way without shad-ing it heavily, and their pink blossoms would add to the general color scheme of the garden. The garden could also be enclosed with tallhedge (*Rhamnus frangula* 'Columnaris'), a fast-growing deciduous shrub that is dense, very narrow and upright, and graceful in habit.

The great English Victorian garden designer Gertrude Jekyll had a garden a bit like this one. She called it her "hidden garden"—hidden only because the path that led to it was not very obvious. It was a spring garden in which she had planted early-blooming flowers in a number of shades, and foliage plants such as wild ginger, ferns, woodruff and hosta. It was surrounded by hollies and other shrubs that she planned to let grow until the garden was completely shaded, at which point she would turn it into a fern garden—a perfect example of how you can sometimes plan carefully to let nature take its course.

Entering a garden through a doorway in a hedge gives you the feeling of discovering something special—in this case a "garden room" at Kellie Castle in Scotland. Within the tall hedge is a central urn and a rose-filled border.

PLAN OF THE GARDEN

The garden presented here is meant to be enclosed. In the illustration it is shown with a dark yew hedge. Whatever you use—a wall, fence or hedge—you can have a little door or gate set into it if you place sturdy posts on either side; these should be sunk in concrete. A brick or flagstone walk and terrace can be constructed according to the instructions in the box on page 165. If you want a patch of lawn instead, consider making an herb lawn out of thyme or camomile. This kind of lawn is fragrant to walk on and will not need mowing. It seems a shame to bring a lawn mower into such a quiet place.

Surrounding the terrace is a formal, symmetrical herbaceous border, composed of perennials. All are hardy except the dahlias, which must be dug up in cold climates and stored over the winter, and the tuberous begonias, which are grown as pot plants. The varieties of plants selected carry out a pink-

This garden is in the center of a Connecticut town, but it is a secret world tucked away behind tall evergreen hedges and filled with old roses, tulips and other flowers, as well as clipped topiary and whimsical statues.

salmon-peach-white color scheme, so that the garden has an old-fashioned romantic quality that would be perfect for this sequestered garden. You can substitute other shades, of course, depending on which ones you prefer and which varieties are available. If you would like a few notes of intense or dark red for accent, use small-flowered plants like coral bells and pinks. The general effect will still be soft and peaceful.

Spring bloom will begin with pink daffodils (actually, white daffodils with pink trumpets) followed immediately by pink tulips and bleeding heart. Through June the garden will be bursting into a mixture of pink shades: pale herbaceous peonies, floribunda roses, pinks, a salmon-colored lily, Carolina phlox and astilbe. These will be accented by white regal lilies and white Carolina phlox. In midsummer come pink dahlias, 'Pink Perfection' lilies, valerian, day lilies in pink and peach shades, the misty, low-growing tunic flower and the tall, wavy white spikes of snakeroot. Later flowers include red speciosum lilies, a sedum with bright pink flowers, delicate cyclamens, a pink astilbe called 'Finale' (not to be confused with astilbe 'Fanal') which blooms longer than other astilbes, and the magnificent gold banded lilies. Some of the earlier flowers will still be blooming at the end of the summer too—dahlias, pinks, roses and valerian. 'Silver Mound' artemisias sit, like soft, silvery cats, at either corner of the walk where it meets the terrace.

You could have fun looking for annuals in this color range to add, but bear in mind that they must tolerate light shade. It should not, however, be necessary to use annuals to fill in gaps, unless you have had losses. There is a steady succession of bloom planned, and in such a manner that the foliage of early bloomers, the bulbs in particular, is hidden by that of later plants such as dahlias and astilbe. Probably the most glamorous pink-and-peach flowers you can find, for part shade, are those of tuberous begonias. I like the simple rose-form kind, but there is also a ruffled variety. Plant one or two in terra cotta pots. They are not winter hardy, and have fragile stems that you will want to keep out of the way of playful pets and stray baseballs and other unguided missiles. (In my fantasy gar-

THE SECRET
GARDEN

PLAN OF THE SECRET GARDEN (MIDSUMMER) ⅜″ = 1′

HEDGE

1 rubrum lily

3 snakeroot

3 pink perfection lily

3 snakeroot

1 rubrum lily

1 gold-banded lily

1 gold-banded lily

12 daffodil

6 tulip

6 tulip

1 floribunda rose

1 floribunda rose

3 pink astilbe

1 rubrum lily

1 rubrum lily

2 coral bell

2 coral bell

3 cyclamen

4 Allwood's pink

3 cyclamen

3 day lily

3 day lily

5 tunic flower

5 tunic flower

6 daffodil

6 daffodil

3 late astilbe

3 late astilbe

6 tulip

6 tulip

tuberous begonia

1 bleeding heart

1 bleeding heart

3 pink Carolina phlox

3 pink Carolina phlox

3 pink Carolina phlox

1 sedum

1 sedum

tuberous begonia

3 white Carolina phlox

6 daffodil

6 daffodil

3 white Carolina phlox

2 coral bell

2 coral bell

BRICK TERRACE

3 day lily

3 day lily

3 cyclamen

3 cyclamen

6 tulip

1 Silver Mound artemisia

1 Silver Mound artemisia

8 daffodil

6 tulip

1 regal lily

4 dahlia

4 dahlia

1 regal lily

peony

8 daffodil

peony

Chinook lily

1 regal lily

1 valerian

1 valerian

1 regal lily

Chinook lily

DOOR

THE GARDEN IN SPRING

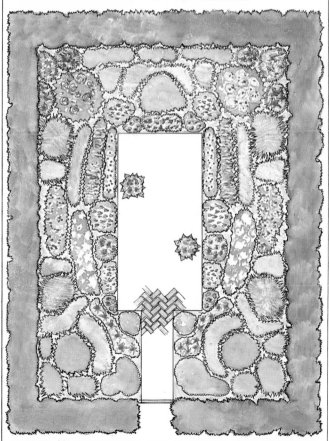

THE GARDEN IN LATE SUMMER

LAYING A BRICK TERRACE

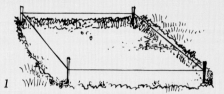

Fig. 1

Grade area level or sloping slightly away from house. Measure area and mark with stakes and taut string. Remove topsoil. In poorly drained areas lay a 2- to 4-inch bed of crushed stone, removing some subsoil if necessary. Dig a trench along the string for edging.

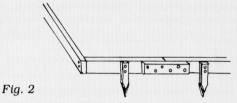

Fig. 2

Construct edging from 2-by-4's made of redwood, cedar or lumber treated with wood preservative. Stake every 4 or 5 feet with 12-inch stakes; splice where lengths meet, as shown. Set edging in place so that top is flush with the ground. Refill outside of trench with soil.

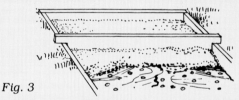

Fig. 3

Lay down heavy plastic or asphalt building paper, with holes punched every foot or so for drainage. Lay a bed of sand, smoothing with a screed, as shown. Allow just enough space above sand so that when bricks are laid they will be flush with the top of edging.

Fig. 4

Starting in one corner, lay bricks in sand, tamping with the handle of a tool, and checking level with screed. There are many different patterns; the one shown is basketweave. For extra stability, bricks may be laid on edge or on end, but you will need many more bricks and a deeper bed. Brush dry sand between the cracks until they are filled, then water with a fine spray.

den, there would be a dozen or so of them in different shades of pink, melon, apricot and white, planted in the pale rose-colored clay pots that are imported from Italy at great expense. I would place them all over—on the table, in the corners of the terrace and so that they cascade over the rose-brick wall.)

SITE

You will need a site where partial shade can be maintained in summer. The need for partial shade is directly related to the color scheme: many pink flowers are intolerant of bright sun. It fades them. Total shade, while it might be nice for a secret garden, will prevent most garden plants from blooming, and a true woodland situation is to be avoided. Lilies, in particular, like a good dose of sun, even though they like their roots shaded. Small trees could be placed near the edges of the garden to provide filtered light. Flowering crab apples, cherries or hawthorns would lightly shade the garden, and also bloom with suitable pink-and-whiteness.

If the proper site is provided this will be an easy garden. Most of the plants in it have similar requirements: a moist but well-drained soil that has been lightened and enriched by adding humus in the form of leaf mold, compost or peat, but not made excessively fertile with manure or other fertilizers. A flat or gently sloping site would be suitable. If you must, however, use a steep grade, build the garden on several levels, using retaining walls.

GROWING INSTRUCTIONS

The best time to begin to prepare this garden would be summer, building the brick walk and terrace, and adding humus to the soil. A surrounding hedge can be planted in fall. Even if the soil is loam of average consistency to start with, add a good two inches of humus, dug in about a foot. If the soil is clay, add sand until the soil does not hold its shape when you squeeze a handful of it. Also dig in bone meal at this time; five pounds per hundred square feet is a good formula. Preparation and planting could be done in the spring if it is more convenient, but fall preparation will give the beds more time to settle. Tulips, daffodils and peonies should be planted in fall. Day lilies, phlox, coral bells and *Lilium* could be too. But the other plants

The "secret garden" at Tyninghame in Scotland is filled with romantic pastel flowers: roses, pinks, delphiniums. In the foreground is a red fuchsia.

should wait until spring. Plant the cyclamens in midsummer for fall bloom.

Keep this garden especially tidy (no one will interrupt your labors), since it is formal, and any weeds will be noticeable. But weeds shouldn't be much of a problem; the planting is full, and there will not be much space between plants. A mulch is not necessary if you have prepared the soil well with humus; in fact some of these plants resent being smothered, and it would be better to grow them without mulch. (The cyclamens, however, will need a winter mulch in cold climates.) Scratch in a little bone meal or 5-10-5 each spring. Water the garden in hot, dry weather; the location should not be so distant and secret that no garden hose can find it.

ADDITIONS AND SUBSTITUTIONS

A few of the plants I have suggested, such as snakeroot and tunic flower, are not very common, though all of them are available from mail order sources. If you cannot find them, substitute varieties that have colors, heights and blooming times that would fit in well with the scheme as a whole. Japanese anemone would be a perfect choice; though rather tender, it can be grown in zones 5 and 6 with sufficient winter protection. Pink columbines would be a dainty addition, or the dwarf white Japanese fan columbine (*Aquilegia flabellata* 'Nana Alba'). Don't get carried away and overcrowd the bed, and remember that some great pink flowers, like pink baby's breath or chrysanthemums or asters, really need a lot of sun. If you insist on a few annuals, spiderflower (*Cleome*) and snapdragon would look very good, or any of the pink shades of impatiens.

If you want to make the garden smaller, plant only one side of it; both sides are identical, with a few minor variations. If you want to enlarge the garden you might plant tree peonies instead of or in addition to the herbaceous ones. They come in many pink shades, some with exotic streakings of lavender, white, purple, peach or copper. My favorite is 'Mystery'—a mauve with rich shadings. One of the very dark maroons would be beautiful here. These plants make large stunning mounds (up to five feet in diameter) in a garden large enough to accommodate them.

If you enclose the garden with a wall or fence, you can train clematis or climbing roses on it. If trees and large shrubs enclose the space, you can train these flowering vines so that they twine or ramble through the branches—a romantic effect for this garden.

PLANT LIST FOR SECRET GARDEN

BULBS AND TUBERS

BEGONIA, TUBEROUS. *Begonia tuberhybrida.* Winter hardy only in zone 10. Pink, salmon or peach shades. Either buy as potted plants or start tubers in February or March in a tray of loose potting medium such as peat moss. Feed with 5-10-5 and repot in successively larger pots as the plants grow. Give plenty of light but not direct sun; to prevent mildew, avoid spattering leaves with water. Feed about every 2 weeks, and bring indoors before frost. Let foliage grow indoors until late fall, then remove tubers from soil and store in a cool, dry place until early spring. Do not freeze.

CYCLAMEN, HARDY. *Cyclamen hederifolium (nea-* politanum). Zones 5–9, zone 4 with protection. Dainty pale pink flowers in fall, attractive variegated foliage. Prefers light shade and rich, humus-filled soil. Plant tubers in midsummer, 2 inches deep and 6–8 inches apart.

DAFFODIL. *Narcissus.* 'Mrs. R. O. Backhouse' or other pink variety. To zone 4. Pink daffodils are white with a large cup, peach-pink in this case. Plant 8–10 inches deep and 6–8 inches apart in early fall, fertilizing with bone meal. Do not cut tops back until they turn brown.

DAHLIA. *Dahlia hybrida.* Winter hardy only in zone 10. Pink formal decorative variety such as 'Gerrie Hoek.' This one is a soft medium pink, 3½ feet tall, but there are many to choose from. Bloom is from June until frost. Plant in late May or early June in North, earlier in South. Dust tubers with fungicide and plant 1½–2 feet apart and 7 inches deep, "planting" a stake along with the tuber for tall varieties. Lay tuber in hole horizontally with the eye up. Fill with soil mixed with 20-20-20. Pinch at 8 inches to induce branching. Dig up after frost and store in a cool, frost-free place in a bag of dampened peat or sand until spring.

LILY. *Lilium.* All zones 5–9. A salmon or orange variety such as 'Chinook.' This one is soft salmon, 4 feet tall, with upright flowers in June and July. Regal lily (*L. regale*): white trumpet with gold throat in July, usually 4 feet tall. 'Pink Perfection': large, dusky-pink flowers in July and August, 6

feet tall. *L. speciosum rubrum:* recurved red-spotted flowers in August and September, 6 feet tall. Gold banded lily (*L. auratum platyphyllum*) has huge, white outward-facing trumpets with gold stripes and dark red spots. It grows 5–6 feet tall and blooms in August. Plant lilies in spring or fall, 6 inches deep, in very well-drained soil. Stake just before blooming. They will not reach their full height until the second year.

TULIP. *Tulipa.* Most varieties zones 4–7. Any form—giant Holland, Darwin, lily-flowered, cottage or others—in a pink shade, or mix several forms and shades of pink and peach, combining early- and late-blooming varieties. Most grow about 2 feet tall and bloom in May. Plant about 6 inches apart in late fall, storing the bulbs below 70° F. Deep planting (10–12 inches) will discourage rodents from eating bulbs and may prolong years of bloom, but tulips will usually need replacing every year or so. Add bone meal when planting.

PERENNIALS

ARTEMISIA, SILVER MOUND. *Artemisia* 'Silver

Mound.' Zones 4–9. Silver-gray foliage, very soft to the touch. Grows 6–8 inches high and about a foot wide. Cut back hard in midsummer when straggly. Prefers well-drained soil, but keep moist during drought.

ASTILBE (GARDEN SPIREA). *Astilbe arendsii.* Zones 4–8. 'Ostrich Plume' is a salmon variety, up to 40 inches tall, blooming in June and July; *A. chinensis* 'Finale' is a pink variety blooming in August and September. Both like rich, damp soil and part shade. Plant 15–18 inches apart; divide every few years. Fertilize with 20-20-20; heavy feeders.

BLEEDING HEART, FRINGED. *Dicentra eximia.* Zones 4–9. This grows about a foot tall and blooms heavily all spring, then throws blooms throughout the summer and fall. It has attractive fernlike foliage and is much more compact than the better-known *D. spectabilis.* Prefers cool regions, humus, well-drained soil, light shade.

CORAL BELLS. *Heuchera sanguinea.* Rose, red or coral

shade. Zones 4–9. Tiny, bright bell-like flowers dangle from wiry stems all summer. Grows 18 inches tall. Very vigorous. Plant 12 inches apart and divide every few years.

DAY LILY. *Hemerocallis.* Zones 3–9. Choose two pink shades such as 'Hall of Fame,' 'Pink Heaven,' 'Swiss Strawberry' or 'Evelyn Claar,' and two peach shades such as 'Premier Peach,' 'Graham Bell' or 'Symphony Hall.' Day lilies are among the easiest perennials to grow, but the clumps will become dense and should be divided about every 4 years.

PEONY. *Paeonia lactiflora.* Zones 3–8. Choose a pale pink fragrant double variety such as 'Mrs. F. D. Roosevelt' or 'Moonstone,' and a pink Japanese type (single) such as 'Dawn Pink' or 'Sea Shell.' Grows 2–4 feet high and as broad; huge flowers in late May and June. Prefers cool nights, well-drained soil, humus. Plant according to instructions in Figure 4, page 19. Plants may not bloom the first year. Division is not necessary.

PHLOX, CAROLINA. *Phlox carolina (P. suffruticosa).* Zones 3–9. 'Miss Lingard': loose white flower heads from

June to September, 2½–3 feet tall, and one of the pink varieties, which are similar. Plant 1½–2 feet apart in full sun or light shade, in moist, rich soil. Thin as needed. Cut spent flowers to encourage long blooming season.

PINK, ALLWOOD'S. *Dianthus allwoodii.* Zones 5–9. Any of the Allwood hybrids would be lovely in this garden. For bright accents plant 'Doris' (salmon), 'Helen' (dark salmon), 'Robin' (vermilion), and 'Ian' (dark red). These are biennials in warmer zones. Usually grow 1 foot tall and bear small, fragrant flowers in shades of pink, red, white and bicolors. Gray-green tufts of foliage should be cut back to keep a tidy appearance and encourage summer-long bloom. Plant 12 inches apart.

ROSE, FLORIBUNDA. *Rosa.* Zones 6–10 but farther north with protection. 'Cherish': salmon buds, shell pink flowers. 'Fashion': coral or peach-pink. Floribundas are usually 3–5 feet tall and have clusters of large blooms from June until frost. See Garden of Old Roses, p. 88 for cultivation.

SEDUM, STONECROP. *Sedum spectabile.* To zone 3. Large pink flowers in August and September, gray-green leaves. Grows up to 2 feet high.

SNAKEROOT, BLACK. *Cimicifuga racemosa.* Zones 3–9. Long, white fuzzy flower spikes, gracefully curving, in July and August. Usually about 6 feet tall. Prefers moist, rich, humus-filled soil, in sun or shade. Water in drought. Plant 1½ feet apart. Division rarely needed.

TUNIC FLOWER. *Petrorhàgia saxifraga* 'Flore-plena' *(Tunica saxifraga).* To zone 3. Makes a dainty mat of fine threadlike foliage with clouds of tiny pink flowers similar to baby's breath, from July until frost. Easy to grow, but needs some sun and good drainage.

VALERIAN. *Valeriana officinalis.* Zones 3–10. Old-fashioned plant with pale pink flowers in midsummer. Very fragrant flowers, fernlike foliage. Grows 3–4 feet tall in sun or shade. Tolerates moist soil. Plant 15–18 inches apart; divide as needed.

A Medieval Paradise Garden

A rose, in the Middle Ages, was not just a rose. In love poetry it was a delicate, blushing lady; a beautiful prize to be won. In religious texts it was the symbol of another beloved lady, the Virgin Mary. The glorious rose windows of the great cathedrals are representations of the mystic rose that, like Mary, contained all of Creation.

The rose was simultaneously a symbol of chastity and of fertility.

The lady of the manor, weaving garlands in her "rosary," or rose garden, wove into them a spell of both purity and allure.

In down-to-earth, daily use, the rose provided many of life's sweetest pleasures. Its red hips were made into jelly, as were its petals. Its flowers were dried and put in chests with clothing as a freshener, or strewn in chambers along with sweet herbs. People washed their hands in rose water and drank rose syrups. They rubbed rose oil on their bodies to cure fever.

But it wasn't just roses that had many meanings and uses. All gardening in the Middle Ages was a symbolic act, and gardeners had special powers they don't have today. The monk tending his cloister garden meditated on the associations his violets had with humility, or the power that his rue had against witches. He pondered these things as carefully as he planned his strategy against cutworms.

Every plant had a symbolic "virtue," or power, along with a host of purely practical functions. Of course, plants were treasured simply for their beauty, as well. Medieval times were grim and dangerous, and people took their pleasures where they could find them.

As we have seen elsewhere, the idea of the garden as a "paradise" came to medieval Europe from the Middle East, as did many important ideas of the time. Eden had always been thought of as an enclosed garden, but now there was also the influence of the Persian *pairidaeza* via the Crusades and the Arab conquests in Spain. The sensual garden of love in the biblical *Song of Solomon* beguiled the Middle Ages, even though the church turned it into an allegory of the soul's union with Christ. Everyone wanted a walled "paradise" filled with fragrant flowers, especially the roses that had been grown so skillfully for centuries by the Persians. Monasteries had "plesaunces"—or "paradise gardens"—in their cloisters; these provided altar flowers as well as places that offered solace for the soul.

Much of medieval life necessarily took place within enclosing walls; even whole towns were walled for protection. Gardens were little enclosures within other enclosures—monasteries, castles, palaces—where the gentlest, most courtly moments were experienced in the midst of a violent age. It is no wonder that so many medieval poems begin with a lover who finds himself in a flowery meadow.

Most people, when they think of medieval gardens, think of herb gardens. But every plant was an "herb" then, and there were several kinds of gardens in which they could be grown: physic gardens for medicinal herbs, vegetable gardens, orchards, and "plesaunces" for sheer enjoyment. Sometimes these gardens were combined. I have chosen to represent the "plesaunce" here because it is less familiar than the others, and because it contains a marvelous feature that was very popular then and has since passed into obscurity: the flowery mead. The mead, or meadow, was something like our idea of a lawn, and was used the way we today use a lawn—for strolling, basking, frolicking or simply gazing at. But it was not like any lawn we know. In medieval times this mead would have been made out of pieces of turf cut from wild meadows; favorite flowers would then be planted in it.

The most beautiful medieval meads that I know of are in the Unicorn tapestries at the Cloisters in New York City. The hunting of the unicorn, which is represented in these magnificent wall hangings, is another version of a favorite medieval theme: a precious prize is sought and captured, a prize that is at the same time earthly and spiritual. According to the unicorn legend, the beast could be captured only in the presence of a virgin. With her help, he is tamed, caught and killed. In the last and most famous tapestry he is miraculously resurrected, like Christ, and in his captivity he rests among hundreds of exquisite blossoms, penned in by a low fence or "rail." Each scene in the series takes place in a flowery meadow, each flower of which was chosen not only for its beauty but for its symbolism.

If you have let your lawn go untended in spring or summer and found it full of flowers—dandelions, clover, violets, wild strawberries—you have actually had the start of a flowery mead. Imagine what it would look like filled with choice flowers, fragrant ones—ones you have planned.

PLAN OF THE GARDEN

First you will need an enclosing wall. Medieval gardeners went to great expense and trouble building walls and other garden structures. You, however, may not want to build anything very elaborate; fortunately there are many different kinds of enclosures that are authentically medieval. Hedges sometimes enclosed a garden, and often such a hedge was trained into a pleached arbor— parallel rows of small trees woven together at the top to make a living roof or tunnel. Brick, stone, wood, wood and straw or wattle (woven branches) were also used for walls. Walls could have towers and turrets, and they could be roofed with tiles. If they were of solid masonry, they could have beds of soil set in the top and filled with turf and flowers. This would be a delightful touch, but a big job. If you want a wall of this nature it would be wise to have a professional mason build it.

For this garden I have proposed a palisade fence that is fairly simple to build and incorporates some other structural features of medieval gardens as well. Raised beds were very popular, as they are increasingly today because they are easy to cultivate. Trellises and "rails" built of wood or branches often surrounded the beds. The palisade fence in this garden has raised beds along it that are supported by low wooden rails. These are anchored to the fence, as is the wooden trellis-work built into the top to support climbing roses. The edging of the paths and of the other beds is also built of wood. All these features can be constructed at the same time.

The main focal point of the garden is the "mead," a twelve-by-twenty-foot lawn edged with low wooden railings. One way to plant an authentic medieval mead would be to sow it in Chaucer's "small, soft, sweet grass" and plant spring-blooming bulbs and perennials in it, then just mow it from the end of June onward as if it were an ordinary lawn. But many flowering plants would not be able to stand the competition from the grass. In this mead there is no grass at all, only flowering herbs and ground covers with small clumps of low-flowering perennials set among them. This lawn will have some bloom all summer, and will need no mowing. It will also be fragrant to walk on—something like the herb lawns which can still be found in England today. It will give you fragrant "strewing" materials as well. Thyme, catmint and camomile have been used, along with some other spreading plants such as ajuga, woolly yarrow and prostrate speedwell (veronica). Spring bulbs will poke up through them—old-fashioned species daffodils, snowdrops, lilies of the valley and others you might care to add. Clumps of low-growing perennials will provide spots of gemlike color: primroses, English daisies, scarlet cranesbill, "gilliflowers," columbines, forget-me-nots, wild strawberries, johnny-jump-ups, sweet violets and a pink speedwell. In choosing varieties of these flowers I have tried to be historically correct and yet choose plants that will thrive and bloom a long time. The catmint *Nepeta faassenii* blooms in late summer. The species daffodils are small and quaintly shaped, not at all like the familiar large-cupped trumpets. For columbines, the common columbine, *Aquilegia vulgaris*, or a modern hybrid would be suitable, but you also might plant an American native such as *A. canadensis* or *A. chrysantha*. For primroses, the native

A "paradise garden" at the Cloisters in New York City. It adorns the Cuxa Cloister, brought from France.

THE MEDIEVAL
PARADISE GARDEN

PLAN OF THE MEDIEVAL PARADISE GARDEN (LATE SPRING)

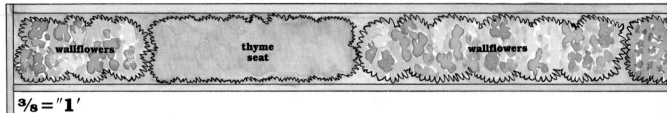

wallflowers — thyme seat — wallflowers

$\frac{3}{8}='' \mathbf{1}'$

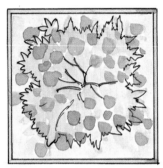 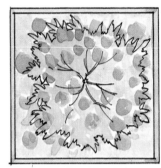

APOTHECARY ROSES IN RAISED BEDS

DOOR

GRAVEL PATH

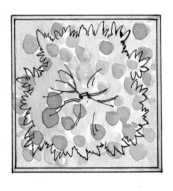 

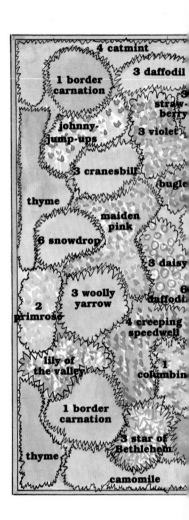

4 catmint

1 border carnation — 3 daffodil

3 strawberry

johnny jump-ups — 3 violet

3 cranesbill

bugle

thyme

maiden pink

6 snowdrop

3 daisy

3 woolly yarrow

6 daffodil

2 primrose — 4 creeping speedwell

lily of the valley — 1 columbine

1 border carnation

3 star of Bethlehem

thyme

camomile

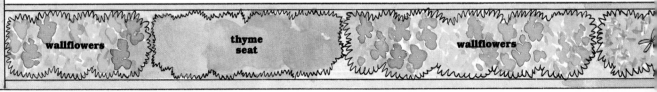

wallflowers — thyme seat — wallflowers

FENCE

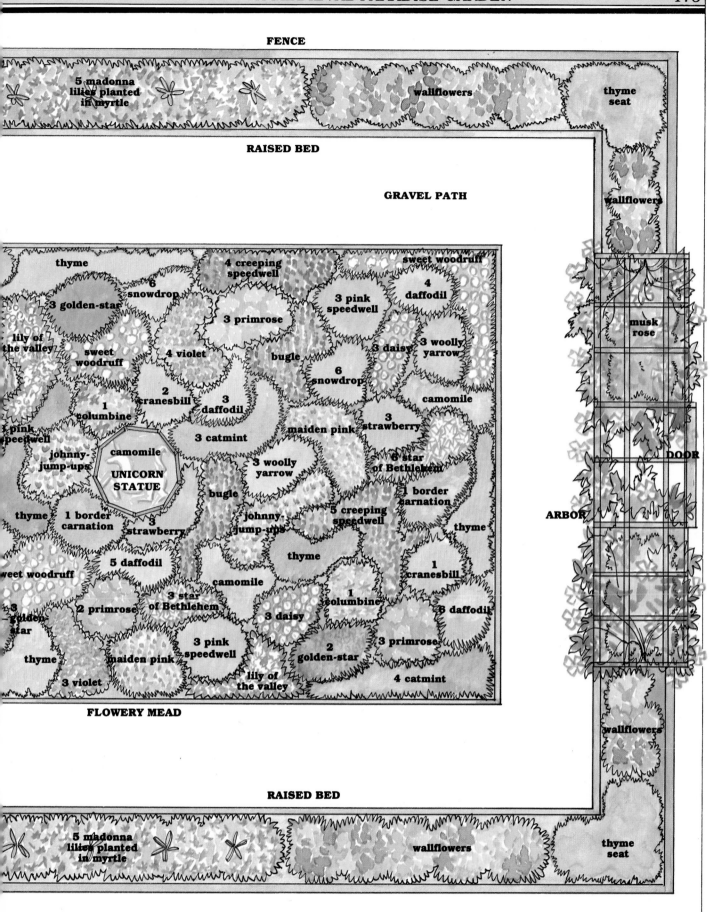

FENCE

5 madonna lilies planted in myrtle

wallflowers

thyme seat

RAISED BED

GRAVEL PATH

wallflowers

thyme

4 creeping speedwell

sweet woodruff

6 snowdrop

3 golden-star

4 daffodil

3 pink speedwell

3 primrose

lily of the valley

sweet woodruff

4 violet

bugle

3 daisy

3 woolly yarrow

6 snowdrop

2 cranesbill

3 daffodil

camomile

1 columbine

3 catmint

maiden pink

3 strawberry

pink speedwell

3 woolly yarrow

6 star of Bethlehem

johnny-jump-ups

camomile

UNICORN STATUE

bugle

1 border carnation

thyme

1 border carnation

3 strawberry

johnny-jump-ups

5 creeping speedwell

thyme

1 cranesbill

sweet woodruff

5 daffodil

thyme

1 columbine

6 daffodil

3 golden-star

2 primrose

3 star of Bethlehem

camomile

3 daisy

3 primrose

thyme

maiden pink

3 pink speedwell

2 golden-star

4 catmint

3 violet

lily of the valley

FLOWERY MEAD

musk rose

DOOR

ARBOR

wallflowers

RAISED BED

5 madonna lilies planted in myrtle

wallflowers

thyme seat

THE GARDEN IN SUMMER

CONSTRUCTING THE MEDIEVAL PARADISE GARDEN

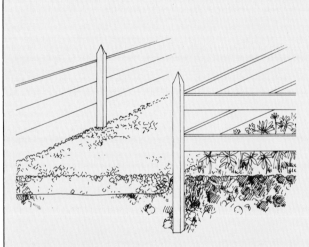

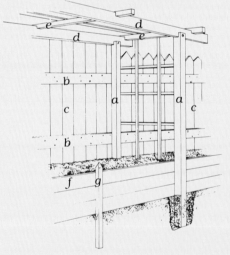

The flowery mead has railings that merely serve as a decorative edging, and there can be spaces between the planks. Sink the corner posts into the ground and nail the planks to them. For the paths, dig out 4 inches of topsoil and add it to the raised beds. Lay down heavy plastic to keep weeds from growing in the paths, and punch holes in the plastic for drainage. Fill to the former soil level with fine gravel or a combination of gravel and sand.

After the site has been graded and any drainage problems solved, the walls should be staked out at right angles. Set 4-by-4-inch posts (a.) at the corners of the small arbor and the 4 corners of the

garden and about every 10 feet in between, sinking them in concrete to a depth of 2 feet. All the wood should be a rot-resistant variety, or treated with preservative, especially parts that come in contact with the soil. To build the fence, nail 1-by-8-inch boards (b.) to the posts horizontally, then nail upright boards (c.) to the horizontal pieces. For the small arbor, notch the tops of the 4-by-4-inch posts; bolt 1-by-4-inch beams (d.) to them, then add 1-by-2-inch crosspieces (e.). Lattice can be nailed to the top and sides. Build raised beds with 2-by-6-inch or 2-by-8-inch planks (f.), anchoring them in back to the fence and in front to small posts (g.) sunk in the ground.

English primroses and cowslips are preferable, but any of the modern hybrids would be so lovely that it is hard to be a purist and exclude them. The subject of gilliflowers is a bit tricky. The flower is usually assumed to be *Dianthus caryophyllus* (called border carnation or clove pink), the ancestor of both our modern carnations and modern pinks, much hybridized in the Renaissance. The name is also applied to several different flowers, among them wallflower and stock. But any of these would lend scent to your garlands and look lovely dotting this meadow.

I have grouped the plants in clusters of three because they grow in small clusters in the wild and because the effect is pleasing.

The rest of the garden has been kept simple, and includes a few other plants very popular with medieval gardeners. There are four apothecary rose bushes in tidy square beds, and a musk rose climbing on a trellis. Both are ancient rose varieties. In the raised beds next to the walls, madonna lilies, that holy flower loved by Mary and dreaded by snakes, are growing, as well as myrtle, another beloved flower, called "joy of the ground." Wallflowers also grow there, a traditional feature. Thyme is planted in the wall beds at intervals to provide soft, fragrant turf seats. Often these side beds were turfed in their entirety and planted with primroses and other flowers, just like the mead. If you have chosen to have a wall topped with beds you can plant these the same way. The wall does not need to be a high one; it should be possible to stand on the turfed seats and look over the wall to see the outside world.

The walks could be brick or stone; they could be sand or gravel. A good treatment would be to lay down gravel (small round stones, not modern crushed stone) and overlay it with sand to make the surface more pleasant to walk on. One final touch: if you can find a statue of a unicorn that suits your taste, place it in the center of the mead, within a wooden railing and your meadow will look just like the one in the tapestry.

SITE

Choose a level site for this garden; make sure it has good drainage and at least six hours of sunlight. Many of the plants, such as pinks and roses, prefer sun. Others are tolerant of some shade, and some, like violets, forget-me-nots, primroses and lilies of the valley, prefer it, but they will grow in sun unless it is blazing hot and the soil is allowed to dry out. This garden could be planted anywhere—near a house, a school, a library, a church, even a castle or monastery. It could be attached to a building at one end, or completely enclosed by it, as with a cloister. It could also stand alone reached by a path from the house.

GROWING INSTRUCTIONS

The mead, like any collection of plants with diverse requirements, should have average soil with a neutral pH and medium fertility. Overfertilizing could cause some of the spreading ground covers to become too rampant. This is a large area to fill with plants, but they may be somewhat sparse at first. The spreaders will soon fill in around the separate clumps. The most important job will be to keep the "lawn" free of weeds, by hand weeding, and to take care that the dainty plants, such as columbine and cranesbill, are not overwhelmed by their more vigorous neighbors. Many of these plants will bloom longer if cut back with hand clippers after bloom, especially pinks, thyme, cranesbill, camomile, speedwell and catmint.

If you do not want to spend a great deal of time supervising the mead, just let the fittest plants survive. You will still have a handsome lawn of ground covers, with plenty of bloom. If it becomes a pet project, however, you may find yourself searching for additions—new spots of color to try out. Don't be afraid to use the mead—not for badminton

This old stone bench planted with camomile is a fragrant and pleasant place to sit in dry weather.

or walking the dog, but certainly for picnics, sunbathing, classes or meetings—and important outdoor activities like garland-weaving and herb-gathering.

ADDITIONS AND SUBSTITUTIONS

Here are a few of the plants you could add to your flowery mead: saffron crocus *(Crocus sativus)*, prized as a source of saffron; sweet william *(Dianthus barbatus)*, as a self-seeding annual; Maltese cross *(Lychnis chalcedoncia)* and rose campion *(L. coronaria)*; dwarf forms of sage and lavender; oxeye daisy *(Chrysanthemum leucanthemum)*; coral bells *(Heuchera sanguinea)*; other low-growing veronicas such as 'Icicle' or *V. incana*; globeflower *(Trollius europaeus)*; pasque-flower *(Anemone pulsatilla)*; cuckoopint *(Arum maculatum)*; feverfew *(Chrysanthemum parthenium)*; borage *(Borago officinalis)*; snow-in-summer *(Cerastium tomentosum)*; Saint-John's-wort *(Hypericum moseranum)*; other *Nepeta* varieties and other thymes. In warm climates grow English pennyroyal *(Mentha pulegium)*—its citron scent is said to keep away fleas and mosquitoes. If your mead is a bit shady, add some form of bluebell such as *Mertensia virginica*, also herb robert *(Geranium robertianum)* which is said to be named for Robin Hood, and other scented geraniums; mints *(Mentha* species); lungwort *(Pulmonaria officinalis)*; woodland forget-me-nots *(Myosotis sylvatica)*. Much of what you do will depend on the size of your mead. If it is tiny, a few ground cover plants will be enough to fill in between the "gems." If it is a big lawn, you would use ground covers extensively.

There are a number of very old roses you can grow besides the two selected—the gallicas in particular (see Garden of Old Roses, p. 88). These are an appropriate height for small raised beds, as is the common moss rose *(Rosa centifolia* 'Muscosa') or the autumn damask, also called rose of Castile *(R. damascena semperflorens)*. As a substitute for the climbing musk you can grow the eglantine, also known as sweetbrier *(R. eglanteria)*.

If you want to expand the side beds into real perennial borders in order to have a better succession of summer bloom, plant foxglove (*Digitalis* species); yarrow (*Achillea* species); tansy (*Tanacetum vulgare*); monkshood (*Aconitum fischeri*); southernwood (*Artemisia abrotanum*) and wormwood (*A. absinthium*) for white foliage accents; mullein (*Verbascum* species) and old-fashioned native European irises (*Iris foetidissima* or *I. germanica florentina*).

Another way to keep the garden colorful would be to plant some annuals characteristic of the period, such as the yellow pot marigold (*Calendula officinalis*)—good in salads and effective against evil—or marguerites (*Chrysanthemum frutescens*). Large pots of sweet bay (*Laurus nobilis*) and rosemary (*Rosmarinus officinalis*) would be handsome, appropriate and useful. So would a few fruit trees espaliered against one wall.

You could also be deliberately inauthentic and fill the beds with a summer's succession of modern lilies and long-blooming modern roses. For you, perhaps, a rose is a rose.

© METROPOLITAN MUSEUM OF ART

A flowery mead is well represented in "The Unicorn in Captivity," one of the famous Unicorn tapestries at the Cloisters.

PLANT LIST FOR MEDIEVAL PARADISE GARDEN

ANNUALS AND BIENNIALS

WALLFLOWER, ENGLISH. *Cheiranthus cheiri.* Grows up to 18 inches tall. Blooms in spring in shades of yellow, red, orange and purple. Sow as a biennial in summer for spring bloom, and sow in early spring to bloom in late summer. Likes cool, damp soil in sun or light shade. Plant 6–12 inches apart.

BULBS

DAFFODIL, NARCISSUS SPECIES. In zones 4–5 plant angel's tears (*N. triandrus*) and dwarf daffodil (*N. pseudonarcissus minimus*). In zones 6–10 add hoop-petticoat daffodil (*N. bulbocodium*) and rush-leafed daffodil (*N. juncifolius*) and others. These are all small-flowered plants, 3–8 inches tall; flowers are yellow and sometimes white. Plant in late summer or early fall, 3 inches deep and 5 inches apart, with bone meal.

LILY, MADONNA. *Lilium candidum.* Zones 3–10. Grows

3–4 feet tall and bears large snow-white flowers in June and July. Plant by covering the bulb with only 1 inch of soil in late summer. Set the bulbs 1–1½ feet apart. Keep the soil damp but not wet. The bulbs develop some leaves in the fall.

LILY OF THE VALLEY. *Convallaria majalis.* Zones 3–7. Tiny, fragrant white bell-like flowers in May. Prefers part shade and moist, acid soil. Plant the "pips," which are not true bulbs but rootstalks springing from rhizomes, in early spring or fall, 3–4 inches apart, 1 inch deep. Clumps will spread quickly. Divide and replant elsewhere. To stop spread of underground roots, sink strip of 2-foot-wide aluminum flashing in soil around clump, or just weed out periodically.

SNOWDROP. *Galanthus nivalis.* Zones 3–9. Single white flowers, and grassy foliage that dies down after bloom. Grows 6–12 inches tall. Spreads, and can be propagated by removing bulblets and replanting. Likes moist but well-drained soil. Plant 3 inches apart, 3 inches deep.

STAR-OF-BETHLEHEM. *Ornithogalum umbellatum.*

Zones 4–10. Clusters of white star-shaped flowers in spring. Grows about 10 inches tall, spreads rapidly. Plant in October or November, 3 inches deep and 6 inches apart.

PERENNIALS AND GROUND COVERS

AJUGA (BUGLE). *Ajuga reptans.* To zone 3. Blue flower spikes 6 inches tall in May and June. Plant 6–8 inches apart. Spreads quickly; if non-spreading variety is desired, plant *A. pyramidalis.*

CAMOMILE, ENGLISH. *Anthemis nobilis.* Zones 3–10. Foliage is bright green, fragrant, feathery, 3 inches high. Flowers are small and daisy-like, recurring all summer if cut. Dislikes lime.

CARNATION, BORDER (GILLIFLOWER). *Dianthus caryophyllus.* Zones 6–7, and farther north with winter protection. Can also be grown as an annual, or plant hardier sorts of *Dianthus* such as *D. deltoides* or *D. allwoodii.* Grayish foliage; grows 1–3 feet tall. Flowers are in many shades, clove-scented; blooms all summer.

CATMINT. *Nepeta faassenii.* To zone 3. Gray-green, spreading, aromatic foliage. Blue flowers from June to August. Sun-loving. Not the variety held sacred by cats.

COLUMBINE. *Aquilegia vulgaris,* the species or its hybrids. Zones 3–9. The old-fashioned blue variety grows about 2½ feet tall and blooms in May and June. Columbines prefer moist soil and tolerate part shade.

CRANESBILL, SCARLET. *Geranium sanguineum.* Zones 4–9. A low-growing European wild flower that bears reddish purple flowers in spring and throughout the summer. Self-seeding and easy to grow. Leaves turn reddish in fall.

DAISY, ENGLISH. *Bellis perennis.* Zones 6–10 as a perennial or biennial. Grows

6 inches tall and blooms in spring. Try to find the old-fashioned single variety with the yellow "eye" (whence its old name "day's eye"). Likes sun and moist, peaty soil.

GOLDENSTAR. *Chryso-gonum virginianum.* To zone 6. Low-growing plant with single yellow flowers on stems up to 2 feet. Blooms all summer. Prefers a site with some shade ad moist, woodsy soil.

JOHNNY-JUMP-UP. *Viola tricolor.* Perennial in zones 6–8. Grow from seeds sown in early spring or fall, or buy started plants. Self-sows freely. Prefers light shade and moist soil, rich in humus.

MYRTLE (PERIWINKLE, VINCA). *Vinca minor.* To zone 4. Dark green ground cover with blue flowers in April. (There is also a white-flowered variety, *Vinca minor* 'Alba.') Enrich the soil with peat moss or leaf mold. Plant 1 feet apart or closer.

PINK, MAIDEN. *Dianthus deltoides.* To zone 3. Foliage

is a low matlike carpet. Flowers are tiny and bright pink, blooming profusely in May and June. Spreads vigorously. Prefers sun and well-drained soil.

PRIMROSE, ENGLISH. *Primula vulgaris.* Zones 4–8. Low clump of broad, bright green leaves with flowers on stalks 6–10 inches high, usually yellow, in mid-spring. Prefers moisture, part shade and woodsy soil.

ROSE, APOTHECARY (RED ROSE OF LANCASTER). *Rosa gallica* 'Officinalis.' To zone 4. Ancient shrub rose, suckering freely when grown on its own roots. It has lush, dark green foliage and semi-double, fragrant, light crimson blossoms in June. Grows to about 4 feet. You may need to prune out the suckering shoots; do this below ground level and give them to friends.

ROSE, MUSK. *Rosa moschata.* To zone 5. Climbing rose, 20–30 feet high. Vigorous and hardy. Bears profuse single white blooms with a musky fragrance in June. Train on a trellis or arbor, pruning back if too rampant.

SPEEDWELL, CREEPING. *Veronica prostrata* 'Heavenly Blue.' Zone 5. Low, spreading mat with bright blue flowers in May and June.

SPEEDWELL, PINK (VERONICA). *Veronica spicata* 'Barcarole.' To zone 4. A vigorous pink variety, 10 inches high. Blooms from June through August. Cut back to encourage profuse bloom and growth. Do not transplant once established.

STRAWBERRY, WILD (WOODLAND STRAWBERRY, *FRAISES DES BOIS*). *Fragaria vesca.* Zones 4–10. Many hybrids are available, such as 'Baron Solemacher.' Hardy perennial. Small white flowers and tiny, oval red fruits all summer. Prefers sun and a dry location. Plant 1 foot apart and divide every few years.

THYME, CREEPING (WILD THYME). *Thymus serpyllum coccineus.* Zones 3–10. Also try lemon thyme, *T. citriodorus*; caraway thyme, *T. herbabarona*; golden thyme, *T. aureus*. All the thymes prefer sun and light, well-drained soil. They are slow to grow from

seed, but you can sow them in spring between established clumps. Best propagated by division, planting a foot apart. Fertilize with bone meal or superphosphate, but not a fertilizer high in nitrogen. Trim the taller varieties in early May. In very cold climates mulch with salt hay in winter.

VIOLET, SWEET. *Viola odorata.* Zones 6–10. Fragrant, usually purple flowers in late spring. Obtain plants from a nursery or a friend.

WOODRUFF, SWEET. *Galium odoratum (Asperula odorata).* Zones 4–8. Dainty, spreading foliage, 6 inches high; used to flavor May wine. Small white flowers in May or June. Grows in sun but prefers some shade. Plant in spring of early fall 10–12 inches apart; divide in early spring or fall.

YARROW, WOOLLY. *Achillea tomentosa.* Zones 3–9. Silvery mat of leaves; yellow flowers all summer. Grows 8–10 inches high. Plant 1 foot apart.

A Grass Garden

L et's say you want a beautiful little garden, but you haven't much time or money to spend on it. You'd like to have something unusual and exquisite, not just a bed of petunias like the one next door. But you simply do not have the time or the disposition to track down a collection of rare and unusual plants, nurse them through the seven plagues, then redo the whole thing the following year.

A grass garden might be just the thing for you. Grasses are easy to grow, and many are available from mail order sources. Ornamental

grasses seem rare and exotic only because few people in your neighborhood are likely to be growing them.

Grass gardening, quite common in Europe and the Orient, is just beginning to be popular in the United States. There are many ways to use grass in gardening. Most people are familiar with the lawn grasses—Kentucky bluegrass, the rye grasses, the fescues. There are also ornamental grasses that can be used to cover areas where the usual ones would be unsatisfactory or boring. There are sea grasses you can use to bind your dunes, hummocky grasses you can plant under your heavy shade trees, and lawn grasses in colors other than "grass green." You can use large and medium-size grasses the way you would use shrubs, as hedges or specimen plants. Many of them will mingle well with annuals and perennials in an herbaceous border as foils or accent plants, and have been used this way for many years in England. Grasses can be grown for their flowers, which are handsome, varied and perfect for dried win-

Though this grass border at Kew has more grass than you might want in your garden, it shows the many foliage contrasts that can be achieved.

ter arrangements. The annual grasses have particularly elaborate and showy ones; their flowers are their sole means of propagation, and must therefore work harder.

What about a garden that is composed only of grasses? Some people feel that grasses massed together look too busy or overwhelming. But on a small scale, and with judicious choices, you can construct a very attractive grass garden that will be perfect for certain situations. Grass has a pure, abstract quality that blends well with modern architecture, for instance. A grass garden usually looks best not surrounded by other foliage, but combined with wood, stone and other hard structural surfaces. The soft, intricate forms of the grasses, the variety in the flower and foliage shapes and the subtle gradations of color will be a welcome contrast. Each grass will be an accent plant in itself.

The grass family, or *Gramineae (Poaceae)*, is a mixture of simplicity and complexity. A grass plant looks simple compared with an orchid or a rose bush, and in fact it has evolved to a marvelously efficient state. It does not need the large, showy, colorful flowers that many plants use to attract insects, because it is wind-pollinated. (Some grasses are even self-pollinating.) All a grass plant needs to do in life is wave in the breeze. These flowers, on the other hand, have their own complexity—parts within tiny parts, and specific hours of the day during which they can be fertilized. The grass family, furthermore, is huge and contains many species, among them most of the world's food supply.

PARTS OF A GRASS

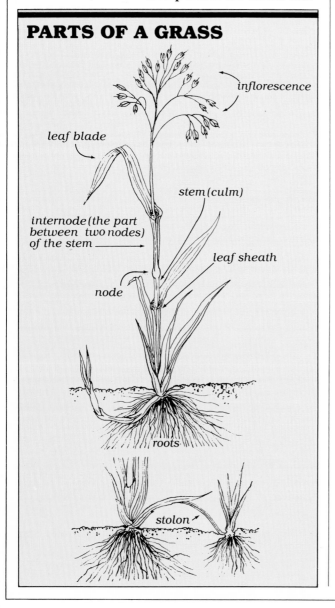

inflorescence

leaf blade

stem (culm)

internode (the part between two nodes) of the stem

leaf sheath

node

roots

stolon

To identify the various grasses and to study their functions often requires a magnifying glass and patience. Some parts of a typical grass plant are shown in the box opposite.

What distinguishes a grass from other plants? All grasses have several characteristics in common: lance-shaped leaves with parallel veins; round, hollow stems; branching roots, never a taproot. Many spread by rhizomes (underground stems) or stolons (horizontal stems just above or just below the ground that creep, then root at the nodes). Within the grass family there is great variation. Some grasses are enormous and treelike, such as the bamboos. Others are soft mats on the ground. Grasses are classified as mounded, upright, arching, open, irregular and combinations of these. They exhibit many different textures and colors in their leaves. The flowers also vary greatly—and beautifully—lacy panicles, stiff brushes, waving plumes. There are also many plants that look like grasses—sedges and rushes, for instance—that are often included in grass gardens.

Every year, more ornamental grasses seem to be available commercially as the interest in them grows. The ones included in this chapter are all sold by some mail order nurseries, and there are more varieties you can buy from the firms that specialize in grasses. You can also, of course, exchange plants and seeds with other ornamental grass enthusiasts.

PLAN OF THE GARDEN

The trick, as with any garden, is to combine a group of plants that not only will look good together but will grow well together. They must share enough of the same requirements so that they can coexist in harmony. For this garden you must exclude certain avid creepers, like the old favorite "gardener's-garters" (*Phalaris arundinacea* 'Picta'), unless you can contain them. You must also reach a compromise on soil and light. A real grass buff could have what would amount to four separate grass gardens: sunny and dry, sunny and wet, shady and dry, shady and wet. But for most of us it is best to pick a location that is well drained and has sun for most of the day, since most grasses prefer or will adapt

This grass garden in Baltimore, designed by Wolfgang Oehme, shows ornamental grasses well adapted to a domestic landscaping situation.

to these conditions. The soil should be kept moist in hot weather by watering and by using a mulch. While some grasses like to have their roots actually standing in water, most do not require it.

The garden I have in mind is composed of seven grasses. The largest, zebra grass, may grow eight feet tall. Maiden grass and switch grass may grow almost as tall. Northern sea oats is a medium-height plant, though its flower stalks sometimes reach four feet. The broad mound shape of fountain grass, in the midborder, contrasts with the upright grasses. Molinia is a fairly low mound with upright-arching spikes, and blue fescue is a low, dense mound. These last two make up the foreground. The seven grasses are grouped within a semicircular area, neatly bordered.

There is as much variation in color in the garden as there is in height. Two have striking yellow-and-green variegation: zebra grass with its horizontal bands and molinia with its vertical stripes. Fountain grass and switch grass have medium green foliage; maiden's is a lighter, bluer green; northern sea oats' is a darker green; and blue fescue's is very blue indeed. Blue fescue and molinia have fine-textured foliage. Maiden grass is fine and gracefully wavy, hence the name. Northern sea oats' leaves are fairly broad. All have interesting flowers, especially fountain grass's coppery brushes, zebra's yellow ostrich plumes, the rich brown nuggets of northern sea oats, and the feathery purple haze of switch grass. All these are properly called "inflorescences," that is, groups or

THE GRASS GARDEN

clusters of many tiny flowers. Most of them will appear from August into fall, but molinia and blue fescue start blooming in June. The fall foliage of these grasses is also very striking: the switch grass and fountain grass turn yellow, the zebra grass becomes orange-brown, maiden grass and molinia change to light brown, and blue fescue remains gloriously blue all year round.

SITE

Choose a sunny location where there is no standing water. If drainage is poor, provide a bed of crushed stone, then add your topsoil mix. A bed that is slightly raised would also contribute to better drainage; it will be easy to tend, and will help to set the bed off as a focal point. In deciding what the soil should be like, bear in mind that zebra grass, maiden grass and northern sea oats dislike dry, sandy soil and prefer soil with plenty of humus. Switch grass and blue fescue like dry, sandy soil. Compromise by adding both soil and humus in equal parts with average garden loam. Avoid clay. Molinia dislikes lime, but a soil of average pH will suit the garden as a whole, as will an average degree of fertility.

All these grasses prefer sun, except northern sea oats, which likes full or partial shade. In full sun it will not have its normally dark color, nor will it grow as tall. However, great height is not required of it in this mid-border setting, and the grasses massed around it will lend it a little shade. Its flowers will be no less effective in sun. They are a good accent, since they have a less feathery quality than those around them.

Fountain grass (Pennisetum alopecuroides) *growing in Washington, D.C.*

It would be best to place this "grass composition" against a dark background, the better to show off the various leaves and flowers. A high wall, fence or hedge will accomplish this, and will also protect the taller grasses from wind. While many treatments are possible, the garden shown here makes use of a dark wooden fence and a gray flagstone terrace. The bed is raised about a foot, with a retaining wall of gray stone. Lay the terrace and the wall in a bed of sand, as for the brick terrace in the Secret Garden (see box on p. 165). Make sure the stones in the terrace are level by stepping on the corners to see if they rock back and forth. The "wall" is really nothing more than one course of natural or cut stone, of a type that will match the stone of the terrace. A dark mulch of shredded bark or leaf mold adds to the dark frame effect and retains moisture and deters weeds as well. The bed could also be placed against a wood or stone building, but remember, if planted in front of a window, the view might be blocked.

GROWING INSTRUCTIONS

While all grasses can be grown from seed, it takes two years or more to have sizable plants. It is much faster to grow started plants from a nursery, potted or bare-root, or small clumps you have obtained from a friend who is dividing mature ones. A good philosophy to have about this garden is to see each plant as an isolated specimen, chosen for itself, even though they are planted in a group. It would be better to have the bed be a little sparse, with dark mulch visible between the clumps to show off the form of each plant, than to have a tightly massed effect. Start with one of each variety, except for the two smallest, molinia and blue fescue. Keep the plot free of weeds to make each plant more visible.

Spring planting is preferable for most grasses. If you are adding more soil to the bed, do it in fall. (You can do this in early spring, then let the soil settle for a few weeks.) Set out your plants, firming the soil around them and watering-in thoroughly. Bone meal will be adequate fertilizer for planting, and a little 5-10-5 each year thereafter.

All these grasses will need to be divided occasionally, some more often than others.

FENCE

1 switch grass

1 zebra grass

1 maiden grass

1 fountain grass

1 northern sea oats

6 molinia

7 blue fescue

PLAN OF THE GRASS GARDEN (SUMMER) ⅜″ = 1′

FLAGSTONE TERRACE

THE GARDEN IN FALL

There are two things to watch for: if a clump looks dead in the center, it needs to have this center removed and the fresh growth broken into smaller clumps and replanted. Or if the plant is growing to the point where it is crowding its neighbors—even if only by its arching foliage—it is time to break it up. Dividing should be done just as the new growth is appearing. This way you will be able to see the new growth, but since the shoots are small there will be little risk of having them wilt during replanting.

In the fall, leave the foliage alone, cutting the flowers only if you want to dry them. How long you leave the foliage on in winter depends on how tidy you want the plot to look. You may want to cut back some of the messier ones early in winter. Most people leave the flower heads on for winter interest until it is time to clear away all the debris in spring. If you do dry the flowers, use the same techniques described for the Gray Garden (see p. 134), except that you may want to dry some of them upright in a vase, to arch the stems. Choose a cool room to prevent the flowers from going to seed.

ADDITIONS AND SUBSTITUTIONS

Here are some other fairly well-known grasses that would look good in this garden: tufted hair grass (*Deschampsia caespitosa*) and feather grass (*Stipa pennata*) for the midborder; plume grass (*Erianthus ravennae*), cord grass (*Spartina pectinata*) and reed grass (*Calamagrostis epigejos*) for the background; for the foreground, bulbous oat grass (*Arrhenatherum elatius variegatum*) or two very good sedges—the variegated Japanese sedge grass (*Carex morrowii*) and the lovely reddish brown leatherleaf sedge grass (*C. buchananii*).

You could also sow a few annual grasses toward the front of the bed, and try a different one each year, especially if you want to experiment with flower drying. Some attractive ones to dry are hare's-tail grass (the *Lagurus* species), the love grasses (*Eragrostis* species), Job's tears (*Coix lacryma-Jobi*), cloud grass (*Agrostis nebulosa*), feather top (*Pennisetum villosum*) and golden top (*Lamarckia aurea*). You could even grow some stalks of ornamental corn (*Zea mays gracillima* 'Variegata'), as annuals, in the background. There are also a great many grasses available for water or bog gardens, and others that are suited to shaded, woodsy situations.

The seven shown here are all hardy through zone 5. In warmer places you can grow some fine grasses as perennials that are not hardy in the North, such as pampas grass (*Cortaderia selloana*), lemon grass (*Cymbopogon citratus*) and crimson fountain grass (*Pennisetum setaceum*, also called *P. ruppelii*). Find out if any local nurseries in your area sell grasses, or would like to.

PLANT LIST FOR GRASS GARDEN

FESCUE, BLUE. *Festuca caesia* (*F. ovina glauca*). Zones 3–9. This is the dwarf variety, which grows 6–12 inches tall, usually 8. Tufted mounds of fine-textured evergreen foliage are usually silver-blue, though there are variants. Small green-beige flowers in June and July. Prefers a cool climate, full sun, dry and sandy soil, no clay. Plant about a foot apart. Cut back in spring and midsummer as needed for fresh blue growth. Divide every few years in spring or fall.

FOUNTAIN GRASS. *Pennisetum alopecuroides*. Zone 5. Grows 2–4 feet, usually 3. Large mound of bright green, medium-fine foliage. Yellow or beige in fall. Reddish brown flowers in August–October; pick early for drying, or the flowers will fall. Likes full sun or part shade, fertile soil, shelter from wind. Divide occasionally and cut back in winter if messy.

MAIDEN GRASS. *Miscanthus sinensis* 'Gracillimus.' Zone 4. Grows 3–8 feet, usually 4. Long, narrow, light silvery-green leaves, upright-arching and curling gracefully at tips. Flowers also curly and silvery, from October to following spring. Likes full sun and fertile soil. Divide as needed.

MOLINIA (PURPLE MOOR GRASS). *Molinia caerulea* 'Variegata.' Zone 5. Grows 1–2 feet, in a tidy mound. Striped yellow and green fine-textured leaves. Small purplish flowers from June on. Tolerates some shade and damp, even wet soil, but fairly fertile and without lime. Stays in tufts; divide occasionally.

NORTHERN SEA OATS. *Chasmanthium latifolium* (*Uniola latifolia*). Zone 5.

Grows 3–5 feet, usually 3. Upright form with medium-broad rich green leaves. Bronze-colored flowers on tall, very thin stems in August, lasting into winter, good for drying. Prefers some shade and fertile, well-drained soil, humus, shelter from wind. Spreads slowly; divide as needed.

SWITCH GRASS. *Panicum virgatum*. Zone 5. Narrow, upright grass that stands up to 6 feet when in flower. Green, medium-textured foliage with many airy flowers that appear in September and last a long time. Yellow fall color. Prefers light, sandy soil and full sun; no clay. Slow to spread; divide when needed.

ZEBRA GRASS. *Miscanthus sinensis* 'Zebrinus.' Zone 5. Upright clump, 4–8 feet tall. Leaves medium texture, green with horizontal bands of yellow, orange in fall. Remove shoots without yellow variegation. Large, showy russet flowers in September that fade to grayish but remain on the plant all winter. Likes sun; growth is weak in shade, especially in fertile soil. Likes moisture. Divide when crowded.

A Victorian Garden

The Victorian era was one of the great ages of gardening. This might come as a surprise to those who think that all the Victorians did was plant jungles in their drawing rooms and stiff little formal beds of flowers outside their houses.

Indeed, there were such beds—stingy efforts at flower gardens dotted amid spacious lawns and stately trees, or winding borders "bedded out" with thousands of cannas, all of the same violent scarlet. But the Victorians, as we know, indulged themselves secretly in many aspects of their lives, and gardening was one of them.

Beyond their great imposing lawns were often more casual yards, and at the rear of these there were sometimes flower gardens, even great sprawling ones. Little paths meandered through informal plantings of shrubbery, leading to arbors and bowers formed by trees; hiding in the seductive shadows one could find little seats of cast iron or rustic wood, or summerhouses and gazebos smothered in fragrant vines.

Victorians took their gardening seriously. It was an age of scientific discoveries, new technologies and forays into exotic lands; all these had an influence on gardening. With a fervor typical of the age, plant hunters scaled peaks and plunged into jungles in search of exotic species. New techniques such as hybridization took hold with something close to mania. Great hothouses and conservatories were built on a scale previously reserved for railway terminals and cathedrals. Not the least of these innovations was the mechanical lawn mower, which made the modern lawn possible and established a pattern of male weekend behavior that is unchanged a century later.

The concept of suburbia was born in the Victorian period. City businessmen began living in rural areas, and they erected enormous, extravagant houses that stood as monuments to their owners' wealth. The great English "landscape" style of gardening of the eighteenth century had lost favor in England, largely because of the inroads of urbanization. Instead of great sweeping "vistas" across parklike grounds or fields, gentlemen now valued their "lines of sight" across lawns of an acre or two, ending in a belt of choice shrubs placed with artful casualness to hide their neighbors' property. People sought and prized land not for farming but simply as a pleasant surrounding to be enjoyed for its own sake. But the grand style had never taken hold very strongly in the United States in the first place; American gardens moved from the essentially Renaissance type of the Colonial period to the Victorian style without much of a transition.

Victorian gardens, however, were really a collection of styles. The "picturesque" style—with its grottoes and bowers—as espoused by American author Andrew Jackson Downing, was a more intimate version of the "landscape" school. This was followed by the "gardenesque" period, in which the flower bed regained its lost legitimacy. The mid-nineteenth century saw a fever of "bedding-out," which was, by an 1885 definition, "the temporary placing out of doors of greenhouse and other tender plants, during the summer months." Often a succession of bedding plants—spring, summer and fall—were planted by the thousands, either a single variety or several in contrasting colors to form elaborate designs or pictures. A special expression of this, called "carpet bedding," involved creating often intricate patterns with very low plants or plants that could be kept low by shearing. Carpet beds were often tilted

A bench nestled in a glade of ferns, among them Nephrolepis cordifolia, *in a California garden.*

toward the viewer, by grading, to be admired the way one would admire a painting or a lacquered tray. Other formal beds were nothing more than little circles with concentric rings of several contrasting flowers, and something rather tropical-looking in the center, trailing out of an urn. Often they were hideous; sometimes they were charming. At the same time, there was much borrowing of styles from other countries, such as Italy, France and Japan. Tasteful gardeners kept to one style, the one that they thought went best with the architecture of their home, and taste was considered all-important.

Toward the end of the nineteenth century, there was yet another option. Led by two great gardening eccentrics of that eccentric era—William Robinson and Gertrude Jekyll—gardeners could renounce "bedding-out" forever in favor of deep herbaceous borders, inspired by the cottage gardens of rural England. The colorful romantic sprawl of these country gardens was turned into an art by Robinson and by Jekyll, and theirs is the style we still practice today, usually in less elaborate scope, when we plan most of our perennial gardens.

The garden I have suggested here is a flower border. In its depth and informality, and its use of foliage plants, it is like a Gertrude Jekyll garden, but several other Victorian elements have been introduced: the arabesque shape, and a tiny enclosure hidden by tall zebra grass and ferns that is reached by way of a mown path that extends from the lawn into and through the border. Inside the enclosure is a bench on which one can sit, smell the flowers, watch the butterflies and not be seen. This garden can be appreciated from several angles: head-on, from either side or from inside the enclosure. At the rear is a grouping of evergreens.

PLAN OF THE GARDEN

The color scheme is blue, yellow, white and green and extends to the foliage plants as well as the flowers. These foliage plants make the garden more interesting than the average border, and help it to look attractive throughout the growing season, much the way annuals do. If well maintained, there should be no time, from spring to fall, when the garden

In the same California garden an ivy-covered gazebo. The lawn is composed of Laurentia fluviatilis.

does not look pretty.

Blue is one of the most difficult colors to sustain in a border. Few of the mainstay perennials are blue, and few blue flowers are long-blooming, so other colors are usually added, as they are here.

The blue in this border begins with hyacinths in April and May. (If you want some more blue in May you can fill in with Siberian iris.) The early summer bloomers follow: Japanese iris, false indigo, *Veronica incana*, delphiniums, flax, scabiosa and the annuals: lobelia and ageratum. The scabiosa and lobelia will continue through the summer, joined by the monkshood in late summer. If you want more midsummer blue, plant some balloonflower (*Platycodon*). Toward the end of the summer, the delphiniums will start to rebloom if you have cut them back properly. Fall will bring blue or purple asters at the back of the border. For blue foliage, you will have 'Boulevard' false cypress, 'Skyrocket' junipers and the rich blue-green of *Hosta sieboldiana*.

Yellow, unlike blue, is easy to keep going in a garden. Many yellow flowers are free-blooming, long-blooming, spreading and vigorous. In this garden we begin with the dainty species daffodils (though any of your favorite yellow or white narcissus would be lovely), followed by the June-flowering lemon lily and joined by the indomitable coreopsis, oenothera and woolly yarrow. From late June onward the heliopsis will brighten the back of

THE VICTORIAN GARDEN

PLAN OF THE VICTORIAN GARDEN (SUMMER) ³⁄₈″ = 1′

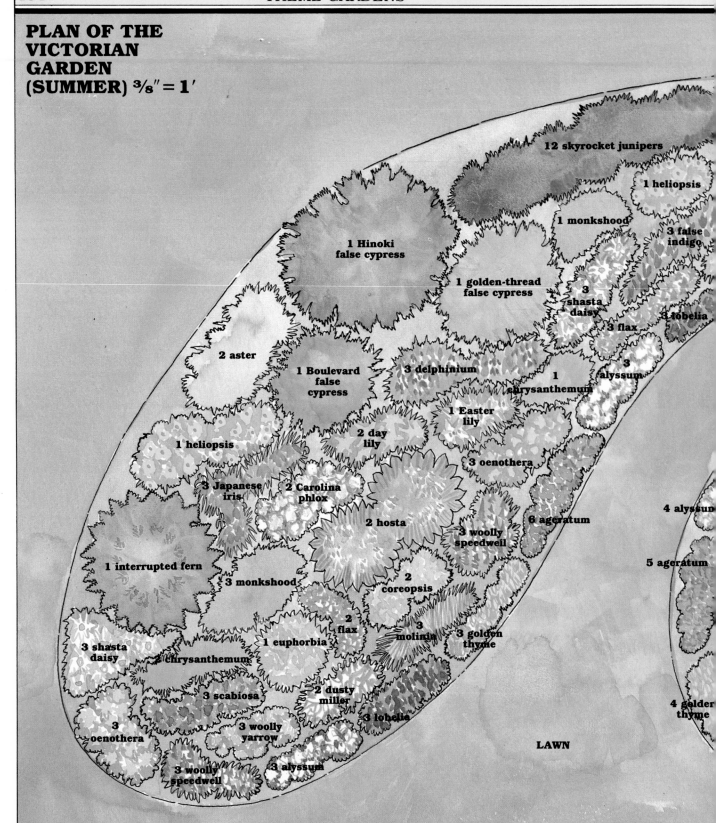

12 skyrocket junipers

1 heliopsis

1 monkshood

3 false indigo

1 Hinoki false cypress

1 golden-thread false cypress

3 shasta daisy

3 flax

3 lobelia

2 aster

1 Boulevard false cypress

3 delphinium

3 alyssum

1 chrysanthemum

1 Easter lily

1 heliopsis

2 day lily

3 oenothera

3 Japanese iris

2 Carolina phlox

2 hosta

3 woolly speedwell

6 ageratum

4 alyssum

1 interrupted fern

3 monkshood

2 coreopsis

5 ageratum

2 flax

3 molinia

3 golden thyme

1 euphorbia

3 shasta daisy

2 chrysanthemum

3 scabiosa

2 dusty miller

3 lobelia

4 gelder thyme

3 oenothera

3 woolly yarrow

LAWN

3 woolly speedwell

3 alyssum

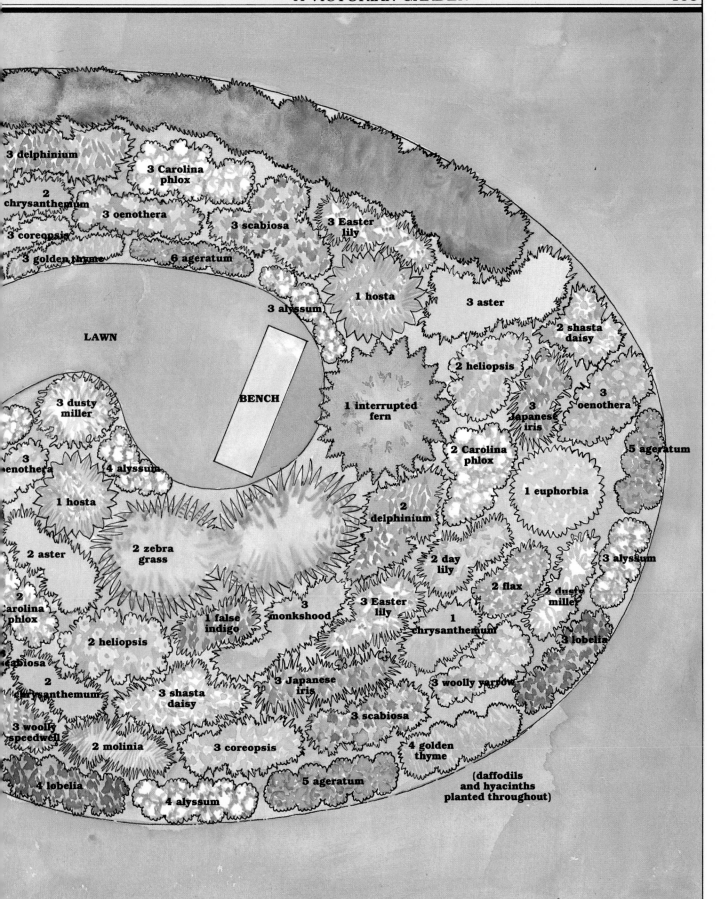

3 delphinium

3 Carolina
phlox

2
chrysanthemum

3 oenothera

3 coreopsis

3 scabiosa

3 Easter
lily

3 golden thyme

6 ageratum

3 aster

3 alyssum

1 hosta

2 shasta
daisy

LAWN

2 heliopsis

3
oenothera

3
Japanese
iris

3 dusty
miller

1 interrupted
fern

BENCH

2 Carolina
phlox

5 ageratum

3
oenothera

4 alyssum

1 euphorbia

1 hosta

2 delphinium

3 alyssum

2 aster

2 zebra
grass

2 day
lily

2 flax

2 dusty
miller

2
Carolina
phlox

2 heliopsis

1 false
indigo

3
monkshood

3 Easter
lily

1
chrysanthemum

3 lobelia

scabiosa

3 Japanese
iris

3 woolly yarrow

2
chrysanthemum

3 shasta
daisy

3 scabiosa

3 woolly
speedwell

2 molinia

3 coreopsis

4 golden
thyme

4 lobelia

4 alyssum

5 ageratum

(daffodils
and hyacinths
planted throughout)

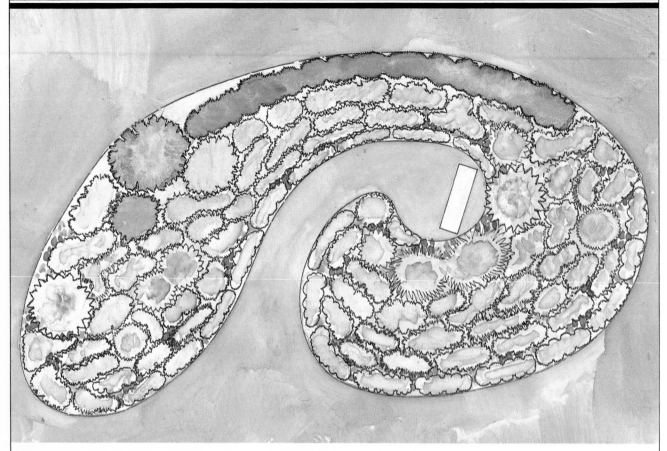

THE GARDEN IN EARLY SPRING

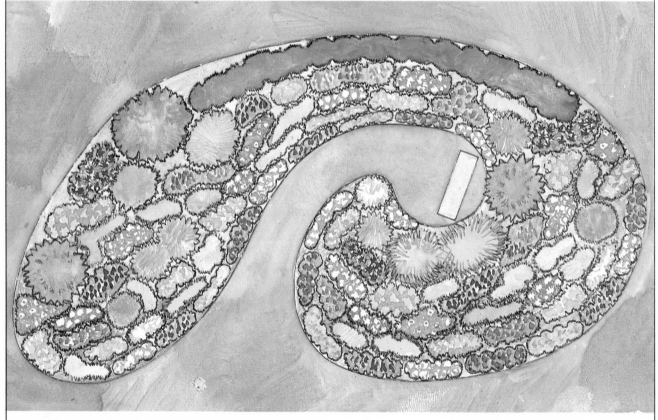

THE GARDEN IN EARLY FALL

EDGING A BED

Fig. 1   Fig. 2

Mark off straight lines with string tied to wooden stakes. With a square spade, make sharp cuts about 4 inches deep at an angle in a smooth, continuous line, pushing sod toward the inside of the bed. For curved lines, lay down a garden hose or thick rope (Fig. 2) and make similar cuts.

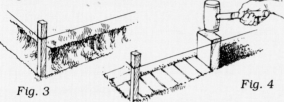

Fig. 3   Fig. 4

For a brick edging, dig a trench slightly wider and several inches deeper than the length of the bricks. With marking string still in place, shovel some loose sand into the bottom of the trench. Lay bricks vertically, as shown, using the string as a guide. Tamp bricks with a mallet so the tops are flush with the surface of the ground, adjusting sand as needed. Fill the trench with sand, tamping carefully around bricks. Laying bricks flat is more economical but less stable. When bricks are laid, you will have a smooth, firm surface on which you can run one wheel of your lawn mower.

Fig. 5

Lay a flagstone edging in the same manner, as above, adjusting the amount of sand under the flagstones and standing on the corners to see whether they rock. Add or remove sand until they are stable.

Fig. 6

For a metal edging, dig a narrow trench deep enough to accommodate a metal edging strip. Lay strip so that the top projects only slightly above ground level, then fill the trench with soil.

Fig. 7

Lay railroad ties in a sand-filled trench so that the tops are just slightly above soil level. The corners can be joined together with metal spikes for extra stability.

the border, lasting well into fall. In addition there is euphorbia, which is really a foliage plant, but its clusters of yellow bracts in late May and early summer resemble flowers. Yellow foliage also shows in the golden thyme, molinia, the yellow-striped zebra grass, and the golden-thread false cypress in the shrub grouping.

For whites, grow white hyacinths and/ or narcissus, followed by Shasta daisies, white Carolina phlox and alyssum. The phlox will bloom all summer, up to the point where white chrysanthemums are ready. White foliage plants include dusty miller (Cineraria maritima) and the leaves of Veronica incana and woolly yarrow.

Finally, there are two green plants for foliage accent, the rich dark green Hinoki cypress, with its lacy needles, and several interrupted ferns. This large fern does well in a border because it does not spread egregiously and does not mind sun. In this situation it also acts as a barrier. When the fern and zebra grass are mature, in midsummer they will hide anyone sitting inside the little enclosure. Ferns were very popular with the Victorians. Indoors or out, they gratified the Victorian wish always to be surrounded—decorously, of course—with forest.

SITE

This garden is too private and informal to be planted in the front of the house. It would be appropriate behind the house or in a side yard. The tall evergreens in the back of the garden could be used as a screen, as the Victorians did, to hide areas where utilitarian work was done.

Wherever you plant this garden it should receive sun for at least six hours a day. A southern exposure would be ideal. Many of the plants here need moist soil, so the garden should not be placed where the soil is characteristically dry, unless you can compensate well for this by mulch and frequent watering. On the other hand, there are plants here, the white-leafed ones especially, that will protest if the soil is too wet, so aim for the average. If wind might be a problem when growing tall plants such as delphiniums or asters, place the garden in such a way that the tall junipers shield it from the prevailing winds.

GROWING INSTRUCTIONS

This bed can be laid out in the fall. If you are doing it in early fall, all the evergreens can be planted too. You would do well to enrich the soil with bulk organic material such as rotted manure, compost, peat moss or commercial humus. Aim for average fertility and an average pH. Then let the garden settle until spring. If the bed is already established, or you are eager to begin in fall, the following can also be planted at that time: veronica, coreopsis, Easter lilies, Japanese iris, yarrow, ferns, hostas, phlox, day lilies and heliopsis. The rest should wait till spring. The whole garden can be planted in spring if you prefer.

Most of the plants should be purchased as started plants or obtained from friends' or your own divisions, but you can grow the annuals from seed, especially alyssum. Among the perennials, scabiosa, flax and Shasta daisies can be sown in summer, and asters in the fall for bloom the following year. The evergreens are not difficult to find in nurseries, though you will probably not be able to buy them in very large sizes, even if you can afford to do so. But they will look good in the border even when they are only two or three feet high, just as do dwarf evergreens. The taller perennials will hide them by midsummer, but they will lend interest to the garden before these others make a show, and in the cold months when nothing is blooming. Prune them as indicated in the plant list, keeping them to a size that harmonizes with the scale of the garden as a whole.

This is quite a large garden, and one that will not look good without maintenance—reduce the weed problem by mulching heavily in the back of the border and around the evergreens. All the perennials there appreciate moisture, and there are large spaces between the plants where grass and weeds could take over. Mulch more lightly in front, especially in places where you expect self-sowing or where you will be growing from seed. Also mulch lightly around the very low-growing plants and the ones with white foliage. The taller plants will need staking with brush or stakes. Many of the plants in this garden require deadheading and/or pinching back (see illustrations, p. 22) back for bushy

plants or repeated bloom, especially delphinium, shasta daisies, coreopsis, false indigo, chrysanthemums and Carolina phlox. The following particularly need water in hot, dry weather: hosta, Carolina phlox, chrysanthemums, heliopsis, asters, monkshood and Japanese iris. The same applies to the evergreens, especially in the first few years of growth.

Since the bed borders a lawn, which is actually incorporated into the bed itself, the grass must be kept tidy and edged after mowing. A strip of brick or narrow flagstones between the bed and the lawn will make mowing easier.

ADDITIONS AND SUBSTITUTIONS

Remember, there are all kinds of Victorian gardens. Pick what you like best about the period. Many nineteenth-century houses have a circular drive leading up to a dignified façade, and a spacious lawn in which stand some fine old trees, probably planted at the

This bedding pattern near the Bridge of Flowers in Shelburne Falls, Massachusetts, is simpler and more appropriate to a home setting. Here the centerpiece is a modest pedestal.

time the house was built. Along the drive you could bed out some annuals or foliage plants in a tidy pattern for an appropriate accent. Formal beds would also look good at the side of the house—in view of a parlor window, perhaps. Shrubs should be in naturalistic groups, not rows, and paths can wind through them or through whatever woods you may have on your property. Period ornamentation can be used for everything from major structures such as gazebos and follies to benches, fountains, statuary, birdbaths, urns and even wire edgings for beds. Rustic window boxes would also be appropriate. But don't overdo this, as the Victorians sometimes did, unless the cluttered look is what you particularly love about that period.

If the garden I've planned here seems too ambitious for you, you could scale it down simply by putting fewer plants in each clump. Just be sure that when you create your secret enclosure you allow enough space for two people to sit comfortably. You want them to feel cozy in there but not claustrophobic.

If you want to add different plants you can easily do so without enlarging the garden. Many flowers have been repeated several times, for the sake of harmony, but here and there you can certainly add a new plant instead of repeating one. You can add many spring bulbs; the less familiar Roman hyacinths would be dainty and unusual mixed in with the species daffodils. Any variety of blue salvia would be a fine addition. So would balloonflower *(Platycodon)*, trollius, lavender, yucca, white or yellow tulips, white or yellow foxgloves, lavender cotton *(Santolina chamaecyparissus)*, the artemisias, other asters such as 'Frikartii,' other veronicas, lilies and delphinium, any of the campanulas, anchusa, feverfew, white or yellow dahlias, blue and white petunias, verbena, white geraniums, old-fashioned fragrant white nicotiana, blue lobelia *(Lobelia siphilitica)*, white peonies and yellow marigolds. Instead of heliopsis you could substitute the old-fashioned double *Rudbeckia laciniata,* 'Hortensia' (golden glow). You can plant another 'dusty miller' similar to the one suggested, but with blue flowers *(Centaurea rutifolia)*, or snow-in-summer *(Cerastium tomentosum)*. You can add any iris—Siberian,

This richly patterned carpet of flowers in Rotterdam, Holland, is a good example of "bedding-out." The tall fern is a typical Victorian centerpiece.

bearded, crested or the Florentine iris *(Iris germanica florentina)*, which the Victorians called orris root and used extensively for face powders and fixatives. Blue fescue would be a fine accent, or some of the hostas that have white or yellow variegation.

Caryopteris, a shrub that bears blue flowers late in the season, would look good right in the border, as would a small blue hydrangea *(Hydrangea macrophylla* 'Nikko Blue'). Victorian shrubs that would be attractive in the vicinity of this garden are forsythia, mock orange *(Philadelphus* species) and any of the larger hydrangeas. There were many popular Victorian trees: ailanthus, paulownia, cedar of Lebanon, Atlas cedar, Norway spruce, weeping willow and flowering almond to name a few. Victorians especially admired pointed trees, because they went well with the points and spires in their architecture.

If you live in a warm climate you can grow most of the plants suggested, but you might want to add some palms and bamboos in the border or off to the sides, perhaps in place of the ferns. They will lend the tropical look so prized by the Victorians, but difficult to achieve in the North except in the greenhouses, conservatories and "crystal palaces" that affluent Victorians delighted in building. Substitutions among the evergreens might include *Juniperus squamata* 'Meyeri' instead of 'Boulevard' false cypress, and one of the columnar *Juniperus scopulorum* varieties such as 'Pathfinder,' 'Blue Heaven' or 'Grey Gleam' instead of the 'Skyrocket' juniper, especially if you live in the West.

While most of the plants in this garden are authentically of the period, you need not be limited by this idea. Instead, be guided by the *tastes* of those times, which often swung from extremes of formality and stiffness to excesses of lushness and variety. Victorian gardeners always had an eye out for the unusual, both in the choice of plants and in the way they combined them. They were playful and full of imagination—perhaps their greatest contribution.

PLANT LIST FOR VICTORIAN GARDEN

ANNUALS

AGERATUM. *Ageratum houstonianum.* Choose one of the dwarf varieties, which grow about 6 inches tall, with a compact globe shape and fluffy, buttonlike, lavender-blue flowers. Rather slow to get started. You may sow seeds indoors or buy started plants and set out as early as frost conditions permit.

ALYSSUM, SWEET. *Lobularia maritima.* White variety. Grows 4–6 inches tall and blooms from late spring to frost. Tiny fragrant blossoms make a carpet. Easily grown from seed by sowing in ground in early spring or starting indoors. Can be transplanted to fill in gaps. Cut back for lusher recurrent bloom. Often self-sows.

DUSTY MILLER. *Cineraria maritima (Senecio cineraria).* Perennial in zones 9–10. Usually about a foot tall, with stark white woolly foliage. Start seeds indoors very

early, or buy nursery-grown plants.

LOBELIA, EDGING. *Lobelia erinus* 'Crystal Palace Compacta,' or another good blue variety. This one is an intense deep blue. Likes moist, rich soil. Start seeds indoors in February and set out after last frost, or buy started plants.

BULBS

DAFFODIL. *Narcissus* species. In zones 4–5 plant angel's tears (*N. triandrus*) and dwarf daffodil (*N. pseudonarcissus minimus*). In zones 6–10 add hoop-petticoat daffodil (*N. bulbocodium*), rushleafed daffodil (*N. juncifolius*) and others. These are all small-flowered plants, 3–8 inches tall; the flowers are yellow or white. Plant in late summer or early fall, 3 inches deep and 5 inches apart, with bone meal.

HYACINTH. *Hyacinthus orientalis.* Zones 4–10. The familiar large-flowered kind, 8–

12 inches high, in shades of blue and white. Plant in fall, 6 inches apart and 5 inches deep. Division not necessary.

LILY, EASTER. *Lilium longiflorum.* Zones 3–10. Grows 2–3 feet tall, and bears fragrant white trumpets in July. Plant in spring or fall, 6 inches deep, in very well-drained soil.

FOLIAGE PLANTS

EUPHORBIA (SPURGE). *Euphorbia epithymoides.* Zones 3–9. Grows 12–15 inches tall. Bushy plant, often 2 feet wide. Clusters of yellow flowerlike bracts in late May and early summer. Foliage turns reddish bronze in fall. Prefers dry, well-drained soil, and sun. Plant at least 2 feet apart.

FERN, INTERRUPTED. *Osmunda claytoniana.* Zones 3–8. Grows up to 5 feet tall in a vase-shaped clump. Fiddleheads covered with white hairs appear in early spring. Short, fertile leaflets covered with brown spores are produced in the middle of the fronds, "interrupting" the pairs of large green sterile leaflets. Likes acid soil (pH 5.5–6.5) lightened with leaf mold and/or sand if your soil is heavy. Can be

propagated by division, but you rarely need to disturb the clump, as it is not fast-spreading.

HOSTA (FUNKIA). *Hosta sieboldiana (H. glauca).* Zones 3–9. Grows about 2 feet tall, and as broad, with huge blue-green striped leaves. Lavender flowers in midsummer on short stalks. Likes moist soil, enriched and lightened with organic matter such as compost or leaf mold. Does best in light shade but tolerates full sun if ground is kept moist with mulch. Plant at least 2 feet apart and divide clumps if necessary in early spring before the leaves are large.

MOLINIA (PURPLE MOOR GRASS). *Molinia caerulea* 'Variegata.' To zone 5. Grows in a tidy mound, 1–2 feet high. Striped yellow and green, fine-textured leaves. Small purplish flowers from June on. Tolerates some shade and damp—even wet—soil, but it should be fairly fertile and without lime. Stays in tufts; divide occasionally.

THYME, GOLDEN. *Thymus serpyllum aureum.* Zones 3–9. There are several yellow-leafed thymes, all of which would be suitable here. This one forms a low, aromatic mat and bears lavender flowers in June that will look good in this garden. Likes sun and well-drained soil. You can sow seed, indoors or out, but growth is slow. A better idea is to grow mats of it somewhere and divide in spring whenever you need some.

ZEBRA GRASS. *Miscanthus sinensis* 'Zebrinus.' To zone 5. 4–8 feet tall. Leaves medium texture, green with horizontal bands of yellow, orange in fall. Remove shoots without yellow variegation. Large, showy russet flowers in September that fade to grayish but remain on the plant all winter. Likes sun; growth is weak in shade, especially in fertile soil. Likes moisture. Divide when crowded.

PERENNIALS

ASTER, NEW ENGLAND. (*Aster novae-angliae*) or **NEW YORK.** (*A. novae-belgii*). Tall purple or blue shades of horticultural varieties or the native species. Zones 5–9. Most varieties grow 3–4 feet tall;

stake in this border. They like plenty of sun, moisture. Bloom is in late summer and fall. To keep clumps vigorous, divide in early spring, discarding center of clump and replanting young shoots.

CHRYSANTHEMUM (HARDY CHRYSANTHEMUM). *Chrysanthemum morifolium.* Zones 4–10. Choose one of the white decorative varieties (the common, tall, large-flowered type). Grows 1½–3 feet tall, blooms August–October. Likes sun, rich well-drained soil lightened with humus and cultivation. Pinch the terminal shoots until mid-July to encourage branching. Some gardeners winter their chrysanthemums in a cold frame and start new plants in early spring by removing stolons with new growth on them and replanting. Others buy new plants each spring (they are inexpensive). Others, by pinching, mulching and good care, keep their clumps going for several years before they lose their vigor.

COREOPSIS (TICKSEED). *Coreopsis grandiflora* or *C. lanceolata.* Zones 4–10.

Grows up to 2½ feet tall. Blooms bright yellow most of the summer if spent blooms are removed. Likes sun, well-drained soil. Spreads and self-sows readily. Divide in spring or fall.

DAY LILY (LEMON LILY). *Hemerocallis liliosphodelus.* Zones 3–9. Fragrant yellow species, blooming in late spring. Or plant a later-blooming fragrant yellow, such as 'Hyperion.' Easy to grow, but divide clumps when they become dense, about every 4 years.

DELPHINIUM, GARLAND. *Delphinium* 'Belladonna' (light blue) or 'Bellamosa' (rich blue). Zones 3–7. *D.* 'Connecticut Yankee' would also be a good choice. Grows 3–5 feet tall, blooms in June and July and again in late summer or fall if you cut the spent blooms. When new growth starts, cut the old stem off close to the ground, fertilizing and watering thoroughly. Delphiniums respond well to good treatment: scratch about half a handful of lime and the same amount of 5-10-5 into the soil around each plant in early spring and several times during the summer. Stake delphiniums to prevent damage by wind.

FALSE INDIGO. *Baptisia australis.* Zones 3–10. Grows 3–5 feet tall. Blue flowers in June with others later if spent flowers are pinched off. Likes sun in cool climates, but prefers a little shade in warm ones. You can grow from seeds sown in spring or fall, to bloom the

following season, or set out young plants. Because mature plants have a deep taproot they resent transplanting.

FLAX. *Linum perenne* 'Heavenly Blue.' Zones 4–9. Grows 1–1½ feet tall and bears bright blue flowers all summer. Likes full sun and well-drained soil. Propagate by seed, not division. Plant 12–14 inches apart.

HELIOPSIS. *Heliopsis helianthoides scabra* 'Golden Plume.' Zones 3–9. This variety grows 3–4 feet tall, but shouldn't need staking. Double yellow flowers from late June until fall. Easy, vigorous plant; prolific bloomer. Likes sun, moisture, rich soil. Plant at least 2 feet apart and divide every few years in spring or fall.

IRIS, JAPANESE. *Iris kaempferi.* Zones 5–8. Choose several blue, white or blue-and-white varieties, and blooming times will be staggered through June and July. Grows 3–3½ feet tall. Flowers are enormous but exquisite, with rich intricate shadings and vein patterns. Likes sun, acid soil (pH 5.5–6.5), moisture. Water

in drought and mulch with composted peat, leaf mold or garden compost. Plant 15–18 inches apart. Division not usually necessary. Generally planted in spring but can also be planted in summer or fall.

MONKSHOOD. *Aconitum henryi (A. autumnale).* Zones 3–8. Ask for 'autumn monkshood' for blue color in late summer and fall. Grows 3–5 feet tall. Likes rich, moist soil, mulch in winter. Do not move or divide.

OENOTHERA (SUNDROPS). *Oenothera fruticosa* or *O. missourensis.* Zones 4–10. Often called evening primrose, though this name refers more accurately to a similar plant whose flowers close for most of the day. This one grows 12–18 inches high and has bright yellow blooms like large buttercups from June through August. Likes sun and well-drained soil. *O. fruticosa* spreads very quickly, but is easy to thin out in spring and give away.

PHLOX, CAROLINA. *Phlox carolina (P. suffruticosa)* 'Miss Lingard.' Zones 5–9. This variety has loose white flower heads and blooms June–Sep-

tember. It grows 2 ½–3 feet tall. Plant 1½–2 feet apart in full sun or light shade, in moist, rich soil. Thin as needed. Cut spent flowers to encourage a long blooming season.

SCABIOSA (PINCUSHION FLOWER). *Scabiosa caucasica.* Zones 3–9. Grows 2–2½ feet tall. Flowers are light blue or lavender and come in summer and early fall. Likes sun and soil enriched with manure. Water in drought. Propagate by division every few years or sow seeds in summer to bloom the following season.

SHASTA DAISY. *Chrysanthemum maximum* 'Alaska' or 'Polaris' (singles) or one of the double varieties. Zones 5–9 (protect with winter mulch in zone 5). Grows 2–3 feet tall. Large daisylike blooms in June–July, and later if cut back and spent blooms removed. Likes sun and good, rich soil. Divide every 2 years for stronger plants. Can be sown in spring for second-year bloom.

SPEEDWELL, WOOLLY (VERONICA). *Veronica incana.* Zones 3–10. Silvery foliage, blue flower spikes a foot

tall. Blooms in July–August. Well-drained soil is important; place gravel under the leaves if soil is too damp. Plant a foot apart.

YARROW, WOOLLY. *Achillea tomentosa.* Zones 3–9. Silvery mat of leaves, yellow flowers all summer. Grows 8–10 inches high. Plant a foot apart.

SHRUBS AND TREES

FALSE CYPRESS, 'BOULEVARD.' *Chamaecyparis pisifera* 'Boulevard' (Cyanoviridis). To zone 4. Grows slowly in a dense, irregular pyramid to 8 feet. Lush, soft blue foliage, brushed with white. Especially blue in winter and early spring.

FALSE CYPRESS, GOLDEN-THREAD. *Chamaecyparis pisifera* 'Filifera Aurea.' To zone 5. Easier to grow than to pronounce. Grows slowly to a 15-foot-wide mound, but more graceful if kept pruned to 6 feet. Weeping, threadlike foliage is gold-colored year round, but needs full sun to keep gold color. All false cypresses like rich, well-drained,

moisture-retentive soil and dislike drying winds. Prune in early spring.

FALSE CYPRESS, HINOKI. *Chamaecyparis obtusa* 'Gracilis.' Zones 4–8. Not the dwarf form suggested for the Winter Garden, but with similar foliage and branching habit. Grows quickly to about 6 feet, but can attain a height of 12–18 feet after many years. Prune to stay at 6–8 feet for this garden.

JUNIPER, SKYROCKET. *Juniperus virginiana* 'Skyrocket.' To zone 3. Very narrow, upright tree that will grow quickly to 18–25 feet, but can be kept shorter if you like by pruning. A variety of the native eastern red cedar, it likes full sun and well-drained soil.

A Winter Garden

Most gardens in winter look like the morning after a good party. Just about the only reminders of past glories are sodden nests of day lily foliage and green bamboo stakes supporting nothing. Except for occasional tussles with the snow shovel, yard care has ceased, and the January thaw reveals a landscape of rotting leaves and lost toys.

It doesn't have to be this way, however. Even if you look forward to the time when your garden is put to bed—and you can rest from your labors, you can still arrange a spot that will give you joy in these somber months, a little island of discreet shadings of green, gray and other tones as well as dashes of color. It can be admired from a window or be a place to sit in when it is sunny and a bit warm.

There are two styles of outdoor winter gardening: the bright and the subdued. The bright style occurs to most people first. A bright winter garden is a triumph over adversity, a magician's act in which vivid colors appear in a drab season, like rabbits out of a hat. There are many plants you can buy for this quality alone. Take bark, for example. You can find shrubs and trees with bark that is bright red (Siberian dogwood), bright

yellow (golden-twig dogwood), bright green (*Kerria*), stark white (birch, or whitewashed bramble) or mahogany *(Prunus serrulata)*, to name a few. There is an equally wide range in the color of berries, many of which stay on the plants until spring. You can grow trees, shrubs, perennials and bulbs that will bloom in the "dead" of winter. The warmer your climate the more you have to choose from, but even in the coldest regions you can trick a few flowers into bloom by growing them in a protected location—next to a warm chimney perhaps. Or you can plant things that bloom very early in mild winters. It becomes a game. When a surprisingly mild day comes you are rewarded with not only the day but also some flowers that give you a taste of spring.

For the subdued garden you must look for subtle beauty in the general bleakness of winter; things that go unnoticed amid the gaudiness of spring, summer and fall. Learn to appreciate bark textures, the shapes of bare trees, the different greens, blues and bronzes of winter evergreens, the earth tones of dried things. Start to appreciate lichens on rocks, seedpods on plants; the different ways that snow sits on trees, the color of bare soil. See the rhododendrons curling their leaves to conserve moisture on days when it is very cold and relaxing them when it is warmer. You may decide that you prefer this muted

A garden at Hyde Hall, Chelmsford, England, in the snow.

landscape that expresses the resting state of the winter world. You might want to combine the special winter colors of several evergreens, or several dry grasses. Or try evergreen ground covers and ferns. You might start your quest with the hope that there must be *some* plant that looks good in winter, only to end up feeling that there are so many you hardly know where to begin.

The winter garden shown here combines both the bright and the subdued approach. There is a small rock garden that displays dwarf conifers and low-growing perennials. Some of the latter have evergreen foliage; others bloom in summer and leave attractive seed heads. There is the texture of the rocks themselves. Elsewhere are bright berries and some early bulbs placed where there is a chance of winter bloom. It is a little sun trap, protected from the winter wind and designed to give shelter not only to the plantings but to the person enjoying them.

PLAN OF THE GARDEN

The garden I have proposed here is an enclosure protected on one side by the house and on two others by a yew hedge. It can be entered by stepping out onto a small brick terrace. Since it is a spot you would use all year long, the plants are a collection that will be attractive in other seasons as well. The single tree, a flowering dogwood, bears white "flowers" in spring, is graceful in summer and gives light shade, has red foliage and berries in fall, and the branches make a pleasant horizontal silhouette in winter, with smooth gray bark and promising little fat buds at the tip of each twig. It is a good tree for birds. They will eat the berries, then stay to perch on the branches, especially if you hang a bird feeder among them.

The yew hedge forms a dense screen. It also has a good rich dark green color, and red berries in winter. It should be allowed to grow high enough to keep the wind out— about seven feet—but should not shield the sun. Under and behind the dogwood is a group of Japanese barberries. This "common" shrub grows wild in many areas, but is nonetheless an excellent year-round garden plant. The small leaves are fiery red-orange in fall, and the red berries last all winter and well into spring. When it leafs out—and it is among the very first plants to do so—the berries are there among the new foliage along with yellow flowers that look like very tiny roses. Buy the *minor* variety if you can; it is more compact. But even the usual larger one can be kept tidy and shapely with pruning.

A bed of myrtle (also called vinca or periwinkle) and early spring bulbs is planted under the dogwood. Even when myrtle covers the ground thickly it leaves enough space for small bulbs to sprout and lets in enough sun to warm the ground for them. The earliest to bloom are the white snowdrops and the yellow winter aconites, overlapping with the blue glory-of-the-snow. The myrtle also has blue flowers in spring. Bear in mind that the blooming times of these early bulbs vary from place to place and from winter to winter. In some parts of the country you will have blooms as early as January, in others February or March. They may even vary from one spot in your bed to another.

The Bar Harbor juniper forms a dense mat on the ground. Its usual blue-green color takes on a purplish tinge in winter. This flat area would be a good place to set up a birdbath to go with your dogwood feeder. Or if you want to display a piece of statuary—a good winter accent to be viewed from the house and illuminated at night—here, against the dark yew hedge, would be a perfect setting. The juniper mat leads into the rock garden, which also contains several junipers.

A rock garden is a natural choice for winter. Many rockery plants are evergreen, and among these are various foliage colors. The rocks themselves provide interest. You can also vary the terrain with a few small "hills" and "valleys," especially if you have a flat yard. The rocks will hold the sun's heat and provide warm patches of earth to encourage the early-blooming bulbs that are set among them. Paradoxically, these same rocks will provide cool soil in summer for plants whose roots like to escape from the heat of the sun. And finally, a rock garden just looks good with snow, perhaps because we associate snow and mountains.

Rock gardening originated as a highly specialized art: an attempt to re-create, in domestic surroundings, the growing condi-

Winter aconites (Eranthis hyemalis) *come up through the snow in late winter or early spring, depending on your locality.*

© PAMELA HARPER

tions of special habitats such as moraines and screes and alpine peaks. A real alpine garden, in the hands of an expert, is a fascinating thing; it is the only way certain high-altitude plants can be grown. But ordinary rock gardening is also very popular and has been well adapted to modern landscaping. Once considered too informal for the proper English yard, unless planted in a special "wilderness" far from the house, a rock garden is now often the pride of the property, especially in New England, where a front yard is apt to have a natural outcropping in the middle of it whether anyone likes it or not. It is a lot of fun to create a rocky landscape that is laced with discrete pockets of soil, filled with choice tufts of foliage and gemlike blooms. Avoid certain pitfalls like painted rocks or masses of garish pink phlox, and you might create something very beautiful.

This rock garden is easy to grow. It contains no tender plants that need to be coddled. Bloom begins with the crocuses and

THE WINTER
GARDEN

scilla, which echo the yellow and blue bulbs in the myrtle bed, but slightly later. White candytuft and yellow basket-of-gold follow in May. Coral bells and wine-leaf cinquefoil begin about then and keep going, joined by woolly yarrow, 'Dragon's Blood' sedum and thyme. Flax will throw bright blue flowers here and there all summer, along with blue woolly speedwell. If you want more summer color, tuck in some little annual portulacas wherever you find an extra pocket of soil. Dwarf asters and the larger sedums will bloom in September and October.

Most of these have winter foliage. The yarrow and speedwell are silvery. Blue fescue and dwarf blue spruce that stay blue. Coral bells and cinquefoil have bronze leaves in winter. Thyme, candytuft and dwarf Hinoki cypress are dark green. Flax has dainty seedpods at the tips of its waving stems. 'Dragon's Blood' sedum leaves stay a red color; the other sedums are deciduous and lose their color when they freeze, but the stems stay erect and keep their handsome red-brown seed heads. The asters have seed heads that are

ROCK GARDEN CONSTRUCTION

Rocks positioned to look like natural outcroppings.

Proper angle at which to set rocks in a slope.

very dark brown, with contrasting tufts of white fuzz. Hen-and-chickens come in many varieties that are fun to tuck into any available corner among the rocks—some stay green; some turn red or brown.

The terrace and walk also lend a warm note of color. Brick was chosen because it is handsome and easy to lay in sand (see box, p. 165). Choose a mellow shade of red-brown that will harmonize with the bronzy reds and browns in this garden. It is worth spending a little extra time and money on the brick, since it is a small area but one you will use often. Old, used brick, with its irregular coloring, is very attractive, though less durable than paving brick. Salvage some, chip away the mortar, and lay it just as you would new brick.

SITE
It is very important to pick the right site for a winter garden. First decide which part of your property already has the most winter protection. Is there a sunny spot where snow melts first and the ground is soft early? Where there is the least amount of wind? If there are several choices, pick the one where you would most like to sit. This will probably be close to the house; most people don't venture far in winter.

Many houses are built so that the largest windows face south, in order to make the most of the sun's light and heat. A winter garden in front of a south-facing window would be excellent. In general, it is most important to protect the garden on the north and west sides because the worst weather—and the least sun—comes from those directions. This garden could be placed on the east side of a house so that it is open at the south end, with the hedge to protect it on the north and east sides. Many variations are possible. Just remember that the garden must be shielded from wind, but let in plenty of sun at the same time.

GROWING INSTRUCTIONS
This garden can be laid out and the terrace built at any time that the ground is not frozen. But all the plants except the bulbs should be planted in spring. Set out the bulbs early in the fall, or sooner, since they are early

The seed heads of this sedum still have a rich color in February in the New York Botanical Garden.

bloomers and need time to put down roots during winter. Plant the dogwood and shrubs with plenty of compost, peat moss or leaf mold among the roots. The soil should stay moist but well drained. Moisture will also please the aconites that are here. Avoid the temptation to mulch this area, however; the myrtle will help to keep some moisture in, and you want the sun to shine directly onto the earth in spring to warm it up. A winter mulch would only keep it frozen. Water the bed in hot weather, especially around the dogwood, which is shallow-rooted. Keep the yew and barberry trimmed to avoid a scraggly look. The dogwood should not need pruning.

The rock garden should be built with care, since whatever you do will be permanent. The result should look natural, as if the rocks were there before you started. As master rock gardener and author Lincoln Foster has said, a rock garden should look good even without plants. Here are the steps you should follow:

1. Clear the entire area of weeds; they will be difficult to remove later.

2. Make sure the site has good drainage; if it does not, remove the topsoil to a depth of at least nine inches and lay a base of four to six inches of gravel. Replace soil.

3. Start with a few large rocks; you may need a crowbar or winch to place them. All the rocks should be the same kind and color—native stone if possible—with the grain of all of them running in the same plane. This way it is possible for a group of movable size to look like the outcroppings of one single, buried stretch of natural rock ledge. Choose angular rocks rather than ones with rounded, flat faces. If you have existing rocks or ledges you can build your garden around these, exposing more surface if needed, but don't try to plant deep-rooted plants on shallow soil that rests on rock. They need adequate moisture, and want to tuck their roots under the rocks. Give them pockets or V-shaped fissures. If you are setting rocks into a slope, tilt them upward so that rainwater will run into the soil pockets, not out of them.

4. Add more topsoil if needed. Most rockery plants like a sandy soil. Sand helps to maintain good drainage and also holds warmth, to encourage early bloom from the bulbs. Equal parts sand, loam and leaf mold is a good formula. Tamp the soil firmly as you go.

5. Bring in a few smaller rocks, but don't make the garden more rocks than plants. Bury them so that about two thirds of the rock is showing. Keep tamping the soil as you go, even if it takes a long time; any air pockets will kill the plants. Water the soil with a hose to compress it further.

Use phosphorus-rich fertilizer or bone meal to encourage root development, but do not fertilize heavily. A slightly poor soil helps rock garden plants stay an appropriately small

Even the spent foliage of a tall ornamental grass can be a winter accent.

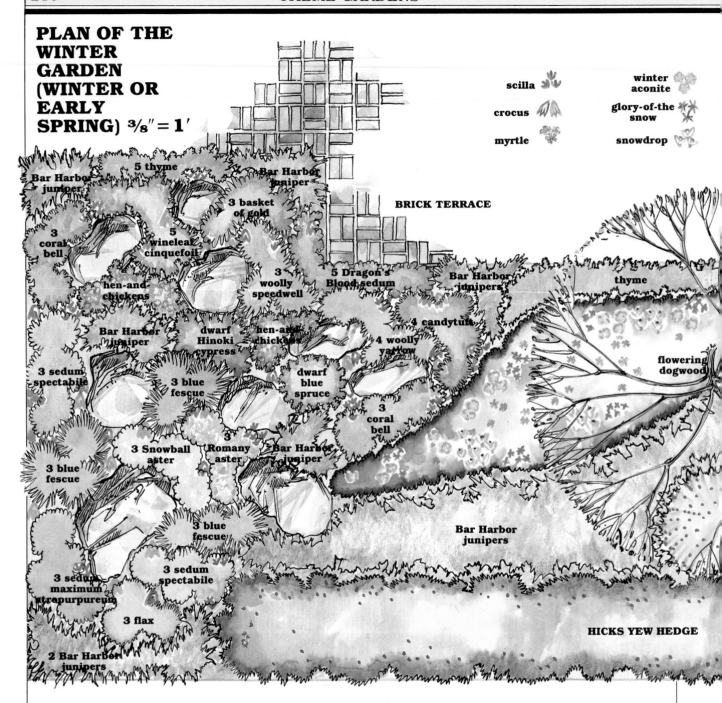

PLAN OF THE WINTER GARDEN (WINTER OR EARLY SPRING) ⅜″ = 1′

scilla

crocus

myrtle

winter aconite

glory-of-the snow

snowdrop

BRICK TERRACE

Bar Harbor juniper

5 thyme

Bar Harbor juniper

3 basket of gold

3 coral bell

5 wineleaf cinquefoil

3 woolly speedwell

5 Dragon's Blood sedum

Bar Harbor junipers

thyme

hen-and-chickens

Bar Harbor juniper

dwarf Hinoki cypress

hen-and-chickens

4 candytuft

4 woolly yarrow

3 sedum spectabile

3 blue fescue

dwarf blue spruce

flowering dogwood

3 coral bell

3 Snowball aster

Romany aster

Bar Harbor juniper

3 blue fescue

3 blue fescue

Bar Harbor junipers

3 sedum maximum atropurpureum

3 sedum spectabile

3 flax

HICKS YEW HEDGE

2 Bar Harbor junipers

size, both for aesthetic reasons and because of the limited space and moisture. It will also discourage rampant weed growth. Weed regularly. Keep an eye on the size of the plant groups and don't let the vigorous spreaders crowd out the others. When fall comes, leave the seed heads and foliage alone. They are part of the picture.

ADDITIONS AND SUBSTITUTIONS

The number of good "winter" plants is so great, especially in warm climates, that it would take

a whole book just to list them. But here are a few variations on the basic theme I have presented. If you have a severe deer problem, substitute Canadian hemlock for yew. Deer will nibble hemlock, but they can totally devour yew. There are many other barberries you can plant, some of them dwarf, some of them evergreen, some with deciduous red or yellow foliage. Another wonderful shrub is *Daphne mezereum,* which has fragrant lavender blooms as early as February. If you have a shady corner in the garden, you can plant

THE GARDEN IN FALL

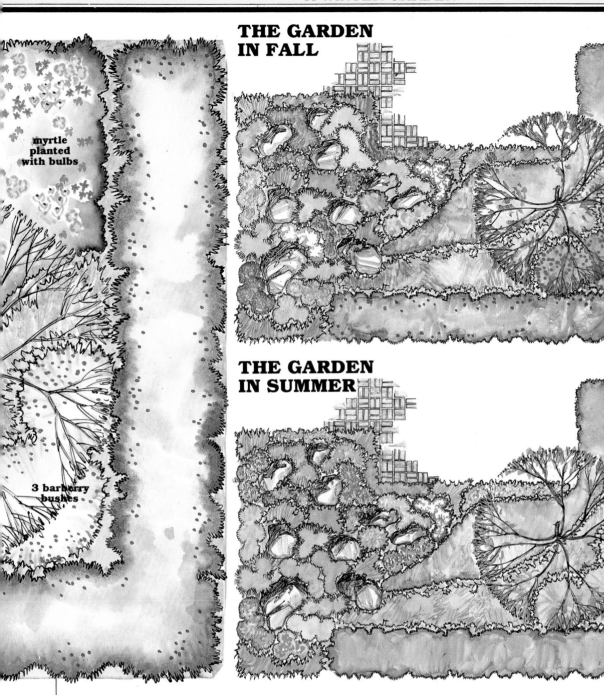

myrtle planted with bulbs

3 barberry bushes

THE GARDEN IN SUMMER

leucothoe or mahonia, both of them broad-leafed evergreens. Other deciduous trees you could include are Washington hawthorn, crab apple, weeping cherry and paperbark maple (where hardy). There are other winter bulbs such as winter crocuses, and winter perennials such as the hellebores and hardy cyclamens such as *Cyclamen purpurascens (C. europaeum), C. coum* or *C. hederifolium (C. neapolitanum).* There is great variety among the sedums and sempervivums, the thymes and the dwarf evergreens. If you decide to

plant more of the latter, be sure they are true dwarfs, however. Among the winter ferns are Christmas fern and the spleenworts. Wintergreen, with its red berries, is a good winter ground cover, as are the evergreen wild gingers: *Asarum shuttleworthii* and *A. hartwegii.*

Another plant worth seeking out is *Clematis integrifolia*, a low-growing clematis with blue flowers in summer and lovely plumed seed heads in fall and winter. Or try mountain cranberry *(Vaccinium vitis-idaea)*, also called red whortleberry, a low-growing broad-leafed evergreen. Another I especially like is snowberry *(Symphoricarpos albus)*, which bears fat white berries for most of the winter. And finally, the staghorn sumac *(Rhus typhina)*, considered common and weedy by some and perhaps inappropriate for a small enclosed garden, but a shrub to remember for winter: it turns a gorgeous red in fall and bears bright red berry clusters that look beautiful against the dark bark, glistening black in rain or contrasting with snow.

If you use the plants suggested, or some like them, your winter yard will be far from dismal, and you will enjoy keeping it in order. Sweep away any leaves to keep the low tufts of foliage visible. The terrace should be kept free of snow, and swept when dirty. Sturdy winterproof yard furniture is a good idea, and it too should be swept off so that when that break in the weather comes your outdoor "room" will be ready and waiting for you.

PLANT LIST FOR WINTER GARDEN

BULBS

CROCUS. *Crocus vernus* (common or Dutch crocus). Zones 3–10. Yellow and purple varieties. Grows 4–8 inches tall, self-propagates. Plant 3 inches apart, 4 inches deep.

GLORY-OF-THE-SNOW. *Chionodoxa luciliae.* Zones 3–10. Blue-lavender starlike flowers in clusters, 6 inches tall. Prefers cold climate, sunny location, well-drained soil. Spreads. Plant 2 inches apart, 3 inches deep.

SCILLA. *Scilla siberica* (Siberian squill) or *S. tubergeniana* (Tubergenian squill). Zones 1–8. Bright blue flowers, 4–6 inches tall. Spreads,

especially if fertilized. Plant 4 inches apart, 4 inches deep.

SNOWDROP. *Galanthus nivalis.* Zones 3–9. Single white flowers, grassy foliage that dies down after bloom. 6–12 inches tall. Spreads, and can be propagated by removing bulblets. Likes moist but well-drained soil. Plant 3 inches apart, 3 inches deep.

WINTER ACONITE. *Eranthis hyemalis.* Zones 4–9. Bright yellow flowers like large buttercups, from small tubers. Soak before planting. Prefers rich, humus-filled soil in protected location, year-round moisture. Plant 3 inches apart, 3 inches deep.

PERENNIALS

ASTER *Aster* 'Romany': purple-blooming dwarf, 6–8 inches tall. Blooms Septem-

ber–October. 'Snowball': white dwarf, 8–10 inches tall. Blooms in September. Both zones 5–9. Plant both 12–15 inches apart.

BASKET-OF-GOLD.(GOLD-DUST) AURINA SAXATILE *(Alyssum saxatilus).* Any variety. Zones 4–9. Bright yellow flowers in May, 10–15 inches tall. Foliage somewhat gray, sprawling. Plant 8–12 inches apart. You can substitute spiny alyssum *(Alyssum spinosum)* for white spiny tufts in winter.

CANDYTUFT. *Iberis sempervirens* 'Autumn Snow.' Zones 3–9. White flowers in spring and again, more sparingly, in fall if cut back. Dark green foliage year-round. Prefers rich, well-drained, sandy soil, full sun. Propagate by cutting. Plant 1 foot apart.

CINQUEFOIL, THREE-TOOTHED (WINELEAF CINQUEFOIL). *Potentilla tridentata.* Zones 3–8. Three leaflets, like strawberry, and white strawberrylike blooms. Bronze-red leaves in fall and winter. 6 inches high. Plant 10 inches apart.

CORAL BELLS. *Heuchera sanguinea.* Zones 4–9. Tiny red or pink flowers on wiry 18-inch stems, from low cluster of scalloped leaves. Blooms all summer. Prefers humus in soil to conserve moisture; must be divided every few years.

FESCUE, BLUE. *Festuca caesia* (*F. ovina glauca*). Zones 3–9. This is the dwarf variety, which grows 6–12 inches tall, usually 8. The tufted mounds of fine-textured evergreen foliage are usually silver-blue, especially if cut back in spring and mid-summer. Small green-beige flowers in June and July. Prefers a cool climate, full sun, dry and sandy soil, no clay. Plant about a foot apart. Divide every few years in spring or fall.

FLAX. *Linum perenne* 'Heavenly Blue.' Zones 4–9. Bright blue flowers all summer. 1–1½ feet tall. Full sun and well-drained soil. Propagate by seed, not division. Plant 12–14 inches apart.

HEN-AND-CHICKENS. *Sempervivum tectorum* and hybrid varieties. Zones 3–9. Prickly rosettes in green and other shades that make 'babies' next to them and send up stalks with usually pink flowers in midsummer. Foliage keeps color (often reddish) in winter. They appreciate a dry, sandy soil. Plant 6 inches apart.

MYRTLE (PERIWINKLE, VINCA). *Vinca minor.* Zones 4–10. Dark green ground cover with blue flowers in April. (There is also a white-flowered variety, *Vinca minor* 'Alba'.) Plant 1 foot apart, or closer.

SEDUM (STONECROP). To zone 3. *Sedum. maximum atropurpureum*, mahogany plant: dark purplish leaves, creamy-rose flowers in August

and September. 18–24 inches high. *S. spectabile*, showy stonecrop: large pink flowers in August and September, gray-green leaves. Up to 2 feet high. Plant both 12–15 inches apart. *S. spurium*, 'Dragon's Blood': carpet of red foliage, which it keeps in winter. 1–2 inches high. Flowers in June and following.

SPEEDWELL, WOOLLY. *Veronica incana.* Zones 3–10. Silvery foliage, blue flower spikes a foot tall. Blooms July and August. Well-drained soil important; place gravel under leaves if soil stays damp. Plant a foot apart.

THYME, CREEPING (WILD THYME). *Thymus serpyllum coccineus.* To zone 3. Best, hardiest thyme for rockery. Dense evergreen mat, bronze in fall. Reddish lavender flowers in late June. Never dry out roots when planting; water-in well. Plant about 1 foot apart.

YARROW, WOOLLY. *Achillea tomentosa.* Zones 3–9.

Silvery mat of leaves, yellow flowers all summer. 8–10 inches high. Plant 1 foot apart.

TREES AND SHRUBS

BARBERRY, JAPANESE. *Berberis thunbergii* 'Minor.' Zone 5. Compact form of common shrub, grows to 5 feet. Thorny twigs, bright red berries. Very easy to grow.

DOGWOOD, FLOWERING. *Cornus florida.* Zone 5. Large white, flat "flowers" in May. Usually white, sometimes pink. Red fall foliage, red berries. Ultimate height as tall as 40 feet (but unusual). Partial shade or full sun. Likes moist, well-drained acid soil. Protect bark of newly planted tree with coarse screening.

FALSE-CYPRESS, DWARF HINOKI (DWARF HINOKI CYPRESS). *Chamaecyparis obtusa* 'Nana Gracilis.' To zone 3. The dark rich green needles have an unusual fan shape and

the plant has an Oriental quality that makes it a perfect ornament for the rock garden. It grows only an inch or two a year and will eventually reach 4 feet. *C. obtusa nana* is an even tinier variety.

JUNIPER, BAR HARBOR. *Juniperus horizontalis* 'Bar Harbor.' To zone 3. Prostrate spreading evergreen, native of Maine. Very hardy. Blue berries in fall, wine-colored winter foliage. Prefers acid woodsy soil.

SPRUCE, DWARF BLUE. *Picea pungens globosa.* To zone 3. A tiny version of the familiar Colorado blue spruce, this keeps its compact, round shape as it grows very slowly to 4 feet.

YEW, HICKS. *Taxus media* 'Hicksii.' To zone 4. Columnar dark green hybrid shrub with dark green evergreen needles. Plant 2 feet apart for hedge. Prefers moist, well-drained acid soil. Prune, thinning from the inside.

PLANT HARDINESS ZONE MAP

Plant zones have been designed to indicate the lowest winter temperature that a plant can withstand. The approximate range of average annual minimum temperatures for each zone is indicated in the key.

PREPARED BY THE U.S. NATIONAL ARBORETUM, AGRICULTURAL RESEARCH SERVICE, U.S. DEPARTMENT OF AGRICULTURE IN COOPERATION WITH THE AMERICAN HORTICULTURAL SOCIETY.

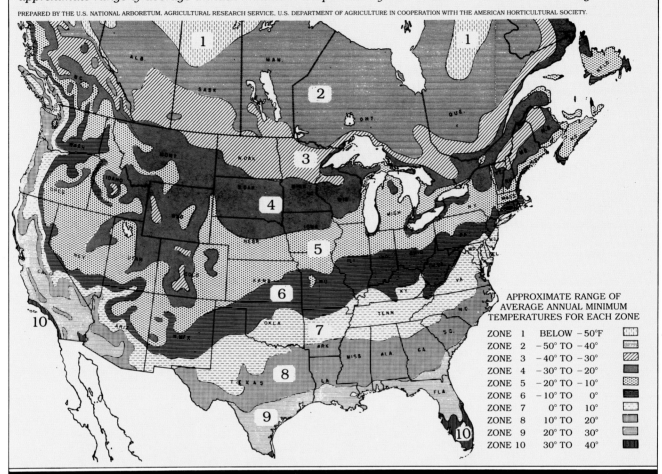

APPROXIMATE RANGE OF
AVERAGE ANNUAL MINIMUM
TEMPERATURES FOR EACH ZONE

ZONE	1	BELOW −50°F
ZONE	2	−50° TO −40°
ZONE	3	−40° TO −30°
ZONE	4	−30° TO −20°
ZONE	5	−20° TO −10°
ZONE	6	−10° TO 0°
ZONE	7	0° TO 10°
ZONE	8	10° TO 20°
ZONE	9	20° TO 30°
ZONE	10	30° TO 40°

WHERE TO ORDER PLANTS

The following is only a sample of the many mail order sources of plants and seeds. In some cases there is a charge for the catalog, but since prices are subject to change, they are not listed.

BULBS

Blackthorne Gardens, 48 Quincy St., Holbrook, MA 02343 (specialty: lilies).

Breck's Reservation Center, 6523 N. Galena Rd., Peoria, IL 61632.

De Jager Bulbs, Inc., 188 Asbury St., South Hamilton, MA 01982.

Rex Bulb Farms, Box 774, Port Townsend, WA 98368 (lilies).

John Scheepers, Inc., 63 Wall St., New York, NY 10005.

Van Bourgondien Bros., Box A, 245 Farmingdale Rd., Rt. 9, Babylon, NY 11702.

FRUITS

Rayner Bros., Inc., Box 1617, Salisbury, MD 21801 (specialty: berries).

Stark Bros. Nurseries, Louisiana, MO 63353.

HERBS

Borchelt Herb Gardens, 474 Carriage Shop Rd., East Falmouth, MA 02536 (seeds only).

Carroll Gardens, Box 310, Westminster, MD 21157.

Greene Herb Gardens, Greene, RI 02827 (seeds only).

Hemlock Hill Herb Farm, Hemlock Hill Rd., Litchfield, CT 06759 (plants only).

Merry Gardens, Camden, ME 04843 (also scented geraniums).

Nichols Garden Nursery, 1190 N. Pacific Hwy., Albany, OR 97321 (also rare plants, gourmet vegetables).

The Rosemary House, 120 S. Market St., Mechanicsburg, PA 17055.

Sunnybrook Farms Nursery, 9448 Mayfield Rd., Chesterland, OH 44026 (plants only, many thymes).

Taylor's Herb Garden, Inc., 1535 Lone Oak Rd., Vista, CA 92083.

Well-Sweep Herb Farm, 317 Mt. Bethel Rd., Port Murray, NJ 07865.

ORNAMENTAL GRASSES

Applewood Seed Co., Box 4000, Golden, CO 80401 (also wild flowers, herbs).

Kurt Bluemel, Inc., 2543 Hess Rd., Fallston, MD 21047.

Garden Place, 6780 Heisley Rd., Mentor, OH 44060.

Horticultural Systems, Inc., Box 70, Parrish, FL 33564 (specialty: seaside grasses).

Windrift Prairie Shop, R.D. 2, Oregon, IL 61061 (prairie grasses).

PERENNIALS

Bluestone Perennials, Inc., 7211 Middle Ridge Rd., Madison, OH 44057.

Lee Bristol Nursery, Route 55, Sherman, CT 06784 (day lilies).

Garden Place, 6780 Heisley Rd., Mentor, OH 44060.

The D. S. George Nurseries, 2491 Penfield Rd., Fairport, NY 14450 (clematis).

Chas. Klehm & Son Nursery, 2 E. Algonquin Rd., Arlington Heights, IL 60005 (peonies, day lilies, iris, hosta).

Lamb Nurseries, E. 101 Sharp Ave., Spokane, WA 99202 (including rock garden plants).

David Reath, Box 251, Vulcan, MI 49892 (herbaceous and tree peonies).

Schreiner's, 3625 Quinaby Rd., Salem, OR 97303 (iris).

Louis Smirnow and Son, 85 Linden La., Glen Head P.O., Brookville, NY 11545 (herbaceous and tree peonies).

Swan Island Dahlias, Box 800, Canby, OR 97013 (dahlias).

Wayside Gardens, Hodges, SC 29695.

White Flower Farm, Litchfield, CT 06759.

Gilbert H. Wild and Son, Inc., Sarcoxie, MO 64862 (day lilies, peonies, iris).

ROSES (MODERN)

Jackson and Perkins, Medford, OR 97501

Stocking Rose Nursery, 785 N. Capitol Ave., San Jose, CA 95133.

Thomasville Nurseries, Inc., Box 7, Thomasville, GA 31792.

ROSES (OLD)

U.S. and Canada:

High Country Rosarium, 1717 Downing, Denver, CO 80218.

Joseph J. Kern Rose Nursery, Box 33, Mentor, OH 44060.

Lowe's Own Root Nursery, 6 Sheffield Rd., Nashua, NH 03062.

Pickering Nurseries, 670 Kingston Rd., Pickering, Ontario L1V 1A6, Canada (no importation permit required).

Roses of Yesterday and Today (formerly Tillotson's), 802 Brown's Valley Road, Watsonville, CA 95076.

Melvin E. Wyant Rose Specialist, Inc., Rt. 84, Johnny Cake Ridge, Mentor, OH 44060.

Europe*

David Austin Roses, Bowling Green Lane, Albrighton, Wolverhampton WV7 3HB, England.

Peter Beales Roses, Intwood Nurseries, Swardeston, Norwich NR14 8EA, England.

Hillier Nurseries (Winchester) Ltd., Ampfield House, Ampfield, Romsey, Hants S05 9PA England.

Ellen og Hugo Lykke, Rosenplanteskole, Hønebjergvej 31, Søby, Voldum, 8900 Randers, Denmark.

*To obtain plants from nurseries abroad, importation permits are required. To apply, write the U.S. Department of Agriculture, Room 638, Federal Bldg., Hyattsville, MD 20782. Permission is sometimes required at the state level as well. You can find out how to contact the plant importation representative for your state by writing the USDA address above.

V. Petersens Planteskole, Ved M. H. Thim, Plantevej 3 - LØVE - 4270 HØNG, Denmark.

SEEDS

W. Atlee Burpee Co., Warminster, PA 18974; Clinton, IA 52732; Riverside, CA 92502.

Comstock, Ferre and Co., 263 Main St., Wethersfield, CT 06109.

Gurney's Seed and Nursery Co., Yankton, SD 57079.

Joseph Harris Co., Inc., Moreton Farm, Rochester, NY 14624.

Herbst Seedsmen, Inc., 1000 N. Main St., Brewster, NY 10509.

Johnny's Selected Seeds, Albion, ME 04910 (specialty: vegetable varieties for northern climates).

Geo. W. Park Seed, Co., Inc., Hwy 254-N., Greenwood, SC 29647.

Thompson and Morgan, Inc., Box 100, Farmingdale, NJ 07727.

W. J. Unwin Ltd., Histon, Cambridge, England CB4 4LE (specialty: sweet peas).

A World Seed Service, J. L. Hudson, Seedsman, Box 1058, Redwood City, CA 94064.

SHRUBS AND TREES

Ferris Nurseries, 811 Fourth St. N.E., Hampton, IA 50441.

Gerard Nurseries, Box 428, Geneva, OH 44041.

WATER PLANTS

Lilypons Water Gardens, 1603 Hort Rd., Lilypons, MD 21717; 1603 Lilypons Rd., Brookshire, TX 77423.

William Tricker, Inc., 74 Allendale Rd., Box 398, Saddle River, NJ 07458.

Van Ness Water Gardens, 2460 N. Euclid, 5, Upland, CA 91786.

WILD FLOWERS

Appalachian Wildflower Nursery, Rt. 1, Box 275 A, Reedsville, PA 17084 (plants only).

Environmental Seed Producers, Box 5904, El Monte, CA 91734.

Far North Gardens, 15621 Auburndale Ave., Livonia, MI 48154.

Gardens of the Blue Ridge, Box 10, Pineola, NC 28662 (including trees and shrubs).

Illini Gardens, Box 125, Oakford, IL 62673 (plants only, including rock garden plants, ferns).

Nature's Garden, Rt. 1, Box 488, Beaverton, OR 97007 (including alpines, ferns).

New England Rootstock Association, Box 76, Cambridge, NY 12816 (plants only).

Putney Nursery, Inc., Putney, VT 05346 (plants only).

Clyde Robin Seed Co., Inc., Box 2855, Castro Valley, CA 94546 (seeds only).

Siskiyou Rare Plant Nursery, 2825 Cummings Rd., Medford, OR 97501 (including alpines and ferns).

J. R. Smith Prairie Nursery, Westfield, WI 53964.

Vick's Wildgardens, Inc., Box 115, Gladwyne, PA 19035.

MISCELLANEOUS

Henry Field Seed and Nursery Co., Shenandoah, IA 51602.

Gurney's Seed and Nursery Co., Yankton, SD 57079.

Kelly Bros. Nurseries, Inc., Dansville, NY 14437.

Mellinger's, 2310 W. South Range Rd., North Lima, OH 44452.

Wayside Gardens, Hodges, SC 29695.

FOR FURTHER READING

The following articles and publications offer useful supplementary information about the theme gardens described in this book.

FRAGRANCE GARDENS

Brownlow, Margaret E. *Herbs and the Fragrant Garden* (Reprint of 1963 ed.) England: Darton-Longman-Todd, 1980.

Genders, Roy. *Growing Herbs as Aromatics*. New Canaan, Conn.: Keats Publishing, Inc., 1977.

McDonald, Donald. *Fragrant Flowers and Leaves*. London: Frederick Warne and Co., Inc., 1905.

Rohde, Eleanour Sinclair. *The Scented Garden*. (Reprint of 1931 ed.) Detroit: Gale Research Co., 1974.

Taylor, Norman. *Fragrance in the Garden*. New York: Van Nostrand Reinhold Co., 1953.

Verey, Rosemary. *The Scented Garden*. New York: Van Nostrand Reinhold Co., 1981.

Wilder, Louise Beebe. *The Fragrant Garden: A Book About Sweet Scented Flowers and Leaves*. (Originally published in 1932 as *The Fragrant Path*.) New York: Dover Publications, Inc., 1974.

COLONIAL GARDENS

American Society of Landscape Architects. *Colonial Gardens: The Landscape Architecture of George Washington's Time*. Washington, D.C.: United States George Washington Bicentennial Commission, 1932.

The Colonial Williamsburg Foundation Staff. *Gardens of Williamsburg*. Williamsburg, Va.: The Colonial Williamsburg Foundation, 1970.

Dutton, Joan Parry. *The Flower World of Williamsburg*. Williamsburg, Va.: The Colonial Williamsburg Foundation. Rev. ed., 1973.

Earle, Alice M. *Old Time Gardens, Newly Set Forth*. (Reprint of 1901 ed.) Detroit: Gale Research Co., 1968.

Favretti, Rudy J., and DeWolf, Gordon P. *Colonial Gardens*. Barre, Mass.: Barre Publishing Co. Inc., 1972.

Favretti, Rudy J., and Favretti, Joy P. *For Every House a Garden: A Guide for Reproducing Period Gardens*. Chester, Conn.: The Globe Pequot Press Inc., 1977.

Garden Club of America, Alice G. B. Lockwood, ed. *Gardens of Colony and State: Gardens and Gardeners of the American Colonies and the Republic before 1840*. New York: Charles Scribner's Sons, 1931.

Leighton, Ann. *Early American Gardens: 'For Meate or Medicine.'* Boston: Houghton Mifflin Co., 1970.

————. *American Gardens in the Eighteenth Century: 'For Use or for Delight.'* Boston: Houghton Mifflin Co., 1976.

Parkinson, John. *A Garden of Pleasant Flowers: Paradisi in Sole Paradisus Terrestris*. (Reprint of 1629 ed.) New York: Dover Publications, Inc., 1976.

Phipps, Frances. *Colonial Kitchens, Their Furnishings and Their Gardens*. New York: Hawthorn Books, 1972.

BUTTERFLIES AND BUTTERFLY GARDENS

Brewer, Jo. "Bringing Butterflies to the Garden." *Horticulture*, May 1979.

————. "An Invitation to the Butterfly Meadow." *Defenders* Educational Supplement No. 53-4-a, from *Defenders*, 1978.

Donahue, Julian P. "Take a Butterfly to Lunch: Butterfly Gardening in Los Angeles." *Terra*, the Members Magazine of the Natural History Museum Alliance, Vol. 14, No. 3, Winter 1976. Available from the Xerces Society.*

Emmel, Thomas C. *Butterflies: Their Worlds, Their Life Cycle, Their Behavior*. New York: Alfred A. Knopf, Inc., 1975.

Heal, Henry George. "An Experiment in Conservation Education: The Drum Manor Butterfly Garden." *International Journal of Environmental Studies*, Vol. 4, 1973.

Klots, Alexander B. *A Field Guide to the Butterflies of North America, East of the Great Plains*. Peterson Field Guide Series. Boston: Houghton Mifflin Co., 1977.

Newman, L. Hugh. *Create a Butterfly Garden*. The Press at Kingsworth, Tadworth, Surrey: World's Work, Ltd., 1969.

Pyle, Robert Michael. *The Audubon Society Field Guide to North American Butterflies*. New York: Alfred A. Knopf, Inc., 1981.

Smith, Alice Upham. "Attracting Butterflies to the Garden." *Horticulture*, August 1975.

Stone, John L. S., and Midwinter, H. J. *Butterfly Culture: A Guide to Breeding Butterflies, Moths and Other Insects*. Poole: Blandford Press, 1975.

CHILDREN'S GARDENS

Dunks, Thomas, and Dunks, Patty. *Gardening With Children*. Santa Cruz, Calif.: Harvest Press, 1977.

Jekyll, Gertrude. *Children and Gardens*. London: Country Life Ltd.; New York: Charles Scribner's Sons, 1934.

MacLatchie, Sharon. *Gardening with Kids*. Emmaus, Pa.: Rodale Press, Inc., 1977.

ROSE GARDENS

Anderson, Frank J. *The Complete Book of 168 Redouté Roses*. New York: Abbeville Press Inc., 1979. Paperbook edition, 1981.

Bunyard, Edward A. *Old Garden Roses*. (Reprint of the 1936 ed.) Pine Plains, N.Y.: Earl M. Coleman Enterprises, Inc., 1978.

Edwards, Gordon. *Wild and Old Garden Roses*. New York: Hafner Press, 1975.

Gibson, Michael. *Shrub Roses for Every Garden*. London: William Collins Publishers, Inc., 1971.

Gore, Katherine F. *The Book of Roses or The Rose Fancier's Manual*. (Reprint of the 1838 ed.) Pine Plains, N.Y.: Earl M. Coleman Enterprises, Inc., 1978.

Harkness, Jack. *Roses*. London: J. M. Dent, 1978.

Jekyll, Gertrude, and Mawley, Edward. *Roses for English Gardens*. New York: Charles Scribner's Sons, 1902.

Keays, Ethelyn. *Old Roses*. (Reprint of the 1935 ed.) Pine Plains, N.Y.: Earl M. Coleman, Enterprises, Inc., 1978.

Modern Roses 8: The International Checklist of Roses. Compiled by the International Registration Authority for Roses, Harrisburg, Pa. Jefferson, N.C.: McFarland and Co., Inc., 1980.

Shepherd, Roy. *History of the Rose*. (Reprint of the 1954 ed.) Pine Plains, N.Y.: Earl M. Coleman Enterprises, Inc., 1978.

*For further information, readers may contact the Xerces Society, an organization founded to "prevent human-caused extinctions of rare arthropod populations." It is named for the Xerces Blue (*Glaucopsyche Xerces*), "the first butterfly species in North America to become extinct as a result of human interference." Write to: Teresa Clifford, Secretary; Department of Zoology and Physiology, University of Wyoming, Laramie, WY 82071.

Staff of Ortho Books, ed. *All About Roses*. San Francisco: Ortho Books, 1977.

Stemler, Dorothy. *The Book of Old Roses*. Boston: Bruce Humphries Publishers, 1966.

Sunset Editors. *Roses: How to Grow*. A Sunset Book. Menlo Park, Calif.: Lane Publishing Co., 1973.

Thomas, Graham Stuart. *Climbing Roses Old and New*. New York: St. Martin's Press, 1965.

———. *The Old Shrub Roses*. Revised ed. London: J. M. Dent, 1979.

Sources for Additional Information on Roses

Other books on old roses may be obtained from Earl M. Coleman, Enterprises, Inc., Publishers, P.O. Box T, Crugers, N.Y. 10521.

The *Combined Rose List*, compiled by Beverly R. Dobson, is extremely useful in verifying rose names, dates and nursery sources. It is available from Beverly R. Dobson, 215 Harriman Road, Irvington, New York 10533.

Readers may also be interested in The Heritage Roses Group, "a fellowship of those who care about Old Roses." For information contact the regional coordinators:

Northeast: Lily Shohan, RD 1, Clinton Corners, NY 12514.

North central: Henry Najat, M.D., Rt. 3, Monroe, WI 53566.

Northwest: Jerry Fellman, 947 Broughton Way, Woodburn, OR 97071.

Southwest: Miriam Wilkins, 925 Galvin Dr., El Cerrito, CA 94530.

South central: Vickie Jackson, 122 Bragg St., New Orleans, LA 70124.

Southeast: Dr. Charles G. Jeremias, 2103 Johnstone St., Newberry, SC 29108.

Editor: Carl Cato, 5917 Hines Circle, Lynchburg, VA 24502.

ZEN AND JAPANESE GARDENS

Bring, Mitchell, and Wayembergh, Josse. *Japanese Gardens, Design and Meaning*. New York: McGraw-Hill Book Co., 1981.

Condor, Josiah. *Landscape Gardening in Japan*. New York: Dover Publications, Inc., 1964.

Herrigel, Gustie L. *Zen in the Art of Flower Arrangement*. (Reprint of the 1958 ed.) Boston: Routledge and Kegan Paul, Ltd., 1974.

Holborn, Mark. *The Ocean in the Sand: Japan, from Landscape to Garden*. Boulder, Colo.: Shambhala Publications, Ltd., 1978.

Murphy, Wendy B., and the editors of Time-Life Books. *Japanese Gardens*. From the *Time-Life Encyclopedia of Gardening*. Alexandria, Va.: Time-Life Books, 1979.

Newsom, Samuel. *Japanese Garden Construction*. Tokyo: Domoto, Kumagawa and Perkins, 1939.

———. *A Thousand Years of Japanese Gardens*. Rev. ed. Tokyo: Tokyo News Service, Ltd., 1955.

Saito, Katsuo, and Wada, Sadaji. *Magic of Trees and Stones*. New York: The JPT Book Company, 1964.

Watts, Alan W. *The Way of Zen*. Reprint of the 1957 ed. New York: Random House, Inc., 1974.

SHAKESPEARE AND RENAISSANCE GARDENS

Bloom, J. Harvey. *Shakespeare's Garden: Being a Compendium of Quotations and References from the Bard to All Manner of Flower, Tree, Bush, Vine, and Herb, Arranged According to the Month in Which They Are Seen to Flourish*. (Reprint of the 1903 ed.) Detroit: Tower Books, Inc., 1971.

Brooklyn Botanic Garden. *William Shakespeare Through His Gardens and Plants*. A Brooklyn Botanic Garden Brochure. Written and compiled by Lucy Chamberlain and Stephen K. M. Tim. New York: Brooklyn Botanic Garden, 1981.

Comito, Terry, *The Idea of the Garden in the Renaissance*. New Brunswick, N.J.: Rutgers University Press, 1978.

Dent, Alan. *World of Shakespeare: Plants*. New York: Taplinger Publishing Co., 1973.

Ellacombe, Henry N. *The Plant-lore and Garden-craft of Shakespeare*. 2nd. ed. London: W. Satchell, 1884.

Gerard, John. *The Herbal or General History of Plants*. (Reprint of the 1633 ed.) New York: Dover Publications, Inc., 1975.

Kerr, Jessica. *Shakespeare's Flowers*. Illustrated by Anne Ophelia Dowden. New York: Thomas Y. Crowell Co., 1969.

Rohde, Eleanour Sinclair. *Shakespeare's Wild Flowers: Fairy Lore, Gardens, Herbs, Gatherers of Simples and Bee Lore*. London: The Medici Society, Ltd., 1935.

Singleton, Esther. *The Shakespeare Garden*. (Reprint of 1933 ed.) New York: AMS Press, Inc.

Strong, Roy C. *The Renaissance Garden in England*. London: Thames and Hudson, 1929.

GRAY-LEAFED AND SEASHORE PLANTS

Foley, Daniel J. *Gardening by the Sea From Coast to Coast*. Philadelphia: Chilton Book Co., 1965.

Menninger, Edwin A. *Seaside Plants of the World: A Guide to Planning, Planting and Maintaining Salt-Resistant Gardens*. New York: Hearthside Press, 1964.

Underwood, Mrs. Desmond. *Grey and Silver Plants*. London: William Collins Publishers, Inc., 1971

LOVE GARDENS AND GARDENS OF THE MIDDLE EAST

Crowe, Sylvia, et al. *The Gardens of Mughal India: A History and Guide*. London: Thames and Hudson, 1977.

Lehrman, Jonas. *Earthly Paradise: Garden and Courtyard in Islam*. Berkeley: University of California Press, 1981.

Moynihan, Elizabeth B. *Paradise as a Garden: In Persia and Mughal India*. New York: George Braziller, Inc., 1979.

Sackville-West, Vita. "Persian Gardens." In *The Legacy of Persia*, ed. by A. J. Arberry. Oxford: The Clarendon Press, 1953.

Wilber, Donald Newton. *Persian Gardens and Garden Pavillions*. 2nd ed. Washington, D.C.: Dumbarton Oaks, 1979.

GARDENS FOR HUMMINGBIRDS AND OTHER BIRDS

Arbib, Robert, and Soper, Tony. *The Hungry Bird Book: How to Make Your Garden Their Heaven on Earth*. New York: Taplinger Publishing Co., Inc., 1970.

Browning, Norma Lee, and Ogg, Russell. *He Saw a Hummingbird*. New York: E. P. Dutton Inc., 1978.

McElroy, Thomas P., Jr. *The New Handbook of Attracting Birds*. Rev. ed. New York: Alfred A. Knopf, Inc., 1960.

MEDIEVAL GARDENS

Alexander, J., and Woodward, Carol H. *The Flora of the Unicorn Tapestries*. Reprinted from the *Journal of the New York Botanical Garden*, May and June 1941.

Freeman, Margaret B. *Herbs for the Medieval Household: For Cooking, Healing and Divers Uses.* New York: The Metropolitan Museum of Art, 1943.

McLean, Teresa. *Medieval English Gardens.* New York: The Viking Press, Inc., 1980.

Sipress, Linda. *The Unicorn Tapestries.* (Based on a study of the Unicorn Tapestries by Margaret B. Freeman.) New York: The Metropolitan Museum of Art, 1974.

ORNAMENTAL GRASSES

Forster, Karl. *Einzug der Graser und Farne indie Garten.* Melsungen: Verlag J. Neumann-Neudamn, 1961.

Grounds, Roger. *Ornamental Grasses.* New York: Van Nostrand Reinhold Co., 1981.

Johnson, Norman K. "Lots of Plant, No Clutter." *Southern Living,* August 1980.

Loewer, H. Peter. *Growing and Decorating with Grasses: A Creative Approach.* New York: Walker & Co., 1977.

Meyer, Lynne. "Ornamental Grasses for Gardens." *American Horticulturist,* Vol. 57, 1978.

Meyer, Mary Hockenberry. *Ornamental Grasses: Decorative Plants for Home and Garden.* New York: Charles Scribner's Sons, 1975.

VICTORIAN GARDENS

Downing, Andrew Jackson. *Treatise on the Theory and Practice of Landscape Gardening.* (Reprint of 1859 ed.) New York: Funk & Wagnalls Co., 1967.

Highstone, John. *Victorian Gardens.* San Francisco: Harper & Row, Publishers, Inc., 1982.

Scott, Frank J. *Victorian Gardens: The Art of Beautifying Suburban Home Grounds.* (Reprint of the 1870 ed.) Watkins Glen, N.Y.: American Life Foundation, 1977.

Van Ravensway, Charles. *A Nineteenth-Century Garden.* New York: Universe Books, Inc., 1977.

WINTER GARDENS

Graff, M. M. *Flowers in the Winter Garden.* Garden City, N.Y.: Doubleday & Co., Inc., 1966.

Lawrence, Elizabeth. *Gardens in Winter.* Baton Rouge, La.: Claitor's Law Books and Publishing, 1973.

Taloumis, George. *Winterizing Your Yard and Garden.* Philadelphia: J. B. Lippincott Co., 1976.

Thomas, Graham. *Color in the Winter Garden.* Boston: Charles T. Branford Co., 1958.

Wilson, Helen Van Pelt. *Color for Your Winter Yard and Garden, with Flowers, Berries, Birds and Trees.* New York: Charles Scribner's Sons, 1979.

FRUITS AND VEGETABLES

Crockett, James Underwood. *Crockett's Victory Garden.* Boston: Little, Brown & Co., 1977.

Raymond, Richard O. *Down-to-Earth Vegetable Gardening Know-How.* New Ed. Charlotte, Vt.: Garden Way Publishing Co., 1975.

Rodale, J. I. *How to Grow Vegetables and Fruits by the Organic Method.* Emmaus, Pa.: Rodale Press, Inc., 1961.

HERB GARDENING

Brooklyn Botanic Garden. *Handbook on Herbs* (A Special Printing of *Plants and Gardens,* Vol. 14, no. 2, 2nd revised ed.) Brooklyn, N.Y.: Brooklyn Botanic Garden, 1973.

Clarkson, Rosetta E. *The Golden Age of Herbs and Herbalists.* (Reprint of *Green Enchantment,* 1940.) New York: Dover Publications, Inc., 1972.

Hylton, William, ed. *The Rodale Herb Book: How to Grow and Buy Nature's Miracle Plants.* Emmaus, Pa.: Rodale Press, Inc., 1974.

Meltzer, Sol. *Herb Gardening in the South.* Houston, Tex.: Pacesetter Press, 1977.

Kamm, Minnie W. *Old Time Herbs for Northern Gardens.* (Reprint of 1938 ed.) New York: Dover Publications, Inc., 1971.

Owen, Millie. *A Cook's Guide to Growing Herbs, Greens, and Aromatics.* New York: Alfred A. Knopf, Inc., 1978.

Simmons, Adelma G. *Herb Gardens of Delight.* New York: Hawthorn Books, Inc., 1974.

NATIVE PLANTS AND ROCK GARDENING

Birdseye, Clarence, and Birdseye, Eleanor G. *Growing Woodland Plants.* (Reprint of 1951 ed.) New York: Dover Publications, Inc., 1972.

Brooklyn Botanic Garden. *Handbook on Rock Gardens.* Brooklyn, N.Y.: Brooklyn Botanic Garden, 1973.

Bruce, Hal. *How to Grow Wildflowers and Wild Shrubs and Trees in Your Own Garden.* New York: Alfred A. Knopf, Inc., 1976.

Foster, H. Lincoln. *Rock Gardening: A Guide to Growing Alpines and Other Wildflowers in the American Garden.* Boston: Houghton Mifflin Co., 1968.

Miles, Bebe. *Bluebells and Bittersweet: Gardening with Native American Plants.* New York: Van Nostrand Reinhold Co., 1969.

Sperka, Marie. *Growing Wildflowers: A Gardener's Guide.* New York: Harper & Row Publishers, Inc., 1973.

Symons-Jeune, B. H. B. *Natural Rock Gardening.* 2nd ed. London: Country Life, Ltd., 1936.

GENERAL READING

Bloom, Alan. *Perennials for Your Garden.* (Reprint of 1974 ed.) Beaverton, Oreg.: International Scholarly Book Services, Inc., 1981.

Brooklyn Botanic Garden. *Handbook on Bulbs.* Brooklyn, N.Y.: Brooklyn Botanic Garden, 1966.

Condon, Geneal. *The Complete Book of Flower Preservation.* Englewood Cliffs, N.J.: Prentice-Hall, Inc., 1970.

Crockett, James Underwood. *Crockett's Flower Garden.* Boston: Little, Brown & Co., 1981.

Cruso, Thalassa. *Making Things Grow Outdoors.* New York: Alfred A. Knopf, Inc., 1971.

Foster, Catharine Osgood. *The Organic Gardener.* New York: Random House, Inc., 1972.

Free, Montague. *All About the Perennial Garden.* New York: Doubleday & Co., Inc., 1955.

Hebb, Robert S. *Low Maintenance Perennials.* New York: Quadrangle/Times Books, 1975.

Hunt, John Dixon, and Willis, Peter, eds. *The Genius of the Place: The English Landscape Garden.* New York: Harper & Row, Publishers, Inc., 1976. (Contains Francis Bacon's essay "Of Gardens.")

Jekyll, Gertrude. *Color in the Flower Garden.* London: Country Life, Ltd., 1908.

Lees-Milne, Alvide, and Verey, Rosemary. *The Englishwoman's Garden.* London: Chatto and Windus, 1980.

Midda, Sara. *In and Out of the Garden*. New York: Workman Publishing Co., Inc., 1981.

Perényi, Eleanor. *Green Thoughts: A Writer in the Garden*. New York: Random House, Inc., 1981.

Pettingill, Amos. *The White-Flower-Farm Garden Book*. New York: Alfred A. Knopf, Inc., 1971.

Robbins, Ann R. *How to Grow Annuals*. Rev. ed. New York: Dover Publications, Inc., 1977.

Sackville-West, Vita. *V. Sackville-West's Garden Book*. New York: Atheneum Publishers, 1979.

Smith, L. Ken. *Do-it-Yourself Garden Construction Know-How*. San Francisco: Ortho Brooks, 1976.

REFERENCE

Bush-Brown, James, and Bush-Brown, Louise. *America's Garden Book*. Rev. ed. New York: Charles Scribner's Sons, 1980.

Chittenden, Frederick J., ed. *The Royal Horticultural Society Dictionary of Gardening*. 2nd ed. Oxford: The Clarendon Press, 1974.

Cronquist, Arthur. *Basic Botany*. 2nd ed. New York: Harper & Row Publishers, Inc., 1981.

The Editors of Sunset Books and *Sunset* Magazine. *New Western Garden Book*. 4th ed. Menlo Park, Calif.: Lane Publishing Co., 1979.

Everett, T. H. *The New York Botanical Garden Illustrated Encyclopedia*. New York: Garland Publishing, Inc., 1980.

Johnson, Hugh. *The Principles of Gardening: A Guide to the Art, History, Science and Practice of Gardening*. New York: Simon & Schuster, 1979.

Lawrence, Elizabeth L. *A Southern Garden: A Handbook for the Middle South*. Revised ed. Chapel Hill, N.C.: University of North Carolina Press, 1967.

Pirone, Pascal P. *Diseases and Pests of Ornamental Plants*. 5th ed. New York: John Wiley & Sons, Inc., 1978.

Southern Living gardening staff and Floyd, John A., Jr. *Southern Living Garden Guide*. Birmingham, Ala.: Oxmoor House, 1981.

Staff of the L. H. Bailey Hortorium, Cornell University. *Hortus Third: A Dictionary of Plants Cultivated in the United States and Canada*. Macmillan Publishing Co., Inc., 1976.

Taylor, Norman, ed. *Taylor's Encyclopedia of Gardening, Horticulture and Landscape Design*. 4th ed. Boston: Houghton Mifflin Co., 1961.

Wyman, Donald. *Shrubs and Vines for American Gardens*. Revised and enlarged ed. New York: Macmillan Publishing Co., Inc., 1969.

———. *Trees for American Gardens*. Revised and enlarged ed. New York: Macmillan Publishing Co., Inc. 1965.

———. *Wyman's Gardening Encyclopedia*. Revised and expanded ed. New York: Macmillan Publishing Co., Inc., 1977.

Index to Plants

A

Achillea, see Yarrow
Aconitum, see Monkshood
Agave, 60
Ageratum, 19, 191, 200
Ailanthus, 199
Ajuga (bugle), 110, 171, 179
Akebia, five-leafed, 74
Allium, giant, 79, 85;
  A. sativum, see Garlic;
  A. Schoenoprasum, see
  Chives
Almond, flowering, 144, 146,
  148, 199
Althaea rosea, see Hollyhock
Alyssum, sweet, 19, 26, 31,
  34, 62, 64, 69, 94, 98,
  197, 198, 200
Alyssum, perennial, *see*
  Basket-of-gold
Anchusa, 199
Anemone, 147; *A. blanda,*
  199, 124; *A. japonica,* 16,
  68, 75, 166;
  A. pulsatilla, 11, 119,
  120, 178
Angelica, 44, 46, 50
Anise, 44, 45, 49, 50
Antirrhinum, see
  Snapdragon
Apple, 48, 59, 120, 178. *See*
  also Crab apple
Apricot, 110
Aquilegia (columbine), 24,
  94, 95, 98, 113, 123, 151,
  171, 177;
  A. canadensis (native
  American), 38, 47, 150,
  156, 157, 171;
  A. caerulea, 98;
  A. chrysantha, 171;
  A. flabellata nana
  (Japanese fan), 68, 69,
  74, 76, 167; *A. vulgaris,*
  98, 120, 125, 171, 179
Arborvitae, 95
Armeria maritima, see
  Thrift
Artemisia, 68, 75, 95, 134,
  135, 199; *A. abrotanum*
  (southernwood), 31, 35,
  44, 45, 52, 178; *A.*
  absinthum (wormwood),
  32, 52, 122, 123, 125,
  178; *A. dracunculus*
  (tarragon), 48; *A.*
  ludoviciana 'Silver King,'
  136; *A. schmidtiana*
  nana 'Silver Mound,' 98,
  136, 161, 167; *A.*
  stellerana (beach
  wormwood), 27, 35, 98,
  136

Arugula, *see* Rocket
Asclepias, see Butterfly
  weed; Milkweed
Asparagus, 144
Aster, 17, 21, 22, 24, 60, 62,
  63, 98, 167, 191, 197–
  199; dwarf, 68, 75, 208;
  New England, 11, 64, 201;
  New York, 11, 64, 201
Astilbe, 13, 15, 74, 161, 168
Atlas cedar, 129, 199
Azalea, 14, 16, 44, 74, 110,
  146, 150, 151, 156, 158,
  160

B

Baby's breath (*Gypsophila*),
  16, 68, 69, 75, 84, 98,
  129, 133–135, 167, 168
Baby's tears, 110
Bachelor's buttons
  (*Centaurea cyanus*), 19,
  84, 129, 134, 136, 147
Balloon flower (*Platycodon*
  grandiflorus), 23, 157,
  191, 199
Balm, lemon, 120, 123, 125
Bamboo, 183, 199
Baptisia, see False indigo
Barberry, Japanese, 204,
  210, 213
Basil, 45, 47, 49
Basket-of-gold, 208, 212
Bay (*Laurus nobilis*), 33,
  121, 123, 124, 178
Bayberry, 135
Bayberry, California, 134
Beach wormwood, *see*
  Artemisia
Bean, 39, 84
Beautybush, 156
Bee balm, 21, 65, 150, 157
Begonia, tuberous, 161, 167
Bellfower, peach-leafed, 47,
  98, 157
Bergamot, 63, 65
Birch, 110, 204
Bittersweet, 84
Black-eyed Susan, *see*
  Rudbeckia
Bleeding heart, 79, 86, 161,
  168
Bluebell (*Mertensia*
  virginica), 178
Bluebell, California, 134
Blueberry, 48, 60, 78, 79, 85
Borage, 44, 45, 47, 49, 60,
  62, 64, 178
Bouncing bet, 33, 38, 47, 75
Boxwood, 33, 44, 110, 120,
  123, 126, 160

Bramble, whitewashed, 204
Broccoli, 84
Broom, 119, 126
Buckeye, 156
Buddleia, 61, 64, 66, 129,
  135, 137, 156
Bugle, *see* Ajuga
Bulbous oat grass, 188
Burdock, 59, 63, 84
Burnet, 44, 45, 50
Butterfly bush, 61, 64, 66,
  135. *See also* Buddleia
Butterfly weed (*Asclepias*
  tuberosa), 23, 62, 63, 65,
  84, 86, 133, 134, 136

C

Cabbage, 84
Calendula, 39, 44–46, 48,
  113, 119, 121, 124, 147,
  148
Camomile, 48, 161, 171, 177,
  178
Campanula, 69, 74, 157,
  199; *C. carpatica, see*
  Harebell carpathian; *C.*
  medium, see Canterbury
  bell; *C. persificola, see*
  Bellflower
Candytuft, 63, 68, 69, 76,
  212
Canna, 189
Canterbury bell (*Campanula*
  medium), 11, 19, 44, 46,
  51, 94, 98
Caraway, 45, 50
Carnation, 31, 32, 35, 94,
  98, 125, 147, 177, 178
Carrot, 62. *See also* Queen
  Anne's lace
Caryopteris, 61, 66, 136, 199
Catmint (*Nepeta faassenii*),
  33, 135, 171, 177, 199
Catnip (*Nepeta cataria*), 44,
  45, 50, 63, 79, 86, 135
Ceanothus, 60, 64, 134
Cedar, red, 135
Centaurea cyanus, see
  Bachelor's buttons
Centaurea rutifolia, 199
Centranthus, see Jupiter's
  beard
Chaste tree, 129, 135, 137
Cherry, 60, 63, 103, 110,
  124, 166, 211. *See also*
  Prunus
Chervil, 45–47, 49
Chick pea, 144
Chickweed, 60
Chicory, 48

Chinese lantern, 79, 86
Chives, 44, 45, 47, 50,
  62–64
Christmas fern, 211
Chrysanthemum, hardy
  (*C. morifolium*), 17, 22,
  24, 31, 35, 68, 69, 74,
  76, 98, 146, 147, 167,
  197, 201; *C. maximum,*
  see Daisy, shasta ; *C.*
  parthenium, see Feverfew
Cimicifuga, see Snakeroot
Cineraria maritima, 129,
  136, 197, 200
Cinquefoil, three-toothed
  (wineleaf cinquefoil), 208,
  212
Citrus, 26, 32, 33, 75, 156
Clary, 48
Clematis, 26, 74, 95, 98,
  150, 151, 156, 158, 167;
  C. integrifolia, 211; *C.*
  paniculata, 27, 33, 36,
  74
Clethra, see Summersweet
Clover, 33, 59, 60, 62, 63,
  65, 84, 170
Club moss, 110
Columbine, *see* Aquilegia
Coneflower, purple
  (*Echinacea purpurea*),
  62, 65, 133, 136. *See*
  also Rudbeckia
Convolvulus, 134
Coral bell, 74, 84, 94, 98,
  150, 151, 157, 161, 166,
  168, 178, 208, 212
Cord grass, 187
Coreopsis, 62, 63, 65, 191,
  198, 201
Coriander, 44, 45, 50
Corn, 39, 60, 84, 87, 188
Cosmos, 19, 68, 69, 75
Cowslip, 119, 122, 177
Crab apple, 74, 110, 115,
  120, 123, 126, 166, 211
Crabgrass, 59, 60, 109
Cranesbill, scarlet, 171, 177,
  179
Cress, garden, *see*
  Peppergrass
Crocus, 48, 74, 77, 79, 85,
  178, 205, 212; saffron,
  120, 124, 178; winter, 211
Crow-flower, 113
Crown imperial, 45, 48, 114,
  119, 120, 123, 124, 147
Cuckoo-bud, 113
Cuckoo-pint, 178
Cucumber, 78
Currant, 48
Cyclamen, 147, 161, 166,
  167, 211
Cypress, *see* False cypress

D

Daffodil, *see* Narcissus
Dahlia, 161, 167, 199
Daisy, 69, 74, 84, 113, 119, 120, 125
Daisy, African, 135
Daisy, English, 171, 179
Daisy, oxeye, 178
Daisy, Shasta, 13, 74, 197, 198, 202
Daisy, turfing, 135
Dame's rocket, 33, 47, 63, 75
Dandelion, 21, 59, 62, 84, 170
Daphne mezereum, 31, 36, 210; *D. odora*, 33
Day lily (*Hemerocallis*), 14, 17, 19, 24, 31, 35, 63, 65, 150, 157, 158, 161, 166, 168, 198, 203; *H. lilioasphodelus* (lemon lily), 44, 52, 191, 201
Delphinium, 68, 69, 74, 76, 94, 98, 99, 139, 151, 156, 157, 166, 191, 197–199, 201
Deutzia, 68, 69, 76
Dianthus 33, 98, 114, 120, *See also* Carnation; Pink; Sweet william
Dichondra, 110
Dictamnus, see Gas plant
Digitalis, see Foxglove
Dill, 44, 45, 50
Dogwood, 16, 60, 74, 203–205, 208, 213
Doronicum, 11
Dusty miller, *see* Artemisia; *Cineraria maritima*

E

Eglantine, *see* Rose
Elaeagnus, see Russian olive
Elecampane, 47
Epimedium, 108–110
Euphorbia, 197, 200
Evening primrose, 68, 75, 202. *See also* Oenothera
Evening star, 75

F

Fairy lily, 75
False cypress (Chamaecyparis), 'Boulevard,' 191, 199, 202; golden-thread, 197, 202; Hinoki, 197, 202, 208, 213
False dragonhead, 47, 150, 157
False indigo, 62, 63, 65, 191, 198, 201
Feather grass, 187
Feather top, 188
Fennel, 48, 64, 113, 120, 124, 147
Fern, 146, 160, 190, 197, 204, 211. *See also* Christmas fern; Interrupted fern; Japanese painted fern; Pacific maid maidenhair;

ribbon brake fern; spleenwort; *Woodsia*
Fescue, blue, 75, 135, 183, 186, 188, 199, 208, 212
Feverfew, 44, 45, 46, 51, 178, 199
Flame-of-the-woods, 64
Flax, 16, 17, 47, 133, 136, 191, 198, 201, 208, 213
Fleabane, 63
Flower de luce (fleur-de-lis), *See Iris pseudacorus*
Flowering moss, 110
Flowering tobacco, *see Nicotiana*
Foam flower, 69
Forget-me-not, 11, 15, 63, 98, 171, 177, 178
Forsythia, 199
Fountain grass, 183, 186, 188
Foxglove, 11, 19, 74, 94, 95, 99, 139, 178, 199
Freesia, 33
Fraises des bois, see strawberry
Franklinia, 44
Fritillaria imperialis, see Crown imperial
Fuchsia, 150, 151, 156, 166
Fuchsia, California, *see* Hummingbird's trumpet

G

Gaillardia aristata, 11
Gardener's-garters, 183
Gardenia, 33
Garlic, 48, 85
Gas plant, 62, 63, 65, 74
Gazania, 135
Geranium, 147, 156, 199
Geranium, scented, 26, 27, 31, 32, 34, 178
Germander, 44
Gilliflower, 113, 114, 119, 120, 125, 171, 177. *See also* Pink; Carnation
Ginkgo, 110
Gladiolus, 74, 75
Globe thistle, 133, 134, 136, 157
Globeflower (*Trollius*), 45, 46, 51, 178, 199
Glory-of-the-snow, 205, 212
Golden top, 188
Goldenrod, 63
Goldenrod, beach, 135
Goldenstar, 180
Gooseberry, 48
Gourd, 79, 87
Grape, 48
Grape hyacinth, 45, 49, 147
Grass, lawn, 44, 147, 171, 182, 191
Groundsel bush, 135
Gypsophila, see Baby's breath

H

Harebell, 124
Harebell, carpathian, 157
Hare's-tale grass, 188
Hawthorn, 112, 121, 124, 166, 211

Heartsease, *see* Johnny-jump-up
Heather, 16, 135
Hebe, 69
Helichrysum, 134
Heliopsis, 14, 17, 24, 191, 198, 199, 201
Heliotrope, 31, 33, 34, 64
Hellebore, 211
Hemerocallis, see Day lily
Hemlock, 95, 135, 160, 210
Hen-and-chickens, 37, 45, 51, 79, 84, 86, 208, 211, 213
Herb robert, 178
Hibiscus, 147, 150, 151. *See also* Rose Mallow; Rose of Sharon
Hinoki cypress, *see* False cypress
Holly, 95
Holly, Japanese, 108–110
Hollyhock, 44, 46, 51, 60, 62, 65, 84, 94, 95, 99, 145, 147
Honesty, 44, 46, 51, 63, 79, 86
Honeysuckle (*Lonicera*), 27, 33, 48, 74, 113, 115, 122, 124, 126, 147, 156
Hop vine, 60
Horse chestnut, 156
Horseradish, 48
Hosta, 24, 68, 69, 76, 98, 135, 160, 191, 198, 199, 200
Hummingbird's trumpet, 151
Hyacinth, 31, 33, 34, 98, 145, 147, 191, 197, 199
Hyacinth, wild, *see* Harebell
Hydrangea, 74, 135, 199
Hyssop, 35, 45, 50, 121, 123, 125

I

Ice plant, 135
Impatiens, 15, 167
Indian paintbrush, 60
Interrupted fern, 197, 200
Iris, 22, 98, 103, 134, 146, 147; *I. cristata* (crested), 199; *I. foetidissima*, 178; *I. germanica* (bearded, German), 19, 74, 121, 125, 129, 133, 136, 199; *I. g. florentina* (Florentine), 32, 125, 178, 199; *I. kaemferi* (Japanese), 68, 69, 74, 76, 191, 197, 198, 201; *I. pseudacorus*, 114, 119, 121, 123; *I. siberica* (Siberian), 74; 191, 199
Irish moss, 110, 135
Ivy, 121, 124, 191

J

Jack-in-the-pulpit, 84
Jacob's ladder, 45, 46, 51
Japanese painted fern, 110
Jasmine, 33, 68, 75, 138, 142, 145–148
Jasmine, star, (*Trachelospermum jasminoides*), 33

Jewelweed, 84
Job's tears, 188
Johnny-jump-up (*Viola tricolor*), 37, 44–46, 52, 122–124, 171, 180
Juniper, 135, 191, 199, 202, 205, 213
Jupiter's-beard, 31, 35

K

Kerria, 204

L

Laburnum, 110
Lady fern, 69, 76
Lady-of-the-night, 75
Lady-smock, 113
Lamb's ears, 68, 98, 128, 129, 133, 134, 137, 139
Lantana, 62, 63, 64
Larch, 95
Larkspur, 11, 19, 44, 48, 94, 98, 147
Laurel, *see* Bay; Mountain laurel
Lavatera, 145, 147
Lavender, 11, 27, 32, 33, 35, 47, 63, 98, 119, 121, 125, 133, 134, 137, 178, 199
Lavender cotton, 27, 33, 34, 44, 75, 113, 135, 199
Leek, 124
Lemon grass, 188
Lemon lily, *see* Day lily
Lettuce, 44, 46, 48, 79, 84, 87, 123
Leucothoe, 211
Lichen, 102, 103, 108, 204
Lilac, 26, 31–33, 36, 44, 52, 60–62, 66, 74, 156
Lilac, Persian, 145, 146, 148
Lily, (*Lilium*), 33, 68, 95, 114, 119, 145, 147, 148, 158, 161, 166, 167, 178, 199; *L. auratum* (gold-banded), 158, 161, 167; *L. candidum* (madonna), 46, 49, 74, 121, 125, 177, 179; *L. longiflorum* (Easter), 198, 200; *L. martagon* (Turk's cap), 47, 124, 147; *L. regale* (regal), 31, 34, 74, 94, 99, 161, 167; *L. speciosum*, 94, 99, 161, 167
Lily of the valley, 33, 74, 84, 147, 171, 177, 179
Lily, water, *see* Water lily
Linden, 112
Lobelia, 95, 98, 191, 199, 200
Long purples, 113, 123
Lonicera, see Honeysuckle
Loosestrife, 62, 65
Lotus, 9, 147
Lovage, 48
Love grass, 188
Love-in-a-mist, 19, 145, 147
Lunaria annua, see Honesty
Lungwort, 178
Lupine, 60, 63, 156, 158
Lyme grass, 128, 135

M

Magnolia, star, 74
Magnolia, sweet bay, 74
Mahonia, 211
Maiden grass, 183, 186, 188
Mallow, 60
Maltese cross, 178
Maple, Japanese, 106, 108, 110, 209
Maple, paperbark, 211
Marguerite, 178
Marigold, 19, 60, 64, 79, 84, 150, 199. See also Calendula
Marjoram, 45, 51, 113, 123, 124, 147
Mary-bud, see Calendula
Meet-her-in-the-entry-kiss-her-in-the-buttery, see Johnny-jump-up
Mignonette, 19, 31, 34
Milkweed (Asclepias), 38, 54, 60
Mimosa, 110, 156
Mint, 25, 46, 48, 79, 113, 123, 125, 178. See also Peppermint
Mock orange, 27, 31, 36, 44, 74, 199
Molinia, 183, 186, 188, 197, 200
Monarda, see Bee balm; Bergamot
Money plant, see Honesty
Monkshood, 44, 52, 124, 178, 191, 198, 202
Moonflower, 68, 69, 76
Mountain cranberry, 211
Mountain laurel (Kalmia latifolia), 160
Moss, 103, 108–110, 124, 160, 209
Mullein, 84, 135, 178
Myrtle (Myrtus communis or latifolia), 121, 124
Myrtle, (Vinca), 122, 177, 180, 205, 209, 213

N

Narcissus (daffodil), 20, 68, 69, 74, 75, 98, 113, 114, 119, 123, 125, 161, 166, 167, 171, 191, 197, 199; N. bulbocodium (hoop-petticoat), 48, 125, 179, 200; N. juncifolius, 179, 200; N. poeticus, 31, 34; N. pseudonarcissus, 48, 179, 200; N. triandrus, 125, 179, 200
Nasturtium, 39, 44, 45, 47, 48, 61, 62, 64, 84, 156
Nepeta, 178. See also Catmint; Catnip
Nettle, 59, 61, 63, 113, 123
Nicotiana, 19, 33, 68, 69, 75, 156, 199
Nigella, see Love-in-a-mist
Night-blooming cereus, 75, 147
Nymphaea, see Water lily

O

Oenothera, 21, 191, 202. See also Evening primrose

Old man, see Artemisia
Old woman, see Artemisia
Olive, Russian, 128, 134
Onion, 144
Oxlip, 114

P

Pacific maid maidenhair, 110
Palm, 199
Pampas grass, 188
Pansy (Viola tricolor hortensis), 11, 19, 86, 98, 113
Papaver, see Poppy, oriental; Poppy, tulip
Parsley, 49, 61, 64, 122–124
Passionflower, 33, 61, 63
Pea, sugar, 78, 79, 87
Peanut, 84
Pearly everlasting, 47, 61, 65, 135
Pear, 48, 49, 135, 178
Pennyroyal, 178
Pentstemon, 158
Peony, 11, 17, 19, 23, 27, 31, 35, 44, 46, 52, 74, 98, 124, 147, 161, 166, 168, 199
Peony, tree, 167
Peppergrass, 44, 47, 50
Peppermint, 86, 125
Periwinkle, see Myrtle
Petunia, 19, 45, 63, 68, 69, 75, 79, 85, 156, 157, 181, 199
Phacelia, 134
Philadelphus, see Mock orange
Phlox, 17, 21, 23, 63, 68, 69, 74, 166, 205; P. carolina, 48, 68, 69, 76, 161, 168, 197, 198, 202; P. divaricata, 48, 74 P. paniculata, 13, 48, 150, 158
Physostegia, see False dragonhead
Pine, Japanese black, 106, 108, 110, 135
Pine, mugo, 135
Pink, (Dianthus), 16, 33, 44, 94, 133, 161, 166, 177; D. allwoodii (Allwood's), 137, 158, 168, 179; D. deltoides (maiden), 179, 180; D. plumarius (grass), 44, 52, 95, 99, 137
Pitcher plant, 84
Pittosporum, 33
Platycodon, see Balloon flower
Plum, 110
Plum, beach, 135
Plumbago, 61, 64
Plume grass, 187
Polemonium, see Jacob's ladder
Popcorn, 78, 79, 87
Poplar, 63
Poppy, California (Eschscholzia californica), 19, 129, 136
Poppy, California, tree (Romneya coulteri), 134
Poppy, horned (Glaucium flavum), 134

Poppy, oriental (Papaver orientale), 17, 19, 129, 137, 146
Poppy, tulip (Papaver glaucum), 144
Portulaca, 79, 84, 85, 86, 208
Potato, 77
Primrose, 48, 113, 114, 119, 122, 124, 126, 171, 177, 179
Primrose, Japanese, 74
Prunus serrulata, 204
Pumpkin, 39, 78, 79, 87
Pussytoes, 129, 134, 137

Q

Quaker ladies, 74
Queen Anne's lace, 49, 61–63, 84
Quince, (Cydonia oblonga), 39, 44, 49, 110, 178
Quince, Japanese flowering, 147, 150, 151, 156, 158

R

Radish, 77, 79, 87
Ragweed, 59, 61
Ranunculus, 145, 148
Raspberry, 48
Red-hot poker, 151
Reed grass, 187
Rhododendron, 16, 74, 158, 160, 204. See also Azalea
Ribbon brake fern, 110
Rocket, 44, 47, 50
Rose, 32, 33, 44, 74, 114, 122, 123, 126, 128, 138, 139, 142, 145, 147, 148, 159, 160, 161, 166, 169, 170, 177, 178; Rosa alba, 89, 92, 94, 97, 99, 100, 114, 126; bourbon, 92, 94, 97, 100; cabbage (R. centifolia), 92, 94, 97, 100, 124; china, 92, 94; cinnamon, 48; climbing, 27, 36, 92, 94, 95, 97, 115, 124, 148, 160, 167; damask, 48, 92, 97, 99, 100, 126, 178; eglantine, 44, 52, 112, 115, 123, 126, 178; floribunda, 88, 161, 168; gallica, 92, 94, 97, 99, 100, 114, 126, 180; hybrid perpetual, 92, 94, 97, 99, 100; moss, 48, 92, 97, 99, 100, 178; musk, 112, 115, 126, 177, 178, 180; noisette, 92, 94; R. rugosa, 89, 92, 95, 97, 99, 135; scotch, 48; tea, 88, 92; wild, 92. See also 88–100 for other rose species and varieties
Rose campion, 178
Rose mallow (Hibiscus moscheutos), 150, 151, 158
Rose of Sharon (Hibiscus syriacus), 74
Rosemary, 11, 27, 32, 34, 98, 113, 122–124, 178
Rudbeckia, 38, 44, 52, 136, 199
Rue, 45, 51, 113, 114, 122, 123, 126, 135, 170

S

Sage, 11, 32, 45, 47, 51, 63, 135, 147, 178. See also Salvia
Saint-John's-wort, 178
Salvia, 151
Salvia, red, 79, 85, 157
Salvia, blue, 135
Santolina, see Lavender cotton
Savory, 113
Savory, winter, 48
Scabiosa, 63, 99, 191, 198, 202
Scilla, 208, 212
Sea buckthorn, 128, 135
Sea holly, 128, 133, 134, 137
Sea lavender, 134, 137
Sea marigold, 135
Sea oats, northern, 183, 186, 188
Sea thrift, see Thrift
Sedge, 188
Sedum, 62, 66, 74, 161, 168, 208, 209, 211, 213
Sempervivum, see Hen-and-chickens
Senecio, 69
Senna, 61, 64
Silene alpestris, 74
Silver king, see Artemisia
Silver mound, see Artemisia
Skunk cabbage, 26
Snakeroot, 61, 62, 66, 74, 161, 166, 168
Snapdragon, 16, 63, 64, 79, 85, 156, 157, 167
Snowball, fragrant, see Viburnum
Snowberry, 212
Snowdrop, 74, 79, 85, 171, 179, 205, 212
Snowflake, 31, 35
Snow-in-summer, 135, 178, 199
Solomon's seal, 38
Southernwood, see Artemisia
Speedwell (veronica), 74, 133, 135, 137, 147, 171, 177, 178, 180, 191, 197, 198, 199, 202, 208, 213
Spicebush, 54, 61, 62, 66
Spider lily, 75
Spiderflower, 167
Spiderwort, 74
Spinach, 48
Spiraea, 74
Spleenwort, 211
Sp eenwort, maidenhair, 108–110
Spruce, blue, 135, 208, 213
Spruce, Norway
Squash, 78, 87
Star-of-Bethlehem, 179
Stephanotis floribunda, 33
Stock (Matthiola), 32, 177; M. annua (common, annual), 27, 34, 64, 94, 98; M. bicornis (night-scented), 27, 33, 34, 68, 75
Strawberry, 44, 45, 47–49, 74, 79, 86, 170, 171, 180, 212
Strawflower, 79, 85
Stonecrop, see Sedum

Sumac, staghorn, 212
Summersweet, 31, 36
Sundrop, *see* Oenothera
Sunflower, 63, 79, 84
Sweet bay magnolia
    (*Magnolia virginiana*), 74
Sweet brier, *see* Rose,
    eglantine
Sweet pea, 19, 27, 33, 34
Sweet sultan, 145, 147
Sweet william, 33, 98, 178
Syringa, see Lilac

T

Tallhedge, 135, 160
Tamarisk, 135
Tansy, 33, 44, 45, 52, 178
Tarragon, *see* Artemisia
Thistle, 61, 63, 147
Thrift, 44
Thyme, 25, 31–33, 35, 44,
    45–47, 51, 112, 119, 123,

126, 135, 161, 171, 177,
    178, 180, 197, 201, 208,
    211, 213
Tomato, cherry, 79, 84, 87
Tree mallow, *see* Lavatera
Trefoil, tick, 59, 61
Trollius, see Globeflower
Trumpet honeysuckle, 156
Trumpet vine, 150, 156, 158
Tuberose, 33, 68, 69, 74, 75
Tufted hair grass, 187
Tulip, 11, 20, 33, 45, 49, 74,
    84, 145, 148, 161, 166,
    167, 199
Tunic flower, 161, 166, 168
Turtlehead, 61, 63

V

Valerian, 31, 32, 36, 63, 161,
    168
Valerian, red, *see* Jupiter's
    beard
Verbena, 74, 98, 199

Verbena, lemon, 32
Verbena, sand, 129, 136
Veronica, *see* Speedwell
Viburnum, 31, 36, 44, 74
Viola, *see* Johnny-jump-up;
    Pansy; Violet
Violet, 26, 31–33, 35, 61, 63,
    69, 112, 113, 119, 122,
    124, 126, 147, 170, 177,
    180
Virginia creeper, 115
Vitex, *see* Chaste tree

W

Wall cress, 135
Wallflower, 26, 177, 179
Water lily (*Nymphaea*), 69,
    144–148
Watermelon, 84
Weigela, 151, 158
Wild ginger, 63, 110, 160,
    211
Willow, 61, 63, 135, 199

Winter aconite, 205
Wintergreen, 110, 211
Wisteria, 26, 61, 66, 74, 68
Woodbine, 113, 115, 122
Woodruff, sweet, 31–33, 36,
    69, 160, 180
Woodsia, 110
Wormwood, *see* Artemisia

Y

Yarrow, 13, 38, 44, 52, 79,
    86, 133, 134, 135, 137,
    139, 171, 178, 180, 191,
    197, 198, 202, 213
Yew, 95, 160, 204, 205, 210,
    213
Yucca, 74, 199

Z

Zebra grass, 183, 186, 188,
    191, 197, 201
Zinnia, 19